THROWN AWA

Jacob's Story

Louise Allen

with Theresa McEvoy

MIRROR BOOKS

m
B

MIRROR BOOKS

2

Published in Great Britain and Ireland in 2021 by
Mirror Books, a Reach PLC business,
5 St Paul's Square, Liverpool, L3 9SJ.

www.mirrorbooks.co.uk
@TheMirrorBooks

Print ISBN 978-1-913406-67-7
eBook ISBN 978-1-913406-68-4

Design and production by Mirror Books.

Printed and bound in Great Britain by
CPI Group (UK) Ltd, Croydon, CR0 4YY

Cover image: Shutterstock
(Posed by model)

No Excuses.

There are no excuses for
child abuse and neglect.

There are no excuses for why a
child is experiencing trauma.

Trauma shows itself both loudly and quietly,
sometimes you would never know it was there.

And no adult who has experienced that
trauma should feel that it is okay to pass on.

A bad childhood is not an excuse.

To those who have influence, power and profession
– you have no excuse allowing it to continue.

To the ones who choose to abuse and
neglect children – you have no excuse.

There are no excuses for the
way we treat some children.

I write my books for those children, whether
still young or grown, who know things that
others don't and hopefully never will.

Contents

The cases I reveal in my books are all based on true experiences, but I have changed names and some details to protect their identities as they go on to build new lives and families of their own.

PROLOGUE

Betty

It was still dark.

Betty woke at her usual time, just a little before dawn, after another very broken night. Two hours seemed to be about the maximum amount of sleep she could achieve uninterrupted, before feeling herself wide awake. What it was that disturbed the night varied. Sometimes it was as simple as her own need to visit the bathroom, but it might be Jacob crying out downstairs, Daisy talking in her sleep or Myrtle in pain. Sometimes it was just Betty's own hurt – a frightening ache deep inside her that no doctor or medicine could cure: the pain of secrets bottled up inside for too long, the agony of mistakes made from which there was no going back.

They were the longest nights.

She sat upright in the darkness, catching sight of her pale face in the tarnished bedroom mirror. The bed was large. Large enough to make it seem very lonely, and she

1

seemed to only take up a fraction of it. It was nearly seven years since her husband Frank had passed away.

And now more than two years since her father had died.

Long, hard, bitter years, all of them.

Disappointment and frustration had eaten her up; now there wasn't time or space even to dwell on those things. The room was cold, with damp creeping its way through the stone walls. There was no protection from outside. The darkness washed over her as it did every morning, and she brushed it firmly away. She had these precious few moments to herself before the household clamoured for her attention. But these were the moments where bad thoughts sneaked in and tried to take root, these private moments morning and evening.

How long did she need to atone?

How much longer could she keep this up?

How much more did she have to give?

It wouldn't be long before Grandma Myrtle called out from the next room, 'Bets, are you there, love?' Betty was always there, of course, though there was little love lost between them. Betty didn't see why she needed to love an old woman who only complained. And she didn't feel loved for her endeavours, only used. But being used made her necessary: necessary for emptying the bedpan, making breakfast, bringing it up the stairs. Necessary for feeding the horses and the chickens. Necessary for doing everything.

She fumbled around in the semi-darkness to get dressed,

pulling on a vest over her thin bones, then an old dress and cardigan that had been slung over the back of a chair. Next came the long socks and old boots. They were Frank's boots, and a little too big for her, so that she had developed a kind of a shuffle when she walked in them. Her muscle memory kept up the shuffle even when she kicked them off at the end of the day.

Downstairs she flicked the light switch before remembering, then struck a match to light the candle. She used its flame to light a taper fashioned from the 'final reminder' of the vet's bill and carried this across to the old wood-burning range to get that going.

'Morning Jacob,' she said, without looking in his direction – already tired of the day before it had even properly begun.

A loud noise startled her. Someone was knocking on the door. It was a strange time for visitors, and it was a rude, insistent knock. She looked out of the window across the yard. A man in a big jacket was standing on the doorstep, with a dog on its lead.

'You ought to be locked up, you know, the way you're treating these animals,' he shouted at the house, though Betty could hear him well enough. He turned away back up the path. 'You won't get away with it!' he screamed out again in the gloom as he made his retreat.

The darkest secrets, the ones the world could never know, seemed to bubble ever closer to the surface in the place where Betty was drowning. She had protected them all, and herself, for so long. What was done could not be undone. There was no going back. Lives had been changed and painful choices made. But perhaps it was what happened next that would determine so much more.

PART ONE

I

Anna

Red sky in the morning, shepherd's warning.

Anna repeated the old saying to herself as she drove across the Downs, enjoying the glorious rosy colours that washed over the undulating countryside around her. It really didn't seem like the sort of day that needed a warning about it. It was still early, before the bulk of the commuter traffic, and she had the road to herself. It certainly looked like a spectacular morning ahead in spite of the old proverb. After a quick check in her rear-view mirror, Anna indicated left and pulled off the dual carriageway onto a slip road. Within a matter of metres that slip road quickly deteriorated into a single lane which twisted and turned round sharp bends, leaving little room to pass. The branches of beech and alder trees met in the space above her so that she seemed to be driving through green tunnels that broke occasionally into open country. There were few residences, and any signs of life or human activity were miles apart. It always surprised her how quickly civilisation could seem a long way away once you turned off a main road.

After a while she could see a large vehicle – a tractor, or some other slow-moving agricultural machine, wending its way in front of her. Just what she didn't need. Her vehicle's inbuilt satellite navigation system said she was still 22 minutes away from Five Stones Farm – but that could soon change if she got stuck behind something crawling along like this. Anna was heading into uncharted territory: a rural location way off the beaten track in a district she'd never heard of – to investigate a complaint of animal neglect on a small tenant farm. It was an isolated complaint so the chances were there was actually nothing wrong. The general public were very quick to misunderstand the treatment of animals, especially farm animals, and often the calls that came in were nothing more than the work of a malicious neighbour seeking retribution after being kept awake by a barking dog.

Anna loved her job as an RSPCA inspector and the opportunity it brought to make a difference to animal welfare every day. For the most part it ended up with helping people as much as animals – often people just needing advice. In the eighteen months since she qualified Anna had only come across deliberate cruelty a handful of times. More often than not she was dealing with ignorance rather than malice in the treatment of animals. It wasn't all rescuing fluffy cats and finding frolicking lambs though; sometimes she did come into contact with aggressive owners who didn't want the help they so clearly needed, and she'd been on the receiving end of fierce words and threats a few times before. Still, the intensive field training she had received when she joined the organisation meant that Anna felt well-equipped to deal with whatever was thrown at her in the course of a working day. The uniform, with its smart tie and shirt epaulettes, helped to give her a sense of authority she didn't always feel.

She was yet to use the 'boat-handling skills' that had been a compulsory part of the training course but she had once had to abseil down a cliff to rescue a fallen sheep, and she had been up and down a ladder more times than she could ever have imagined. The kit and equipment she carried also prepared her for every eventuality – though today's case appeared very routine.

The original alert had come from a concerned dog walker and had been phoned through to Anna from the national call centre. According to the notes, he had taken a new, longer walking route the previous night which had taken him past a dilapidated farm for the first time. He described starving horses and sheep in the fields, and falling-down buildings, but was most concerned about two dogs standing with their heads down, tethered to a metal gate at the farm entrance. The report said they looked 'skinny and dejected', and there was no obvious shelter or water for the animals. Anna didn't like the sound of that, but perhaps it might not be too bad in the grand scheme of things. A farmer fallen on hard times perhaps, not able to keep his animals as he once did. Well, she'd soon find out, if she could find the room to overtake the combine harvester or whatever it was in front of her.

She decided to just enjoy the extra time that was being handed to her, meandering her way through the Downs more slowly and savouring a chance to observe her surroundings, rather than being cross about her journey slowed, or risk life and limb getting past a tractor on these narrow roads. Sure enough, the vehicle indicated left and disappeared up a dirt track, leaving her still nearly four miles from her destination, according to the sat-nav.

The countryside around was rich and green, somehow still lush and verdant after the long summer. The first suggestions of autumn were making themselves seen in the trees, though not yet obviously in the weather. Little golden highlights were just beginning to start their graduated crawl across the foliage from the fringes of outer leaves and it was these that the last traces of the red in the morning sun picked out. Not for the first time Anna acknowledged a feeling of gratitude for the fact that she lived in such a beautiful part of the world. She kept a slow pace, even without a vehicle blocking her path now, enjoying the vista of the hills crisscrossed by ancient chalk paths that carved up the tracts of downland.

The little chequered flag on the dashboard screen that marked the end of Anna's journey was less than a mile away. She indicated into a right hand turn that almost seemed like a gap in the hedge rather than a genuine road and made her question the accuracy of the sat-nav. The caller had described it as a 'remote' spot and he wasn't wrong. After another few hundred yards the hedgerow gave way to a lower stony wall, behind which Anna glimpsed four horses. It was only a flash through the car window and she didn't yet know if this was part of the property she was headed to, but their demeanour gave her a first frown of concern.

The sun was fully up now, all traces of the pink dawn rubbed away by the time Anna finally pulled in to Five Stones Farm, or what she guessed must be that address from the position of the little pin on her digital map, since no signage at the property confirmed it. Her frown intensified. A very skinny dog was tied up near the front gate, just as the passer-by had described. It was a cream-coloured lurcher-cross. There was no obvious supply of water, or anywhere to shelter. Near it, another dog was lying down, totally unresponsive to the arrival of a stranger – as if too weak to stand. It was a black and white border collie, but its white socks were mud-matted and there looked like open sores near its tail. Being squeamish was definitely not on the job description, but Anna put her hand up instinctively to cover her mouth as these first signs of terrible neglect presented themselves to her. Perhaps today did need a warning, after all.

Anna reached for her phone. Already she knew this was not a case she was going to be able to handle alone. The two dogs would fit in the van, and could travel back with her, but the horses she had seen in the next field would likely need attention and the few chickens scratching in the yard were moulting so badly they looked practically oven-ready, not that you'd want to eat anything that scrawny. Six ragged sheep clustered together in a fenced-off area to the left looked well overdue for shearing, leaving them open to the possibility of flystrike. Many of these animals looked like they had just been left to fend for themselves. And she hadn't seen inside the house yet. Who knew what else she might find? Already she felt out of her depth and wished she hadn't come all the way out here on her own. She definitely needed some back-up. Something was very, very off.

'Hi Dave, it's me. I'm out at Five Stones Farm – which really is in the middle of nowhere. That dog-walker who called about some starving animals? He wasn't wrong. It's bad, Dave. Really bad. I don't think I've ever seen anything like it. This is big. I'm a little out of my depth. I'm going to need every car we have.'

Once she had relayed the details as best she could, and given Dave the heads up about the remoteness of the location, Anna took in the rest of the details around her. On the left hand side of the dirt track which led towards what must be the farm house, an old bus stood parked at an awkward angle. There were bricks in front of the wheels, listing over to one side because of perished tyres. Leaves heaped up beneath wheel arches, nettles thrust their way through the front bumper, the curved bonnet was rusted to a lace lattice. Two of the windows were broken, gaffered up with black bin-liner, with mossy growths forming in the seams of the remaining panes. What a shame to let a vehicle like that fall into disrepair, thought Anna, admiring the curved styling of a bygone age.

She returned her gaze to the dogs and took a couple of quick snapshots of this scene of abject misery. She thought about her next move, knowing that it would be some time before the support vehicles began arriving at the property. She wanted to help the poor dogs straight away, but she knew that she should first check out the house and confront the owner before she administered any treatment or made any intervention. And now she had a bad feeling about this place. She approached the front door of the main farmhouse with caution: a farmer on a property like this would no doubt have a gun. She didn't want to be facing down its barrel if he took exception to her arrival.

She called out in her brightest, friendliest voice, 'Hello? Hi there? Is anyone home?'

The house was a simple squat stone building, but the

windows were too filthy to see through and the wooden front door had rotted away at the bottom to leave a tattered hole over the stone front step. There were signs of occupancy though: a bag of refuse by the front door, flies buzzing around it; an old Land Rover parked nearby, its windows down and keys dangling from the ignition, some grey tea towels flapping on a washing line, a laundry basket half-full. Anna was trained to observe the detail and she took in the scene with a growing sense of unease.

Her friendly calling out was met with stony silence, though Anna had a feeling that she was not alone. Dare she try the door? As yet there had been no chance to execute a warrant under the Animal Welfare Act, but what she had witnessed so far would be more than enough evidence to get one. She knocked loudly and called out once more.

'Hello? Is anyone there? My name's Anna. Could we have a quick chat about your animals? It won't take long.' It was slightly disingenuous; this whole case would require far more than a quick chat, but Anna was determined to keep things as friendly as she could, especially as she didn't know quite who she was dealing with. The farm was registered to a 'Mr P Prenderghast', according to the quick checks she'd made earlier. She decided to try the name.

'Hello? Mr Prenderghast? Are you in there?'

'No, he's not,' came a gruff, female voice. 'Ha'nt been for some time, neither.'

Anna spun round to find a middle-aged woman

12

emerging from one of the nearby outbuildings, walking towards her while wiping her hands on a grubby apron.

'What do you want with him?'

Tread carefully, Anna cautioned herself. This could go either way.

'Oh, good morning – I didn't see you there. My name's Anna. Are you resident here? I've come about the dogs.'

The woman kept moving, lumbering purposefully towards the washing line, as though her day was too busy to be interrupted, then bent to pick up the next items from the laundry basket which she began pegging out next to the tea-towels. The woman's disembodied voice floated over the washing.

'The dogs, is it? What's the problem? They don't bother no one.'

Anna felt disconcerted as she suddenly found herself communicating with a large, well-worn and patched sheet that had appeared between the two of them.

'Well, we've had a suggestion from a passer-by that they might need some medical attention. I'm here to help.'

'Help? Is that right?' The woman laughed unkindly. It was a question, but one to which she evidently felt she knew the answer. Her ruddy face appeared between two hanging cloths. Grey hairs escaped from an unruly ponytail. Anna guessed that she must be in her early sixties, though she had the careworn, weathered features of someone who hadn't been dealt an easy hand in life. Maybe she was younger.

Anna wasn't good at judging age. The woman's lips formed a thin line and Anna braced herself for the tirade that she felt sure was about to be unleashed. Instead the woman sighed, as though the fight had gone out of her. 'Had to happ'n sooner or later, I s'ppose. You'd better come in.' She pegged out the last of the washing and hoisted the empty laundry basket onto her hip.

Anna followed her back to the rotten front door, and stepped over the threshold with a mixture of relief at being invited in and some trepidation at what she might find. It was dark inside the cottage and difficult for Anna to see where it might be safe to tread. Again Anna's hand went to her mouth involuntarily. This time it was a reaction to the overwhelming stench of ammonia that hit.

'Could we turn on a light?'

The woman laughed again. 'You'll be lucky. No electricity here. Not for months now.' She pushed open a door in the gloom, then added, as if it was an afterthought, 'You get used to it.'

Through the door to the left was the kitchen, though not one that would pass any kind of food hygiene standards. There was a little more light in here, able to filter through because one of the windows was broken; enough to see that the flagged stone floor was crusted in a layer of mud and filth, as though it was simply an extension of the farmyard exterior. It was mud-thick and tar-like in places. Anna knew she occasionally left it too long to mop the Lino in her own kitchen, but this was no missed cleaning day: the sheer amount of dirt on this floor took it to a whole new level.

'Tea?' the woman asked.

Anna eyed the woman's gnarled hands, also thick with dirt in every crevice, and fingernails black with trapped grime.

'No, you're alright. Please don't put yourself to any bother on my account.'

'Oh, it's no bother. Time for a cuppa myself, and I've got to do one for Myrt anyway. You relax and make yourself at home.'

Shuffling towards the sink, the woman began to rummage amongst a pile of washing up for some mugs. The room was dominated by an enormous wooden table that seemed to serve as a repository for just about anything and everything, much of which didn't seem to have any place in a kitchen. Pots and pans and papers and tools were piled up on it. There was a trug filled with potatoes, some gardening gloves and a pair of secateurs. An empty milk bottle, a roll of wire netting, and a dustpan and brush sat next to what looked like part of a car engine. A pile of dirty plates and cups, a pot of paint, a dried up paintbrush and some turps, a bag of flour and a box of red mite powder nestled at one end. It was an astonishing combination of items.

An ancient sofa stood against the wall to the left of the table. It was piled with coats and blankets, but in the absence of other chairs Anna headed towards it, though she was reluctant to sit anywhere in this festering chaos. 'Oh!' The exclamation was out before she could help herself. Underneath a greying duvet on one half of the sofa was another dog, apparently as limp and lifeless as the ones she had encountered at the farm gate. She could just about see the dog's cream and brown coloured head above the top of the cover: a little fox terrier, perhaps – though its coat was so matted it was difficult to identify the breed. At first she thought it was dead. It was certainly in a worse state than its poor counterparts tethered outside. The eyes were closed and sunken and at first it didn't seem to be moving, but then she noticed the rise and fall of a shallow breath. Anna touched the sofa next to the dog. It was soaking wet: part of the source of that ammonia smell that had choked her on the way in.

'Oh, don't mind him. That's just Prince. He won't hurt you,' the woman said, as she busied herself with filling a rusty kettle and finding some cups.

Anna leant over and lifted Prince's cover. She put her hand over his little body. Bones seemed to protrude from everywhere: hips, ribs and spine prominent. He opened his eyes at her touch and she could see that they were glazed over. He seemed completely unable to move. There was nothing princely about his condition.

'What's wrong with him?' Anna asked, though she was already making her own assessments.

It was clear that this dog needed help urgently.

'Age,' the woman said. 'He's near the end now, poor fella. But he's had a good innings – he's nearly eighteen years old.'

He might have had a good innings, but he certainly wasn't having a good end. This was an animal that needed urgent medical attention, pain relief and quite possibly putting out of its evident misery.

'Look, Mrs…' Anna paused for a moment, not quite knowing how to address her host, 'Prenderghast?'

'Tillyard, actually. Betty Tillyard. Though Prenderghast was my maiden name. Mr Prenderghast – Pete – was my father.'

'Was?'

'Yes, he passed away at the end of last year.'

'Oh, I'm sorry to hear that. Sorry for your loss.'

'Thank you. We've had quite a time of it since then. As you might imagine.'

'Indeed, yes.'

'Three generations of women running a farm – or trying to. Not a man about the place. And Myrt in her eighties now, and with her hips not being able to get down the stairs, and Daisy worse than useless and needing supervision for everything, so the reality is it's just me, trying to do it all.'

'Yes, I can see how that would be difficult.' Anna swallowed. She was feeling more and more uncomfortable. More and more sorry for this poor woman trying to manage without support. Still, it wasn't an excuse for keeping animals in the terrible state that they were in. She wondered how much longer it would take Dave to get here.

'Mrs Tillyard, I should explain properly. I'm here from the RSPCA. We have some welfare concerns about the animals on the farm. The dogs outside are in a terrible condition. And Prince here. The horses I saw. They all need attention. Some are starving.'

Betty narrowed her eyes and looked less kindly at her visitor. She became defensive once more – a not untypical reaction as Anna had discovered in her relatively short experience with the organisation.

'Like I said, times are hard. It's a struggle to make ends meet. I'm doing the best I can. Some days there isn't room to think. All my time is taken up with caring for Myrt, and Daisy's no help, poor thing.'

'I understand that it must be hard without support. Especially if you are caring for people, too. So Myrt, Mrs Prenderghast, is your – mother?'

'That's right, and Daisy's my daughter. Though the beasts in that field out there have plenty more sense than she does in her little head.'

As if on cue, at exactly that moment a younger woman pushed open the door to the kitchen. 'Ma?'

'Ah, Daisy, there you are. Now I need you to give me a hand with a few things.'

Daisy's age was difficult to quantify. Her features had an

absent quality that obscured something essential. She could have been any age from fifteen to forty. Her eyes stared, unseeing, and her jaw fell open slackly, as if it wasn't wired properly. Anna quickly surmised that she wasn't quite 'all there', as her father might have said.

But Daisy's entrance did seem to bring a little movement from beneath the kitchen table that registered in the corner of Anna's vision. She had been so preoccupied with Prince on the sofa that she hadn't noticed another little dog bed with a blanket across it. The rise and fall of something breathing or shifting beneath it could just about be made out in the shadows beneath the table.

'Excuse me, Mrs Tillyard, but what's that underneath there in the basket? Have you got another poorly animal down there? Do you mind if I take a look?' Anna was already making her way towards the bundle of whatever it was.

'That? Oh no, that's just Jacob.'

Anna knelt down, reached underneath the table and gently pulled back the cover. There was a tuft of matted fur – no, more like hair.

No boat-handling, abseiling, climbing or veterinary training had prepared her for what she found there. Curled up in the dog basket, amidst the mud and faecal matter that caked the kitchen floor, was not another farm pet.

It was a human child, perhaps four or five years of age, sleeping.

II

Anna

The child seemed as scrawny, underfed and unresponsive as the animals at Five Stone Farm. All the clattering around of the pots and pans and kitchen junk hadn't disturbed him at all. What was going on? What was wrong with him?

From feeling out of her depth a few moments ago, Anna plummeted even further away from knowing what she was doing. Today's 'shepherd's warning' needed yellow tape across it, not a few red clouds in the sky. This case had spiralled into something she had no idea how to handle.

'Is he...?' she tailed off. 'I mean, who...?' she tried again. 'Why is he...?' She didn't know how to form the myriad questions that needed to be answered here.

'Oh, don't fuss about him. Truly, little Jacob's the least of my worries about the place. The little man's no bother to anyone, bless him. He's good as gold. We barely know he's there.'

Anna swallowed, and found the words to finish the last question she had tried to form. 'But why is he curled up in a dog basket?'

'He likes it,' Betty Tillyard said simply, as though that were explanation enough. She placed a cup of stewed tea in a chipped tea cup in front of Anna. 'Now, get that down you. You'll feel better.'

There were a thousand other things Anna wanted to know, like who this child belonged to, and how old he was, and what exactly was wrong with him, because something wasn't right here.

He looked old enough to be in school, for starters, and it was a Monday morning in term time. Anna wrapped both hands around the cup, not even registering its crusted rim that might have put her off a few moments ago. She was in shock.

Betty filled the silence while Anna struggled to work out what to say and do next. 'I suppose it might seem strange to some folk, but that's his favourite place to be. He's happy there because he feels safe and secure. Jacob's not quite – well, he's not like other children. You'll see what I mean when he wakes up.' She glanced up at a large clock that hung on the wall. 'Perhaps in an hour or so. He's just having his morning nap.'

'Isn't he...' Anna suddenly realised that she knew nothing about children and their sleeping habits, but something didn't add up about this whole set-up. 'Isn't he too old to be having a morning nap. Isn't that something that babies do? I mean, shouldn't he be at school or nursery or something?'

'Schooling's not going to help this poor mite,' Betty smiled, sadly. 'And no nursery would take him. Not with his needs. No, underneath the kitchen table's quite the best place for him.'

'Right.' It was an entirely inadequate response, but Anna was still reeling from what she was seeing and hearing. She felt as if she had stepped into some kind of alternate universe. Betty Tillyard spoke and acted like a sane, reasonable, even kindly person – and yet here she was explaining that she thought it was no problem to keep a child in a dog bed as if it were one of her farm animals. It didn't make any sense.

'Can I ask – whose child is he?'

'Well Daisy's, of course,' snapped Betty – as if the answer to the question was obvious. 'She's his mother – though as with everything else on the farm, I do most of the work.'

And even in the sleeping features of the child Anna could see the family resemblance between Jacob and Daisy, who still stood open-mouthed in the doorway and was yet to say a word. She certainly didn't leap to any defence of herself in the wake of her mother's criticism.

'And, um,' Anna swallowed again, going way beyond her remit as an RSPCA inspector, 'Is Jacob's father h...?'

She tried to choose her words carefully. She was reluctant to ask if he was 'here' and quickly changed the question to, 'Is he – a help?'

Betty Tillyard snorted, 'Fat chance. No, he's long gone. A farm hand who took advantage of Daisy and didn't stick around to finish what he'd started.'

Anna looked over to Daisy, wanting to express her solidarity and support for a fellow female, victim in an age-old tale of women's woe. But Daisy just looked down at the kitchen floor and made circles in the dirt with the toe of her boot, refusing to meet Anna's gaze.

'Oh, I see.'

There was another long silence. Anna wished herself anywhere but here in this filthy kitchen with its pungent smells, ominously ticking clock and growing list of problems that felt overwhelming.

'What other animals have you got on the farm?' Anna asked, in an effort to change the subject and bring her back onto safer territory. It was only later she realised that her question made Jacob, too, sound like an animal.

Within the next half an hour various support teams began to arrive and fill the drive and yard at the front of Five Stones Farm. The lights and evidence of modernity next to the dilapidated bus only emphasised the extensive decay. Betty Tillyard saw Anna looking at it.

'That was Frank's. He bought it to save it from the scrapheap and do it up. He always thought he could save everything. Fix everything. He never managed to, of course. Never managed to do anything to it all.'

Anna's colleagues at the RSPCA began the process of removing all the livestock from the farm, as well as the domestic pets. Dave was as shocked by the conditions as Anna had been, and politely but firmly turned down Betty's offer of a cup of tea. Neither of them were entirely sure about what to do about Jacob, and handed over responsibility to the local police as soon as they could. Given the scale of the animal neglect and the possibility of prosecution, the police would need to be involved anyway. Anna escalated the case and alerted the authorities – implementing procedures she'd never had to follow before.

'I'll take Prince,' Anna offered, still feeling hopelessly out of her depth and needing something else to do, but wondering if the poor creature would actually make the journey back to headquarters. At least she felt on firmer ground dealing with a sick animal. The weather had turned while they were inside and rain lashed down on the farmyard as they did what needed to be done. That old weather warning was right, Anna thought, as the farmyard now puddled into mini lakes that spattered mud as she walked. Betty wavered between anger and resignation as her life was dismantled in front of her.

Pieces of Betty's sorry narrative found their way to Anna as she busied herself securing Prince in the little van. Mr Prenderghast, Jacob's great grandfather, had passed away just over two years ago. Since then, the women had been trying to keep the farm going but with increasing difficulty. It had been hard to keep pace with the changes to government subsidies and agricultural policy and they had been struggling to make ends meet for months. The elderly great-grandmother, Myrt Prenderghast, had a range of physical care needs that had continued to grow since her husband's death, and Jacob's mother, Daisy, had learning difficulties. Betty had spent more than two years trying to hold the family, and the farm, together.

Anna had to give a statement to the police before she was allowed to leave the site. She heard the police calling children's social services before warning Daisy that given the conditions, the social workers would very likely remove young Jacob.

'It's probably for the best, love,' Anna heard Betty comfort her daughter. 'Something had to give, in the end.'

What a day.

Anna couldn't help but feel that she was somehow responsible for the break-up of this family. It was she, after all, who had been first on the scene and escalated the case so that other authorities became involved. Anna was almost inclined to wait with the great-grandmother, grandmother, mother and little Jacob until a social worker arrived. She was invested in this story now, and felt sorry for Betty Tillyard – but Prince needed urgent attention.

'I could come back later and see how you are getting

on?' Anna offered, suffused with guilt as they dismantled the farm around this struggling family.

Dave, just back from rounding up the chickens and still on the phone to a local charity more used to rehoming ex-battery hens past their useful laying life, overheard her. 'Excuse me one moment,' he apologised into the receiver, pausing one conversation to interrupt another. 'Anna, we're going to be flat out this afternoon. You won't have time to come back.' He gave her a warning glare which she understood. Switching back to the telephone call, he said, 'You can take all fifty? That's great news and will be a big help, thank you.'

'How am I to keep going without the income from the eggs?' wailed Betty. 'Do you really need to take all of them?'

'You've seen the warrant, Mrs Tillyard. We'll make sure that they're well taken care of.'

Out of earshot of Betty, Dave whispered, 'And anyway, Anna, they're not your responsibility. Do what you've been trained for and concentrate on the animals. Jacob will get the care he needs. It's your job to make sure that Prince and the others get what they need. Stay out of it. You can't do any more here. You've done a good job today. Let social services do their bit now.'

Anna knew that he was right, of course. The animals that they had removed today would have a far better life and find access to the caring homes they needed as a result of the intervention of the RSPCA. Though she just couldn't help wondering quite what would be left behind on Five Stones Farm. Betty Tillyard would be likely banned from keeping or owning any animals for a number of years and perhaps ordered to pay costs.

But when she did find time to return a few days later, she didn't know if she was relieved or horrified to find that Jacob hadn't been taken into care at all.

'I just popped by to see how you were all doing,' Anna explained.

'Ah, that's nice of you.' Betty Tillyard didn't seem to notice that it simply wasn't possible to 'pop by' Five Stones Farm with its poor road access. The squalor hadn't improved in the time that Anna had been away. Even without the farm and domestic animals to take care of, cleaning up didn't seem to be high on Betty Tillyard's priorities. Prince's sodden sofa had begun to dry out, and the pricking aroma of ammonia that had been so overwhelming a few days before was replaced by a sickly, cloying stale animal smell that caused less smarting but was no more bearable. Nevertheless, Anna found herself with another cup of tea in her hands that she didn't want, as Betty explained.

'There's nothing left. They've taken all the animals.'

'But what about Jacob, and social services?'

'Jacob's still here. No change there.'

Jacob was sitting a little more upright in his dog bed, but didn't respond to Anna's smile and wave.

'They were here for two hours in the afternoon, the

social services lot, after you all left. Two hours of observing, and poking into this and that,' Betty oscillated between being cross, upset and complacent about all the changes. 'Mind you, he was on the phone for most of the time. He said that the setting and conditions are good enough and he was leaving Jacob here, with his family, where he belongs.'

'Oh, that's good,' said Anna, automatically – thinking that perhaps it was actually anything but.

'They did arrange for a health visitor to make an appointment to come back and see Jacob though. I wrote the date down somewhere.'

'Right.'

Anna looked around the room, disturbed that anyone could live like this; moreover could *choose* to live like this. 'Each to their own' was one of her father's favourite sayings, but still. How could conditions not be fit for farmyard animals, but be fine for a school age child? Not just that, but a child with serious learning disabilities who wasn't getting an education and wasn't getting anything much in the way of nurture and care beyond being tucked up in a dog basket in the kitchen? He was being treated worse than the animals. Who could think that it was okay for him to live like this? They were questions that Anna just didn't have answers for, and they continued to bother her as she went through the rest of her working week – one of the toughest of her career so far. She did her best to detach herself from the Tillyards and what she had seen, but it was brutally hard.

She lived for her work, but for once, Anna was looking forward to the weekend, a night out, a few drinks – and most importantly, forgetting about the hellish scenes at Five Stones Farm. In sensible moments she managed to convince herself that Dave and the rest of her colleagues were right; it really wasn't her problem, or indeed her fault. Having initially felt responsible for getting social services involved and potentially breaking up a family, she was now experiencing feelings of anxiety that little Jacob *hadn't* been removed and taken into care. It was all very confusing.

She decided that make-up was in order for tonight, though she didn't have occasion to wear it often. Still, it was a good friend, Hetty's, 25th birthday and six of them were heading out to a smart new restaurant to celebrate so she ought to make an effort. Ro, who lived nearby, came round early so that they could share a taxi into town.

'How's your week been, then?' Ro asked.

'Don't ask,' said Anna.

'That good, eh?'

Anna knew that it would be unprofessional to go into the details – and anyway, the idea of tonight was to block out the terrible images of animal neglect that she had witnessed this week: poor Prince had, as Anna had suspected, had to be put to sleep within a couple of hours of arriving at the RSPCA headquarters. The combination of old age, chronic kidney disease that had been left untreated and the prolonged neglect meant that there was no other option for alleviating his suffering. Benny and Giant, the two dogs that she had encountered first upon her arrival at the farm, remained in a terrible state, both suffering with dental, claw and conjunctivitis issues; the rest of the farm animals were where possible being treated, cared for, rehomed and returning to a quality of life. But it was the thought of a little child in a dog bed that plagued her the most. It wasn't a subject for discussion on a celebratory night out.

'Yeah. But nothing a couple of glasses of wine won't sort out,' countered Anna, with more conviction than she actually felt.

'Nothing you want to talk about, I suppose.'

Ro worked for the local newspaper as a court and crime reporter, and was well-positioned to understand the various issues faced by the local community. She might even know already about what had been discovered at Five Stones Farm since prosecutions for animal cruelty made for good headlines. It also meant Anna being more on her guard. She knew she should watch her tongue in case she let something slip. Although perhaps tonight might be an occasion when it might work in her favour.

'Let's have a drink here, shall we? Just while we wait for the taxi.' Anna reached for two wine glasses from the kitchen cupboard.

'Why not?'

She poured two generous servings and as she wiped away a drop that had spilled onto the kitchen counter she thought again of the filthy conditions she had seen in the farm kitchen.

The evening passed by, with Anna becoming less discreet as the alcohol loosened her tongue. One way or another, whether it was Ro's persistence or Anna's desire to make something happen, it didn't take long for the local press to get hold of the story. Outraged headlines about the child left in 'squalor and poverty whilst animals are removed' soon abounded. Anna felt a momentary pang of alarm, quickly followed by guilt, particularly when the story was picked up by the nationals. Was she instrumental in creating this tsunami of distanced outrage? What else could she have done? As pressure mounted on social services to remove the child, Anna felt vindicated – especially when she heard the news via social media that Jacob had at long last been placed into emergency care, and was finally now living 'with a couple known as experienced foster carers'. Loose lips may have sunk ships in days gone by but perhaps this time they may have helped to save a life.

She chalked it up to experience, considered that it was all for the best, decided that there was nothing more that she could have done, and tried to put Jacob out of her mind.

But the image of a little boy, twisted round to fit within a filthy dog bed, refused to go away.

III

Mary

Mary sipped her lukewarm matcha green tea, trying not to allow her face to make the expression of disgust such a brew deserved. One might, Mary reflected ruefully, consider that after her hippy heyday she should be used to a concoction like this, but she still wanted to wince as the liquid touched her taste buds. She was envious of those other, younger members of the 'looked after children' (LAC) team who were sipping their lattes and cappuccinos with the same enjoyment and careless abandon that she had once known. *Enjoy it while you can*, she thought, grimly. Her own ageing body with its mounting litany of failings meant that diet had become supremely important to her wellbeing, and caffeine in any form that tasted good was off the menu – especially if she wanted to continue working and see out these final months before her scheduled retirement, not to mention the beyond that was on the horizon. Mary was on a mission to do one last good piece of work before she retired and moved to the Shetland Isles to take over her recently deceased brother's croft.

She smoothed out the creases where denim had bunched across her thighs. She deliberately went to work in her jeans, making the concession to wear black ones only when she had to appear in court. Teamed with the rainbow socks were coloured Doc Martens – partly because she liked them, and partly because she well knew that they annoyed Callum, her latest manager.

In spite of, or perhaps because of her long history with the department, she knew that the others saw her as 'past it' – particularly those who didn't know her very well. And, given the high turnover of staff in the team, that was a good few of them these days. Mary's recent health problems had compounded this perception, and had catapulted her into the unfamiliar territory of being classified as an 'old woman'. Colleagues had begun treating her with a deference that was both isolating and patronising: vacating the comfortable seating in a meeting for her benefit; waiting longer than necessary to hold open a door for her while she came puffing and panting down a corridor; abruptly halting conversations about sexual exploits on wild nights out for fear of offending her; and, worst of all, using a gentler register and slightly higher-pitched tone of voice with her that she recognised as being specially reserved for the 'elderly'. She had been guilty of using it herself when her mother spent those last months in a nursing home. Mary very much regretted that now, and made a firm resolution never to employ the 'talking to old people' voice mode in the future. Unless it was reserved for people she really didn't like. But her recent treatment had made it abundantly clear that nearly forty years' experience in social services counted for very little.

Given that the average time for someone to remain in frontline social work in this particular team was six to eight years, Mary knew that she was considered something of an anomaly with so many years under her belt. She'd had her brushes with more senior roles, but had also happily relinquished them, choosing to step aside from management back into working directly in the community. This was the place where she felt she could do the most good, and genuinely help those that society might otherwise malign. The reasons that she had first joined the profession, in fact. Not to mention feeling that she had had enough of being bullied for a lack of 'compliance' which, to Mary's mind, translated to simply insisting the needs of the children came before budgets and personal reputations. She was not popular with senior management as a result. But moving from a more senior position back into working directly with children and families was also somehow seen as career suicide – which was a bizarre perception when you considered that it was what social workers trained to do in the first place. Mary had retained her passion for people and belief that she could make a difference, but unfortunately, to some, that was perceived as a form of failure.

'Good morning, everyone. Let's make a start, shall we?' said Callum, interrupting Mary's train of thought.

Callum was the LAC team leader, and Mary tried very hard to be charitable about whatever merits he must possess to have secured that eminent position. He had been in post for about three months and she found his 'collaborative' style of management annoying and ineffective. Not only was she years older and far more experienced, she was probably significantly older than Callum's parents, she reflected ruefully. He had called the meeting for new allocations, but began with a rather insipid, 'So, how's everyone doing?' as he folded his long fingers together and balanced them on top of his clipboard.

In that group environment it seemed something of a rhetorical question. 'Everyone' was doing just fine – attested to by neutral smiles and nods – and anyone who wasn't would be unlikely to want to discuss the finer details in front of their colleagues, taking up precious group meeting time with an individual issue. 'Good, good, good,' Callum clapped the tips of his fingers together in thanks, momentarily releasing his hold on the clipboard which slid almost to the floor – saved only by a desperate, last-minute snatch. 'Nearly lost it!' he exclaimed cheerfully. Next he offered an 'invitation to raise any concerns that anyone might have at the moment.'

Mary wondered idly how he would react to her catalogue of observations of casual ageism if she chose to raise them – which of course, she never would.

He was such a runt of a man-boy that his inferiority complex around women was evident for all to see. Women of course made up most of the team – and that was how Mary explained to herself why he seemed so uptight most of the time.

Following updates from each member of the team about developments on their caseload, and a quick discussion of outcomes from recent training , they finally reached the main business of the day: the new allocations to discuss and share out.

'As you know, we have a number of new referrals this week and I thought it would be good for us to come together and discuss them, collectively and collaboratively to decide between us who might be best-placed to work with these children and their families.'

Or, alternatively, this meeting could be re-titled, 'Let's get the team to do your work for you,' Mary thought, again more unkindly than she was naturally disposed to be. Back when she had led a team, she had always agonised about which child to place with which team-member based on their experience and existing caseload – wanting to spread complexity fairly so that no one person was burdened with dealing with too many teenagers liable to go missing, or time-sucking court proceedings, or devastating domestic abuse cases that could wear you down. Callum seemed to be advocating a free for all where he who shouted loudest got the least.

There were four new cases to be distributed amongst the team this week, or four families and carers 'up for grabs' as Callum put it. He read out a truncated version of the case descriptions and each of the assembled social workers, apart from Mary who stayed silent, accepted or protested, basing their decisions variously on ease, proximity and experience. Each, apart from Mary, already had a bigger workload than they could easily manage.

'First up is a transracial adoption case.'

This was an area that Mary certainly did know about. She had five grown-up children, two of whom were adopted after she had got to know them in one of the children's homes she managed. The two girls were from Caribbean parents who had been part of the Windrush generation in the fifties. When their mother died and their father couldn't work on the buses as well as look after two children, Mary had taken them in. She first fostered, then adopted the girls and stayed in regular contact with their dad who came to see them every weekend; they became the greatest of friends, forming a lifelong bond. He had introduced Mary to the music of Lord Kitchener, Calypso and Soca. She had many happy memories of them all dancing in her little rented house in Hackney back in the day. She was surprised to hear of a transracial adoption these days, though. Black children were still significantly overrepresented in the public care system but plenty of concerns had opened up about adoptees' racial and cultural identity and the suitability of white parents to raise children from other races. It was a political hot potato these days.

In fact, none of the cases seemed straightforward. It wasn't surprising really. A good friend of Mary who worked in the child protection team – the first port of call for a child in need – had recently been told to increase the benchmark for what actually constitutes a child in need, due to unprecedented demand for their services. That higher benchmark, in Mary's view, just exacerbated problems further down the line. Mary's colleague had joked that at this rate a child would have to be found dead before they were helped. They had both laughed, but it was a tired, desperate laugh – the kind you give when there is no other response to make.

Back in the here and now there was one case left: Jacob Tillyard. Callum gave Mary a meaningful glance as he paused at the first mention of Jacob's name, holding her gaze for long enough to suggest encouragement. Instead it served to show that the case was effectively already allocated – the 'collective and collaborative' discussion was actually a foregone conclusion, Mary suspected. This one had her name on it. The team leader explained a little about the background to the case, which some of Mary's colleagues recognised from the recent unsavoury media coverage.

'Oh, he's the one they're all calling Dog Boy.'

Callum diplomatically ignored that but offered a raised eyebrow in response – managing to both collude and communicate disapproval simultaneously. It was quite an art. 'Jacob's needs are certainly complex and funding cuts mean that specialist care in a home is out of reach,' he continued, glancing in Mary's direction once more.

'It sounds complicated,' someone said on the other side of the room.

Evidently, nobody else was going to be grabbing at the Jacob Tillyard case.

'He's currently in emergency care with the Hallidays,' Callum cleared his throat, 'since being removed from the farm.'

'Oh, that's miles away from where I live,' another colleague chimed in, with evident relief. 'It would make it quite tricky for me.'

The Hallidays, a couple in their late forties with grown-up children of their own who had now left home, were well-known to the team for all the wrong reasons. They were foster carers who were often available, but would never quite be top of the list to use if there was any choice in the matter. This was partly because the independent fostering agencies, the IFAs, were more expensive to use, but this particular couple were also known to have a somewhat lackadaisical attitude towards policy and a tendency to do things their own way. There was also a widely-held perception that they were only in it for the money. Consequently they had a reputation for being difficult to manage and were avoided where possible. The trouble was, the ever-present problem of a shortage of foster carers meant that it wasn't often possible to be so choosy.

Mary had never worked directly with the couple, but since their reputation preceded them she knew, as everyone else did, their supposed shortcomings. She also knew without any doubt that this one was coming her way since her caseload was lighter currently, yet to build up to the near-unworkable levels it had been before she went off sick – plus she had the magical 'experience' that Callum suddenly seemed so keen on.

'And the IFA is Pinnacle,' said Callum meaningfully.

The assembled company knew what that meant, too. They belonged to an independent fostering agency (or IFA) trading as Pinnacle Fostering. It was a small, independent fostering agency originally set up as a business by a couple. He was in the building trade and she was a social worker. It was started in the 1970s with good intentions as a solution to the need for more and better quality foster placements. But over time the couple became greedy, and their foster carers received a much bigger allowance than the local authority ones. And, because referrals went out firstly to the in-house carers, the IFA often ended up with some of the more challenging placements.

'Ah. It will be very work-intensive then' said Greta,

sitting next to Mary, picking fluff from her jumper, avoiding Callum's eye and saying what everyone else was thinking. 'And I've got no experience with special learning needs, so I wouldn't want to take this one on at the moment.'

'Might have the press sniffing round, given the circumstances – watching our every move. Could be controversial – it sounds a bit like the Carroway case,' said Kirsty.

Mary knew that Kirsty was referencing a child that the department had had on their books a few years ago, a child who had died. It was a big scandal as well as a tragedy at the time because the child had been diagnosed with severe disabilities that the carers were ill-equipped to deal with. Mary listened with interest but did not comment. She had been working with a different local authority at the time. The little Carroway girl had died of complications relating to her disabilities and it had turned out to be a major safeguarding breach.

'Remember? The carers were actually arrested.'

Callum was evidently uncomfortable talking about anything that might be viewed as a departmental failing – even though the case was long before his time in charge.

'I don't think we need to rake over old coals, Kirsty. But it would suit a more experienced member of the team,' Callum agreed, putting undue emphasis on the word 'experienced'.

Mary said nothing, just continued to sit quietly,

patiently, waiting to receive Jacob's file. She put herself in Greta's place, or Kate's. In her twenties, perhaps she might have tried to avoid this one, too.

'So...' said Callum, swivelling in Mary's direction once more.

Mary smiled. 'I'll make a call this afternoon to set up a visit as soon as possible.'

Her colleagues breathed a collective sigh of relief.

'Marvellous. That's sorted then. Have a good day everyone,' said Callum, signalling that the meeting was over. He shunted the file across the desk to Mary and snapped his clipboard shut.

'Thanks, Mary,' said Greta, seeming genuinely grateful, as they rose to leave the room.

Mary was not quite as good as her word. To be fair, she did the first bit – she tried phoning straight after lunch. A couple of times, in fact, to make contact with Mr and Mrs Halliday, but the rings went unanswered. So, instead of waiting to book a mutually agreeable appointment time as Callum would no doubt have wished, she decided instead to head straight over to their house. She wanted to meet Jacob as soon as possible. When she had first studied Social Work at Ruskin College, Oxford, in the early 1970s the emphasis had been firmly on the emotional wellbeing of the child. As a student she had been taught that her primary objective was working directly with families and children – whereas these days actually going to see a child seemed to be almost actively discouraged by managers who were more interested in tick-boxing for Ofsted and playing the system to avoid any controversy. But Mary embraced the rebellious streak that clung on from her Greenham Common days.

The Hallidays' address was in one of the more salubrious neighbourhoods on the upper side of town in a leafy street with plenty of parking – a newer estate, but a very luxurious, desirable one, and a far cry from Mary's own terraced property a couple of miles away where early evening parking disputes were the norm. She was glad of the shade. Menopause still played havoc with her temperature management even after a decade, and climbing back into a car that had been sitting in full sunlight wouldn't help. She locked the car and walked across the pavement. In front of her an imposing gate led to a detached property in substantial grounds. There was no answer from the buzzing doorbell at the impressive front door, flanked by imposing pillars. It was always a gamble if you made an unannounced visit, and the unanswered calls had already suggested that they might not be around. She noticed a camera in the corner of the porch, a CCTV sort of device, with a red light beneath suggesting that it was recording. Was that even legal, she wondered. She resolved to put another call through this evening and then to return in the morning, smiling brightly into the little lens as if to say, 'Don't worry, I'll be back.'

Just as she turned to go back down the steps she heard a sudden burst of laughter from the rear of the house. It wouldn't hurt to see if there was anyone there, she decided. It was a nice day after all, somewhat unexpectedly and unseasonably warm after all the rain and heralds of autumn in recent weeks; a real Indian summer. Perhaps the family were all outside and couldn't hear the doorbell – or the phone – from the back garden.

She made her way via a paved path down the left hand side of the house, ducking a little to avoid the branches of a low hanging apple tree still bearing plenty of its fruit. It was a gorgeous garden, or it would be when it was more well-established; the landscaping was recent. There was plenty of lawn, but the garden was also zoned with bushes and borders so that it was impossible to see directly to the end of it, but there was another burst of laughter, and what sounded like several voices. Perhaps it was a little party of some sort – welcoming Jacob to their home.

Just beyond the apple tree, she stopped. There on a rug, in full sun, all by himself, with no toys or books, was a little boy. He was lying as a baby might, arms and legs pointing towards the sky – and wriggling a little, as though he didn't yet have a great deal of control over his limbs.

'Hello there,' she said, 'you must be Jacob.'

Jacob turned his head a little at the sound of her voice, but not in quite the right direction. He didn't seem able to locate the origin of the words. His dark eyes were quite vacant and unseeing – and Mary noticed that he wasn't squinting in the sunlight as she herself was, shielding her eyes with her hands and regretting not bringing sunglasses with her.

Eye test, she thought, mentally adding it to the list of assessments that would need to be made. Good grief, and was he wearing a nappy? He was dressed in shorts and a t-shirt, but above and below the fabric of the shorts a bulky telltale band of plastic protruded, and his t-shirt had rolled up a little so she could see the suggestion of a rash.

His pale skin was already turning red from the sun. Perhaps he wasn't wearing any sunscreen, though it was hot enough to warrant it, and there was a great deal of sunshine left in the day: the back of Mary's colourful shirt was sticking uncomfortably to her skin. Jacob seemed very exposed.

'Hello Jacob, it's nice to meet you. My name is Mary,' she tried again, a little more loudly.

He seemed to search again for the source of the words, but said nothing in return and was still unable to focus on Mary directly.

'You stay there, and I'll be back in a moment.'

Mary continued along the path, following the laughter that floated across to her from the other end of the garden. She crossed a stretch of lawn and shrubbery before she found the source of the sound; it was a long way between the child and where his carers sat, apparently having a relaxed barbecue with friends – Mary counted eight in the group, lounging on rattan furniture in the late stages of the meal.

'I'm *ever so* sorry to interrupt your little gathering,' said Mary – even though she wasn't in the slightest bit sorry. 'My name's Mary Waters. I'm here to meet Jacob – as his new social worker. Delighted to meet you.' She wasn't, under the circumstances. 'All,' she added after a pause.

A cork popped. It was an incongruous percussion to an awkward moment.

'Ah, right. Well, we weren't expecting you. I mean, we didn't know...' said a man in a white linen shirt with a corkscrew in one hand and a now open wine bottle in the other. 'You can't just come barging in here when you feel like it.'

Mary assumed this to be Mr Halliday.

'I did try phoning. Several times.' Again the deliberate pause that indicated her disapproval. 'Is Jacob enjoying the party, Mr Halliday?' she asked, with a raised eyebrow and feigned politeness. Belying her rebellious appearance somewhat, Mary had been educated at a well-known Catholic ladies college; her father was a diplomat and her mother a nurse. Mary was quite capable of turning on her 'cut glass' English accent at the drop of a hat when the occasion demanded it: usually when she was cross or needed to put someone in their place. The occasion definitely demanded it today.

'Jacob is...'

'By himself, with nothing to do, getting sunburnt.' She cut him off. Mary knew that her judgmental tone might be considered unprofessional, but she couldn't help herself. Perhaps this was another of the side effects of ageing and feeling as if she had nothing to lose.

'Well, we thought that he would be bored by the adult conversation,' said a woman in white shift dress.

'Bored, he certainly is. Did you forget that he's by himself over there, in direct sunlight, with no lotion on? Good job I turned up really. Shall we bring him over to join us now?'

The Hallidays' other guests began to make polite allusions to imminent departure, replacing Prosecco glasses on the table.

'No, no, please stay,' pleaded the woman in white, who Mary judged to be Mrs Halliday, 'this shouldn't take too long.'

'Oh, I wouldn't be too sure of that,' Mary took great delight in responding. 'There's a child at the heart of this. We might take all the time in the world.'

She cleared her throat importantly. 'Looking after a child isn't meant to be a Halliday, Mrs Holiday.' She didn't bother to correct herself. 'Oh, and you don't mind if I take a little photograph of your party, do you?'

Without waiting for an answer Mary took a snap of wine glasses, champagne flutes and empty bottles.

'Now, hang on a minute. You can't just...'

'I just did, Mr Halliday. We can argue about it later.'

Within a few minutes the party was dispersed and Jacob became the real centre of attention. Mary lost no time in social niceties with the Hallidays – this wasn't a relationship that she felt she was going to be sustaining for very long. For once this had nothing to do with high staff turnover in the LAC department, and everything to do with the Hallidays' evident unsuitability for looking after Jacob.

After a stern admonishment to the Hallidays about the extent of their caring responsibilities (that might well provoke a complaint, along with taking the photograph – but she would deal with that later) Mary left the property. She wondered if there were other CCTV cameras located around the site that might have caught their exchange. She decided not to worry about it. If the Hallidays chose to complain about her slightly unorthodox interruption then someone could have fun deciphering the footage and trying to put a script to the images on screen.

She contemplated her next move.

The exchange in this morning's meeting had made it quite clear that everyone, Callum included, was perfectly aware of the Hallidays' reputation for bad practice. She would be announcing nothing new there – even if she brought up the fact that she had found him laid out on the grass in the hot sun as if he were a sundried tomato. But careless drinking around a minor? Would that be enough to get Jacob removed from these carers? There were plenty of wine bottles open, and not that many adults to balance the ratio. In fact, Mr Halliday had been in the process of opening another when she had interrupted them.

And she had the photographic evidence to prove it. She wanted Jacob out of there.

But Jacob's was an extreme case and a suitable carer was always going to be difficult to find. Even without a medical opinion it was clear that Jacob's needs were many, and they were complicated. He was certainly physically limited, with major visual impairment, and who knew what degree of specialist learning requirements. No doubt the Hallidays had happily taken the extra money on top of the allowance but did nothing to see what could be done about his eyesight or his muscular weakness. They couldn't even keep him out of the bloody sun while they had a party. Mary knew that Callum would certainly prefer not to have to fund the cost of a residency which could more than quadruple the cost of the placement. Not only would Jacob not be a priority due to the many other emergencies going on around them, she would simply be told that the numbers of children coming into the care system was increasing.

Back behind her steering wheel she breathed a big sigh – the only response to an unsolvable problem. Mary was not impressed with the new wave of younger managers like Callum who seemed to want to be known for rescuing budgets rather than children. Trying to break this kind of mentality was one of the reasons why Mary had once entered management, but she had soon found out that the problems were systemic and she didn't have the magic wand to change the system. She was going to have to work this one from the inside. She would have to make a watertight case against the Hallidays to persuade Callum that they were unfit to look after Jacob.

IV

Mary

Mary well knew that social workers were not allowed to look at information about foster carers unless they had a very good reason for the request and had consulted the manager for permission. Still, she felt as though she could do with a little bit more on the Hallidays. Back at the office, Mary checked out amongst her team, in as casual a way as she could manage, just how relaxed or enforced that data protection rule was in the department.

'Oh everyone's at it,' said Kate, cheerfully. 'I've even used the system to look up colleagues. I'll bet you can't guess which one of us had a difficult childhood and came from the care system to become a social worker? Talk about coming full circle...' she trailed off as she saw Mary's face.

'Don't you think that's their business, and not yours?' Mary countered.

'In my day there were clear rules and ethics for social

workers that had to be adhered to – but these days, well.'
Mary stopped, realising that any utterance that began with
the words 'in my day' was bound to fall on deaf ears, and
perhaps deservedly so. And, she had to remind herself,
she had only spoken to Kate because she had intended to
use the data for her own purposes – just as Kate herself
had done. She could hardly blame her young colleague,
though she could see that Kate was simply being nosey, and
this infuriated her. The ethics seemed to be down to the
individual. Mary would play it straight for now. One of her
friends called the team the 'Wild West'. Mary thought that
perhaps after all this was a good description of the chaos
she found herself working in.

She put her case together, calling for the immediate
removal of Jacob from the family, copied Callum in rather
than going through him for authorisation, and hit 'send'.

Mary's next priority in taking on the Jacob Tillyard case
was to arrange a visit to the local hospital to see the senior
paediatrician and get an accurate picture of what Jacob's
needs really were. It was time Jacob had a full assessment.
So far in his file she had seen nothing but speculation and
uninformed comments about his health. Though 'unable
to keep his head held up' might be an accurate description,
it wasn't a diagnosis. Mary believed he could be helped
enormously if he received the right dedicated care.

Mrs Halliday, who Mary continued to think of as 'the
woman in white', even days after the barbecue when the

weather had broken and she was wearing much more muted tones, reacted reluctantly to the suggestion of a visit to the hospital.

'Are you *sure* that you need one of us there with you?'

Yes, I'm very sure, Mary thought.

'I mean, we'd be very happy for you to take him and report back.'

I bet you would. Aloud she said, 'Given that this is a child in your care, I think it's probably a good idea that you are physically present. After all, you should know the details of his medical and physical needs.' Mary wanted her there to hear what the paediatrician had to say and for them to be able to work together to create a robust care plan – something that Callum, her manager, was not hot on.

And you're not getting out of it, however much you might wriggle. I'm not letting you off the hook, she thought, grimly.

In preparation for the trip Mary had cleared out her car, removing the dog's cage that took up most of the boot and finally making the trip to the charity shop to drop off the boxes of books that cluttered up the back seat. She made it as empty as she could because she wanted to see how Mrs Halliday did things: she would let the woman in white take the lead.

When she arrived at the Halliday property for the second time in a week, Jacob was lying down on a blanket in the front room with a rainbow bridge of toys to amuse him. They were evidently new and this gave Mary cause for hope. Perhaps a leopard could change its spots after all. Mary would give everyone a chance. She watched Mrs Halliday pick Jacob up off the floor with all the finesse of a bulldozer. He went limp like a rag doll, and his head fell backwards. *Or perhaps not,* Mary thought. She did everything to not rush over.

Mrs Halliday carried him out to the car, complaints spilling from her mouth the whole time. 'Goodness me you are a weight. Such a big boy.' She laughed. 'It must be all those pies you ate.' If anything, Mary could see that Jacob was probably underweight for his age and needed feeding up. He was only a 'big boy' if you were treating him like a baby. She wondered if Mrs Halliday was just covering her tracks in making these comments, designed to suggest how well she was feeding him.

'Does Jacob have anything to keep him amused on the journey?' Mary asked, ignoring all the negativity.

By way of response Mrs Halliday huffed and disappeared back indoors, returning a few moments later with a children's book.

Mary rolled her eyes. *Well, he could throw it at us I guess*, she thought. Mary's first instincts about Mrs Halliday and her husband were being all too readily confirmed. In spite of their long history with the IFA, these carers were not specialists who could use their expertise to support Jacob's evident physical and emotional needs.

Mrs Halliday went to get the car seat from her Audi.

Mary noticed that it was new and that there were two more cars on the drive – also new and expensive. She had read that the Hallidays used to run a coach company until it went bust in the last recession. Then they became foster carers – for an easy life, perhaps. Mary smiled to herself, knowing from both her personal and professional life that there was nothing easy about working with children from the care system. Nothing was easy financially, either, in spite of the vast sums of money that changed hands. Foster carers, even unscrupulous ones like the Hallidays, became easy targets for some of the more ruthless fostering agencies who will manipulate their allowances after they have been recruited. Holiday pay and Christmas and birthday allowances are often the first things to be cut, the foster carers expected to pick up the tab out of their own money. But once again, it seemed that there was no shortage of cash for this family. Just a shortage of moral responsibility, perhaps.

The next thing that Mary noticed was that the car seat Mrs Halliday was clumsily manoeuvring was not appropriate. It was a baby seat, not suitable for a child with disabilities. She suspected that the agency would have told the Hallidays to pay for any equipment requirements out of their weekly allowance – which, to be fair, would not have paid for a car seat. Mary guessed that they must have already had the standard seat or been given it. She only just managed to avoid shaking her head in a gesture of disapproval. She waited as patiently as she could for Mrs

Halliday to strap Jacob in the car. It was a pretty painful process to observe, and clearly had not happened very often as she kept muttering to herself and asking where the strap went. While all this was going on Jacob turned his head to Mary who was doing her best to look on and not interfere. She gave him a little wink, which he caught and smiled back. He seemed to have greater focus today than last time.

When Mrs Halliday finally finished fussing and the last clips were clipped, she made a big show of waving goodbye to Mr Halliday – who had been studiously 'pretending' to be busy indoors, or so Mary suspected.

He's terrified of her, was Mary's mischievous conclusion. Good. She was as indisposed towards him as she was towards Mrs Halliday. The pictures from the day she had first met Jacob were stuck firmly in her mind. She could still hear the sound of him laughing as he popped open another bottle of Prosecco while she rounded the corner and happened upon their little gathering, and could still feel the hot flush of her own angry response to the scene.

Once they were all in the car and the adults also strapped in safely, Mary tilted the mirror to see Jacob. She caught him looking at her with a look in his eye that was bright as a button. In spite of all his communicative complexities, Mary had a feeling that he understood plenty of what was going on. She was intrigued by him, she admitted to herself, feeling that there was way more to this boy than met the eye. She could not help but smile – at him, and their exclusive shared moment that was testament to all sorts of potential. He just needed to be in the right place – and that place was not with the Hallidays. They were superficial and uninterested in meeting even his basic needs. Mary didn't need any data protected records to tell her that.

As they eased out of the parking space, Mary turned the car stereo on. She had the Beatles *Yellow Submarine* CD playing, left over from when she had taken two of her grandchildren out to the beach for the day at half term. She put it on partly to drown out the awkward silence with Mrs Halliday – and also to see if Jacob would respond to it. Though concentrating on the road, she watched him in the mirror as much as she could.

He seemed to be listening to the lyrics. *In the town/where I was born/lived a man who sailed the sea.* Mary couldn't think of a better start of a story to a little boy whom she suspected had been listening to many things from the dog basket under the kitchen table. When they reached the repetition of the lines in the chorus, *We all live in a yellow submarine, a yellow submarine...* Mary watched him sway and smile whilst looking at the fast-moving countryside out of the window. The roads were clear and they reached the hospital in good time. Again Mary watched Jacob for reactions. He looked amazed as the arm of the parking barrier let them through. Mary decided that he needed and loved stimulation, something in her mind the Hallidays could not, and would not, offer. They found a space to park, and then Mary let Mrs Halliday take the lead once more. It amused her to see what would happen next. Mrs Halliday had evidently been giving this some thought during the journey, but not enough to come up with any answers.

'So, how shall we, er...?'

'Transport Jacob inside? Like this. I've brought a pushchair for now.'

Mary had arranged for the pushchair, borrowing from her daughter since she had recognised that Jacob seemed incapable of walking. But it was a tight squeeze given that he was five years old and, although small for his age, it was a thing designed for a toddler. The catalogue of physical issues went way beyond not walking. It was difficult to strap him in – perhaps Mary had been a little harsh on Mrs Halliday about her efforts with the car seat. What didn't help was that he didn't seem to have good control over his core muscles: he was more like a baby learning to sit up for the first time. He also couldn't speak, though he could form some sounds and Mary was delighted that he seemed to refer to her as 'Mm'.

'Like the character in James Bond,' Mary joked to Mrs Halliday, but it seemed to go beyond her.

To Mary's mind, the issue was not just how severe they were, but what was causing these developmental delays: what were the underlying health causes, and did they go beyond being left to languish in a basket underneath a kitchen table for the first five years of a life.

When Mrs Halliday went to take the arms of the buggy, Jacob made a fuss. When Mary took the handles, he relaxed again. He evidently wanted Mary to push him – and had found a firm means by which to communicate his preference. Mary obliged, chatting to him all the way. They all went up the long and winding ramp to the entrance of the hospital, passing the signs on the pole by the League of Friends shop, which they stopped to look at for Jacob's benefit before heading to the lift. Again Mary noticed that Mrs Halliday was now surplus to requirements: she and Jacob locked eye contact and smiled as they went up in the lift. He laughed and moved about in his pushchair as if doing a little dance.

They checked in at the reception and waited to be called through to the doctor. Mary passed Jacob some toys that were on the floor in the children's play area. He laughed and threw them back on the floor – but there was communication and interaction: a good sign. Mary wished she could say the same for Mrs Halliday. Though she tried her best, Mrs Halliday's lips remained pursed – it was as though having been forced to be here she was determined to make it as uncomfortable as possible for all three of them, and to punish Mary for her interference. After about twenty minutes of awkward stop-start conversation, Mary gave up. *Have it your own way*, she thought. She was delighted when Jacob's name was finally called and wheeled Jacob enthusiastically into the consultant's room. Both women sat down as the consultant, a very thin, efficient-looking woman, smiled and gestured to the chairs.

'So, which one of you is his mother?' she asked.

Mary's back went up straightaway. The doctor's neat appearance belied an inefficiency. She clearly hadn't read Jacob's notes and had no idea at all about the situation they were dealing with. Mary explained, a hard edge creeping into her voice.

'So, you understand our desire to have an assessment conducted as urgently and *thoroughly* as possible,' she finished.

'Of course,' murmured the doctor, choosing to ignore Mary's tone – or perhaps she was impervious to it.

The doctor crouched down next to Jacob and spoke to him as if he was an imbecile. That patronising tone again that was reserved, Mary realised, not just for the elderly but also for the very young. The doctor examined him, poking and prodding and twisting him round, while failing to explain the purpose of the succession of different instruments she used to gauge and measure. Jacob hated the whole experience, becoming increasingly defensive and withdrawn.

Mary – as experience had taught her – had some sweets in her bag to offer as a consolation to the probing and pulling. Eventually the doctor sat back down, her notes and charts complete. She sucked in her breath. 'Keep going on the bottled milk and with the nappies – essentially he's not much further developed than a newborn. And might never be.'

The consultation was over quickly with little further advice to follow. The doctor's chilling pronouncement as she washed her hands at the sink in the corner of her consulting room was simply, 'This child will never amount to anything. The best you can do is to keep him warm and dry.'

Mary was furious. *And you get paid for that, do you?* She wanted to say. Y*ou cannot simply write off another human being.*

Out loud she said, 'Thank you very much for your time. We'll be leaving now. Come on Jacob,' and busied herself with securing the push chair.

Before they were even out of the building, Mrs Halliday spoke. 'I think I ought to let you know that we'll be giving notice on the placement.'

That 'we' was interesting, Mary considered. She couldn't have had a chance to speak with her husband yet. This was clearly a foregone conclusion – perhaps regardless of what the paediatrician had said.

Perhaps she was right and the Hallidays *had* been seeing this as easy money – though the property they lived in didn't particularly suggest that they were short of a bob or two. The realisation of the work now needed for Jacob and the multiple associated challenges that would no doubt lie ahead under the scrutiny of Mary were enough of a deterrent.

'Oh, I'm sorry to hear that,' Mary said breezily, not even bothering to argue. Inwardly, she was delighted – mostly because she knew that this would be the first step towards getting Jacob out of the Halliday household and into an environment more conducive to his needs.

That boy had potential to be far more than the doctor suggested, and she would be instrumental in proving it. Even if that meant raising her head above the parapet and making herself even more unpopular than she already was.

In the afternoon, when Mary returned to the office, she was called in to see her manager before she had even managed to sit down at her desk.

'He said *straight away*,' Greta urged. 'Don't upset him.'

Mary sighed, more amused than concerned.

When she had first begun social work all managers had an open-door policy where they encouraged a natural and helpful dialogue amongst a team. Now the doors were closed and, in case she hadn't got the message from her colleague, there was a post-it note stuck to her computer in Callum's fair hand.

Mary had the distinct feeling of being sent to visit the headteacher. She wondered idly what sin she might have committed as she logged onto her computer. These days it was difficult to tell – the possible transgressions were so vast. Maybe she was about to get her wrist slapped for spending too much time with a child and not enough time on paperwork – which mostly consisted of bureaucratic form-filling to feed the privately owned business support team. Had she submitted her appointments log a little late last month, or incomplete, maybe? It was another arse-covering piece of paper that was filled in retrospectively, thereby taking her away from more important aspects of social work. Its only purpose was to make sure that every moment of her time was accounted for. Perhaps it was that. Mary had also been known to commit the odd data protection violation by 'forgetting' the BCC option on an email – her philosophy was why shouldn't everyone know who was involved in any given piece of communication? It seemed deceptive if they did not, and she usually got away with the 'forgetful' excuse. Various thoughts along these lines swilled around in Mary's head as she took her time putting together the referral for Jacob.

'I'll get there,' she promised Greta, though she only moved to Callum's glass cubby hole in her own sweet time.

She headed along the corridor, guessing that in reality her poor manager was probably quietly terrified of her. Although there was power in this knowledge, Mary knew that it was a potentially dangerous position for her to be in as he might, like many inadequate managers who feel threatened, use his authority to do something unpleasant to manoeuvre Mary away and punish her.

Still, Mary was relatively safe in the knowledge that

retirement loomed, her union membership was fully paid up and she frankly didn't give two hoots about other people's insecurities. Besides which, she had taken on a case that no-one else wanted, so she was actually doing Callum a favour. But it was an imposition that had since become more of a mission. Mary kept focused on her priority to get Jacob to a good place – even if that meant working 'creatively' around the constraints of the system.

Callum was suspiciously friendly when she finally put in an appearance at the glass cube.

'Mary, good to see you!'

He took a surreptitious glance at his watch, but shook his wrist away and evidently decided not to pass comment on how long it had taken her to arrive at his office.

'So. How are you getting on with Jacob's case? I see you're unhappy with the level of care being provided currently. Can you give me a little update?'

'Sure. You've read my report. I witnessed him being neglected and endangered. Not only that, I was at the hospital with him this morning, accompanying Mrs Halliday...'

'Hmmm. Mrs Halliday, yes, exactly.' Callum interjected, cutting Mary off before she had a chance to 'update' him on anything.

'I'm sorry?'

'I'm afraid that I have some bad news. I heard from the Hallidays' supervising social worker at the agency this morning, and the couple have decided that they can't meet Jacob's needs. They've served the 28-day notice on him.'

Mary smiled inside. They had moved fast. This had happened even more efficiently than she had hoped. For Callum she forced her features to form a concerned frown.

'And they've put in a complaint about you in response to your allegations.'

'Oh dear, I wonder what I did to prompt that?'

'Don't play innocent with me. You charged in there, like a bloody bull in a china shop...'

'To rescue a child with severe disabilities that was being burned in the heat of the midday sun because his carers were busy quaffing wine and having a party.'

'The agency aren't very happy with them either – or with us.'

No, thought Mary, *I bet they're not.* Jacob would have been a nice little earner – potentially long term – for the agency and the carers.

'So you'd better put a referral together just as soon as you can.'

Mary smiled. She had already put the finishing touches to it just moments before. 'No problem, I'll get straight to it.'

'Obviously we're here to support you.'

Not obvious at all, but Mary stopped short of saying that.

'And Mary? Play this one by the book. Stay out of trouble.'

V

Mary

Mary had been honest and factual in the referral. Sometimes writing referrals could feel like a strategic marketing campaign for a social worker – especially when a child had the kind of extreme issues that Jacob did – issues that most foster carers could not manage. Mary had to remind herself that most foster carers were simply regular people responding to ads in papers or on the backs of buses with heart-tugging headlines: *Have you got a big heart and a spare room and want to make a difference to a child's life?*

Back at her desk she launched a one-woman quest to get Jacob in the right place. She began by emailing the placements team who were responsible for sending out the referrals to carers who have empty beds or are known to have the skills to support a child such as Jacob. If no in-house carers picked up the referral then it would go out to the independent fostering agencies. There were fewer of these now than in the past because the truly independent ones had been bought up by large venture capitalists seeking financial gain in a lucrative sector. Mary had seen the spreadsheets when she was a manager. Eye-wateringly large invoices and payments to private fostering companies that made her dream of a simpler time when local authorities delivered their own services. Her hours filled up with searches across the national and regional adoption agencies.

'Don't stay too long, will you?' said Greta, anxiously. 'Do you want a light on in here?' Mary hadn't noticed how dark it had got. She shook herself to get the blood flowing through her limbs once more. She had been hunched over this computer for long enough.

'No, don't worry. I'm heading off now. I didn't realise how late it was. I'll call it a day.'

But Mary didn't call it a day. Once she got home the laptop was out and she was back on her mission. In one night she sent dozens of emails up and down the country seeking adopters who might be able to help Jacob. She didn't disguise the complexity of the case; rather the opposite in fact: she didn't want to pull any punches. She knew that might do more harm than good in the long term. She had also never put so much effort into finding a home for one child before.

'It's probably futile, you know,' Greta said, when she enquired as to how Mary was doing the next morning. She meant it kindly.

'You never know.' Mary suspected it was a long shot, but she had to do everything in her power for Jacob – who so far had been let down by the adults in his life. Some of her other colleagues were less kind than Greta, but the sniping, negative comments of her team became Mary's inspiration to try harder. She contacted anyone in her network across the country who might be able to dig around and help, calling in favours from across the years and across the miles.

This became the pattern for an entire week, with evenings filled as urgently as the days.

But her intense focus on Jacob's case and thorough paperwork trawl had also elicited some other worrying information. There was no birth certificate for Jacob, and no record of the birth. There was no official evidence that this child had even existed before he was discovered by an RSPCA inspector. It was a puzzle with no easy solution. Something was very, very off thought Mary, unconsciously echoing Anna's words from her first encounter with the Tillyards.

Mary was not a religious person, but as she sat at her old pine dining table on Sunday evening, a table decorated with piles of paper pertaining to the case, and two purring tabby cats helping to arrange it, she closed her eyes and prayed to the gods that Jacob would find a family to love him.

She had set everything in motion to make that happen. She had left no stone unturned in the search for a long term placement for Jacob.

But she also had a very immediate concern. Until the right family came forward – and they would, they would, they would – but *until* they did, she needed to find a temporary foster placement urgently now that the Hallidays had served notice. This one could not be anything like the Hallidays. Mary needed to locate a family who could be bothered to support Jacob properly to help him develop a bit more in the short term – and could see the magic in this child that she had already observed. She adapted the text to create an interim referral document and sent it to her own fostering shortlist. She stopped short of crossing her fingers.

The next morning Mary woke with renewed hope and optimism, believing that somehow the universe would look after Jacob. By the time she had parked her car and walked across two shopping car parks to her building, she had convinced herself that a new week would bring good news. She opened the entrance door with gentle determination to get more things in place for Jacob. Acquiring the right wheelchair was near the top of the list. As she logged on, Mary was pleased to see that she was first in. She often had the first hour of the day to herself before the desks around hers filled. Some of her younger colleagues had to drop their children off at school first before beginning their working day. Mary remembered those days fondly, but also enjoyed the feeling of stealing a march and getting on with things. She was more efficient at this time of day.

Once her computer had been through its motions, she was disappointed to see that her inbox remained frustratingly empty in spite of all the legwork she had put in. Where was the perfect in-house carer going to magically appear from?

She headed to the kitchen, hesitating briefly over the detested green tea box before making herself a cup of Earl Grey instead. She savoured the perfumed brew as she carried it back to her desk. How much harm could one cup do? She heard voices in other parts of the office. At the end of the corridor she overheard one of the visiting Looked After Children team social workers talking about a foster carer who had helped a little girl through a difficult time.

'She's an artist and very unconventional – does things a bit differently, you know.'

Mary hovered in the corridor and continued to listen.

'Louise and her family have a bit of magic – I can't really describe it. That something you just need sometimes. She – Louise – grew up in care herself, so she really gets the children.'

Mary poked her head around the door. 'Sorry to interrupt – couldn't help overhearing you talking about an artist, you say? She sounds interesting. I'm interested in purchasing some art. What's her name? Louise something?'

'Louise Allen.'

'Great, thanks. I might look her up.'

Mary flew back to her own desk and did a quick Google search on the name. She knew the rules about searching foster carers online files without good reason but hadn't noticed anyone else abide by the rules, and it had already stood her in good stead to have some background information on the Hallidays.

She looked up the Allen family in the system, looked at the photographs of their home and was intrigued. Louise's house was full of chaos, colour and clutter. There were interesting things in each room and on every wall, original artworks and artefacts, and giant plants and sculptures standing tall – not at all like the spotless but characterless home of the Hallidays. Mary sat back in her chair and brushed her hair away from her forehead. Could she have found what she was looking for?

Mary began to look at the numbers of children already in the Allen household. Two birth sons, one long-term foster girl and a teenage girl on short-term placement. A lively household indeed. Busy, though. She looked at the teenage girl, noting that her placement was due to end in two weeks. Mary smiled. 'Bingo.' How perfect that timing would be.

There were still two and a half weeks to go on the Hallidays' 28-day notice – Mary had been crossing them off in her calendar. This might just work. She read back over all the information: Louise and her husband Lloyd had been approved to look after children of school age only because both worked from home – they were not keen to look after babies and toddlers. Maybe not, but some people are more flexible and easily persuaded than others, Mary consoled herself.

'Just going for a quick breath of fresh air,' she announced, to no one in particular.

'You haven't drunk your tea,' Greta said, with a tone of mock accusation.

Mary shrugged. She had forgotten all about it. She walked over to the other block where the placements team was and introduced herself. She needed a route to Louise Allen. She had to be careful how she did this; timing was crucial. She wanted the Allen family to receive the referral ahead of their current placement ending. Most foster carers like a little break between placements, if at all possible. Mary assessed the various members of the placements team, wondering who she was likely to get on best with – fully aware that this was not the way things were done these days. She didn't have her manager's permission to approach the team directly, and she was certainly unlikely to have his blessing. The thought made her smile. She spotted an older woman wearing thick glasses. She had her hair pulled back into a loose bun and looked a similar age to Mary. Maybe she, like Mary, had been doing this long enough to understand that sometimes the system just needs a little nudge to get it going in the right direction.

'I can see you're busy there. But I don't suppose you've got a minute to listen to a rather bizarre tale?'

Mary had made a wise choice.

Thick Glasses listened carefully to Mary – who talked about Jacob and the dramatic way he had been found. Mary turned the RSPCA inspector's role into a heroic one, adding flourishes as if she had been there. She decided in the telling that she might quite like to meet this Anna one day. Mary listed Jacob's understandably complex needs – and also explained her desire that foster carers were found 'in-house' after the problems with the Halliday family.

The woman told Mary that she had a brother in New Zealand who had a son with similar needs to Jacob. 'Though he had had a very different start in life, thankfully.'

On such coincidences does the world turn. Thick Glasses nodded sympathetically as Mary added more details. She was all heart – and seemed to warm to Mary's earnest telling, and her very specific request at the end of it. The referral went out again urgently to the foster carers with empty beds – and this time also to the artist, Louise Allen.

PART TWO

Louise

Chapter One

I'm in my studio working on the corrections for my new book on adoption and enjoying a rare moment of peace at home when a rather odd email drops into my inbox. The children are all at school and my husband Lloyd is away on business, meeting a new client with his design team in Romsey. He is working away much more than he has ever had to before. He has a new client who is very demanding. Consequently he has been working flat out – alongside his copywriter and photographer – and we have been like ships passing in the night.

They all stay in a hotel and have a long dinner before propping up the bar and talking shop all night. I know the drill and I am glad to be out of it – delighted that he is enjoying himself but relieved that I am not there. My days as a smiling, chatty, but highly-bored employee are over, for a while at least. These days my colleagues – if that is even the right word for them – are scattered amongst publishers and galleries as I straddle the art and writing worlds. I no longer have to endure dull meetings or attend networking sessions. But in the past, when I still taught at the University, I can remember all the staff in my department receiving a three-line whip to attend an evening event hosting local and regional businesses. I vividly recall standing by the buffet table, carefully eyeing up the meagre crisps and dips, when I was interrupted by an older grey-haired man in an expensive pinstriped suit.

His genius opening gambit was, 'hello,' as he stood too close to me.

I remembered my instruction that I was there to network. My job was to get business cards off people and to make sure that I called them within two days to stop the contract from 'going cold'. I really couldn't see the point of calling lots of these people myself because I taught art and had no connection with the world of business. My hawk-eyed university dean was in the corner watching from the other side of the room so I swung into action and began talking to the man. Or at least tried to. He was 'very important in IBM', apparently. Those weren't his exact words but they were the gist. I stood politely for more than half an hour whilst this man talked about himself, barely pausing for breath in his self-congratulatory monologue. I smiled and nodded until I could control the muscles in my face no longer. As soon as a colleague walked within spitting distance I introduced him to the man and scarpered. I was still in earshot when I heard the businessman remark, 'What a fascinating young woman!' to his new victim.

I loaded up my plate with free carbohydrates and vowed to avoid 'networking' at all costs. So I don't envy Lloyd his swanky hotel and meal – he is welcome to it.

The solitude of my studio is much more preferable. I have tonnes to do too. I'm itching to start a new sketch book that will be a series of experiments for a few paintings. I am close to having my first solo exhibition: big news and very exciting, especially as I had to wait and put my art on hold (or literally in a cupboard for a few years while I worked full-time and looked after my adopted mother and the boys). I used to feel so sad because I wasn't doing my own work. The narrative that society thinks a woman should give up or wait till she is 'free' still seems to prevail. When are we free? I decided nearly ten years ago now that not making art and being creative was too much of a price to pay. Now I get up earlier and go to bed later to fit it all in.

But this email has caught my eye. It is from the placements team. That's more than a bit odd, because I still *have* a foster placement currently, a teenage girl, so I don't have an 'empty bed' – and they obviously know that; but nonetheless I open it up. I could certainly do with a break to distract me from the tedious business of editing.

I begin to read the referral. Anyone watching me would see me blow my cheeks out with utter disbelief. A paragraph in and I am upset and outraged. I have had some challenging placements in the past, but – wow.

I read on.

I know that children like this are not wanted. That thought alone makes me want to do something – but I absolutely can't. It would be ridiculous. I have too much work on at the moment, a deadline looming, new work coming in, an exhibition to organise. I don't have time to support this child. But for some reason I don't delete the email. Instead I find myself reading and re-reading, over and over again. It would be so hard. And yet. A boy called Jacob clouds my thoughts and means I can't concentrate. I break for an early lunch, or that's what I tell myself.

Instead I phone Dara. She is my supervising social worker, and has been for a record amount of time now – about eighteen months. I admire her attitude, and we have become firm friends after the way she handled difficult moments with Eden, a former child in my care. She is on my wavelength and I know that she 'gets' me. Her no-nonsense way of speaking appeals to me, and is charmingly framed in the traces of her Eastern European accent. I am sure she will talk me out of the wild possibilities that are forming in my brain.

Dara answers within a couple of rings, and doesn't bother with 'hello'. Before I have a chance to speak, she asks, 'Have you received the referral?'

I make a huffing sound which she echoes, and I can't help but start to laugh. She knows what I'm thinking. I am not going to be persuaded to do anything via guilt. It's an emotion you can choose to feel or not. I don't like it to be used as a tool to encourage me – or anyone else – to take on tricky children. But I don't feel this. There is something about the way this referral has been written that has captured my attention and my imagination.

'So?'

'So.'

More laughter. I know – as Dara does – that this is both crazy and important.

'Look, seriously, Louise. I know next to nothing about this case – I was only copied into the referral email the same as you.'

'But?'

'Bu-ut...'

'What have you done?'

'I have managed to call the social worker for Jacob.'

Okay, perhaps I knew that I wasn't really ringing Dara to be talked out of this.

'I think that you need to meet with her. Mary, her name is. Before you reach any decision and say yes or no. I think this is the best solution.'

'What's she like?'

'I don't really know. I didn't speak to her for very long. She sounds very English and very posh!'

I send Lloyd a quick text, telling him to check his email for a referral 'that he should look at' when he has the chance. He will understand that Allen household code and know what I am thinking. I need him to be fully informed.

I fidget my way through the afternoon, achieving little until the children come home.

Dinner tonight is flour wraps with spicy chicken and salad for most of us – and vegetarian Quorn chicken for Lily. Lily is my longer-term foster child, who has now been a vegetarian for more than two years. She greatly enjoys reminding me about my 'lack of faith' in the early days of her vegetarianism – as though her continued commitment to the cause is a personal triumph over me. This is but one part of her metamorphosis into 'early teenager', a multifaceted role which also incorporates Oscar-worthy eye-rolling tendencies as well as undisputed mastery of the full-on sulk.

Vincent and Jackson are my birth sons, and they gobble up their tea with little fuss and less conversation. Casey, the teenage girl and our current foster placement, is actually at her mum's just for this evening. There are still two weeks to go before she returns home full-time to her mother, and part of the condition for that return is a staggered integration. It started with the odd day, then night and now it is three nights a week. It's working well. Casey seems happy and she has been an easy placement, though one of those that look terrible on paper.

Her family situation was fraught with problems and yet she has been nothing but delightful: helpful and polite from the word go. I can't tell her mum enough how wonderful Casey is, and I am confident that she is well on her way to a more promising next phase of her life. But in many ways it is good that she is not here tonight – timely. I sit down to eat with the children and, when the plates are clear, explain about Jacob's referral. They understandably have many questions.

'Why hasn't he learned to speak?'

'How can he still be in nappies?'

'Will he learn to walk?'

'In a dog basket – seriously?'

But the overall view is that he definitely needs to come here and be looked after. I'm proud of them.

Now for Lloyd. I wait until the children are all upstairs to find out his views. Because of the necessity of not wasting any networking time, this has to be done via text, but he sneaks away to reassure me.

'Do it. He should come and stay with us. You know that you can rely on me and the children to help. And it's always a two-way street. Maybe we will all gain from spending time with Jacob.'

It's a supportive attitude like that which has got me into

all sorts of trouble over the years. But he's right. I have a feeling that Jacob will challenge, and maybe change us.

In the morning I set to business with an enthusiasm and purpose that was entirely lacking in my writing yesterday. It is the thought of Jacob that has given me this renewed vigour. I wake up earlier than usual, and the first emails to Mary and texts to Dara are sent before breakfast.

I'm not making any promises at this stage, I caution in my email to his social worker, *but I would love to invite you here to the house to talk about Jacob.*

My phone rings almost as soon as I have hit send. Mary introduces herself. I am struck by her old-fashioned, almost aristocratic English accent. She sounds ever so rich and ever so posh, and I wonder quite what I am dealing with. No, old, posh and *poor*, I decide. If she was rich she wouldn't be a social worker.

'Absolutely, yes of course,' I find myself saying, in a voice I don't quite recognise that echoes her well-spoken tone, to her question of a visit later today.

On the dot of 2pm, as arranged, the front door bell rings. *Unusually punctual for a social worker*, I think to myself. I open the door to Mary and instantly feel as if she is somehow familiar. Something about her appearance reminds me of some of the women I knew back when I was growing up in Oxford. In the space of a second, a picture forms in my head. There is a hippy vibe to her, not the full stereotype but one that is associated in my memory with good women – the women's libbers who wanted to improve women's lives and fight for social justice back then.

'Good to meet you, Louise. I appreciate you giving up your time today.'

She is relaxed and low key and I warm to her even further when she speaks. Sometimes all you need is a connection and I feel instinctively that we have one. My own inner hippy keeps me caring and finding a balance with the world's madness.

Before I have time to analyse too much, Dara appears behind Mary. 'Have you got the kettle on, Louise?' she calls.

'Give us a second,' I laugh. We head into the kitchen. There are a few, necessary ice-breaking comments and Mary steers the conversation to my artwork. She seems genuinely interested. I am touched. Mary can have no way of knowing it, but although I can always find the space in my head to be creative, I have been struggling with my identity as an artist of late. Sometimes I can live with creative ideas turning over in my head for days while getting down to the practical business of looking after three or more children, cleaning and maintaining a large, slightly derelict old house with its big, demanding garden.

When most people say they are busy I feel that I have sometimes achieved a full day's quota of chores before breakfast – as do so many women I know. I am very often amused – and occasionally annoyed – by how the men I know moan that they are busy. It's as if their male conception of 'busyness' is busier and more important than women's 'busy'. I spent years and years waiting for my painting and writing to take off, and some days I feel sad that after fighting so hard to go to college and get a job my life still seems to have boiled down to laundry and dishwasher emptying and making packed lunches and cleaning and all the things that constitute 'women's work'. I try to explain some of this – and how I am flattered that this social worker values the 'artist' as well as the 'carer'.

But within a few minutes we are talking about Jacob – as we should be. Mary doesn't hold back and somehow I find her honesty more inspiring than alarming. A discussion of the possibilities seems quickly to have become an assessment of the practicalities. All three of us know that this is a done-deal.

'This will be one of the hardest things you've ever done,' Mary says, blowing on her tea to cool it.

'Then that makes me more determined to help him.'

'He's still in nappies.'

'Well, he won't be for long, if I have anything to do with it.'

We say goodbye like three warriors going into battle and somehow I feel as if this *is* extremely important. Jacob is loved by me before he has even met me. Sometimes you just get a feeling about a child, and I have that feeling now.

Back in my studio I begin to pack away paints and

brushes, and tightly roll up canvasses to place them against the wall. I am shutting up shop in preparation for the arrival of Jacob. I have a feeling that there is not going to be much in the way of time for artwork – at least not the kind that sits on an easel. And, in spite of my earlier rant, I feel at peace with this for the time being.

Chapter Two

Today Lloyd comes back from his work trip and I'm going to have to level with him about the reality of what lies ahead. We haven't really had the chance to talk properly beyond a few hastily exchanged text messages, and now that I have had the opportunity to find out more, I wonder if he is fully aware of what having Jacob here really means. I feel nervous and a bit sick, to be honest. Sometimes I wonder if I let myself get carried away with the challenge. I do so love a challenge, in fact I thrive on them, but that means I occasionally bite off more than I can chew.

I know that Lloyd, if left to his own devices, would far rather opt for an easier life than the one I give him. Whatever else it might be, fostering is not the easier life – there is no doubt about that. I'm well aware that if we didn't foster children then our lives would be calmer, far more straightforward and we would be financially far better off. I dread to think how much of our own money we have spent over the years on other people's children – doing the job of propping up the children's social care system. I also know that our lives are infinitely richer because of the work that we do – but those rewards are never material ones.

I'm thinking about money for two reasons today. The first is that, drum roll please, we are about to receive a 'pay rise'. Don't get too excited: our hard work in supporting children as foster carers is to be rewarded with an extra five pounds a week! Hold me back before I blow it all on an all-inclusive trip to the Caribbean. Five pounds. Are they serious? Children seem to grow a foot a month – or at least they do while they are at my house – I suppose five whole pounds might buy a foot of fabric. Sometimes I wonder what planet these people are on – the ones who work out the modern cost of raising a child.

I guess I *could* spend all day cutting out coupons and surfing the internet for clothing and shopping deals but, to be honest, I have a life to live, as do all foster carers – and nowadays none of us can really afford not to work. I remember back when we first began fostering: we were told that one of us *needed* to be at home. I also remember getting cross that the assumption was that I, the woman, would give up my career to look after children who are after all, remember, wards of the state, for less money.

Although things have moved on, they haven't moved on enough, and sometimes I think it may indeed need a woman to overhaul children's social care and organise it in ways that feel fairer and more equal. The idea of the mental load borne by women is fascinating. Here I am worrying about Jacob's arrival – fair enough, but also trying to carefully 'manage' the way others in my household are going to respond. Lloyd is probably merrily travelling back from his work stay, not yet giving any of this a thought.

The other reason that money is at the forefront of my mind today though is because I am only too aware that this child in particular – Jacob – has complex needs that will be expensive to meet. He will require extra funding – but, as ever, all my extra labour will be free.

I carry on with some of that free labour in the meantime: tidying up the kitchen after the children have left for school. Casey is still in her room doing her eyebrows and something that she calls 'contouring'. It takes her ages and sometimes her eyebrows don't look entirely equal but what do I know? I admire her persistence anyway. It's funny what goes through your mind when you clean and tidy the kitchen.

I know that Jacob needs to wear nappies. That in itself is not a problem to me. Like most parents who have children and animals, cleaning up excrement is just part of the role. It's second nature and doesn't bother me – though I know Lloyd can't pick up the dog mess and I have a memory of him retching while changing Jackson's nappy. But, I wonder if that was a tactic to get out of doing the job – a bit like night time with babies years ago. I seem to remember he slept through most of that, too. I shut down that unhelpful train of thought before I get too cross and resent Lloyd. I need to remember all the lovely things he does do, that I am simply not capable of − like sort out all the electronics. That is how a partnership works. I'm just feeling a little overburdened today and I need to put those feelings into perspective.

I set the dishwasher off with a satisfied twist of the dial when I get a text from Mary.

When can I come round to talk through putting together Jacob's care plan with you?

She's keen, and it is a good idea. I already get the impression that any care plan she writes will be both honest and ambitious. I approve of both sentiments, but I'm not quite ready yet. I text back with a holding message, the suggestion that I meet Jacob first so that he gets to see me and I can make an assessment for myself. Not that I really know what I'm assessing − I haven't looked after a child with such big needs before.

When I was a waitress years ago I remember the wine bar where I worked raised money to help a member of the team who needed a respite break from her disabled son. The money was to help fund carers to look after him whilst she worked or had some down time. I was in my early twenties and spent most of my time partying when not working. Even though this event has stuck in my mind I had no idea what it meant and how important it was for that mother to have a break. I think I may need a break here and there; I am old enough and experienced enough to know that none of us are robots and that to give good care I need to be emotionally and physically in a good place.

I will factor respite into the care plan, though I know that some social workers don't think we need a rest; some have actually said that foster carers are rejecting their foster children if they need time to themselves – or that needing a rest suggests that they aren't coping. Don't get me started on a response to that.

There's another text from Mary: *Good idea, I've arranged for us to meet Jacob at the Hallidays' house, here is their postcode, see you there at 11.30am.*

She's fast working. Oh I do like a 'can do' social worker.

I dash round the park with the dogs, Dotty and Douglas. My two little Jackawawas won't get their full walk this morning, but one shortened day isn't going to hurt them, and anyway, they only have little legs. That's my excuse and I'm sticking to it. I get the wind through my hair and the colour in my cheeks, albeit briefly, and the all important opportunity to pick up a bit more poo.

Back from the walk, I rush upstairs to see Casey. She is going into school a bit later today because she is in Year 11 and is on study leave with an exam this afternoon. I tell her how gorgeous she looks. She laughs at me.

'Yeah right, Louise.'

I sing back to her, 'Yeah right, my darling, you're stunning.' I know she pretends to not accept my compliments but I also know that they mean a lot. Her self-esteem has rocketed since I took her to the hairdresser and bought her some trendy new clothes.

I am long enough in the tooth to know never to rely on a teenager to look after the dogs or lock the back door, so I run round putting the dogs into their cage with lots of cushions and turn off the bedroom lights that have been left on before locking up. I grab my bag, throw in my phone and head out of the front door to the car, leaving Casey to it. 'Good luck this afternoon – you've got this one.'

I key the postcode into the sat-nav and can see that I am going to get to the Hallidays' address with only minutes to spare – and I need petrol. To stop myself becoming stressed I listen to Classic FM. Once I have the petrol and a packet of mints I turn on Radio 1 and sing all the way to the Hallidays' house. I see which house it is because I recognise Mary's old dark green VW car, so recently parked outside my home, now pulled onto the drive. There is no room for me on the drive so I find a space on the road. I walk up to the front door. It's a pricey new build and its neatness reminds me of the houses I saw in Australia, houses purpose-designed for modern living and a world apart from my sprawling Victorian property, not quite living up to its former glory.

Something about this place makes me think of a hotel or a holiday home rather than a regular house – everything is very ordered. There's not enough 'stuff'; no detritus of domestic life.

I ring the doorbell and notice that it's not a 'normal' doorbell: it's one of those I have seen on TV with CCTV and a connection to your mobile. I suspect that they are people who also control the heating and fridge content from an app. Evidently we inhabit very different worlds.

The door opens and I am face to face with Mrs Halliday. She is wearing a stripy, Breton-style t-shirt underneath a mauve fleece with what appear to be excessively ironed jeans and white, unblemished trainers. Her hair is blond and cut into what I call a 'headteacher's bob'. (When I used to visit schools in my old job I thought this particular cut came as standard.) She wears a sensible amount of daywear make-up, managing that 'effortlessly natural' look that ironically requires a great deal of effort. I admire this ability in other women because I can't achieve it myself. If the mood takes me I can end up looking like a cross between old Hollywood glam and Widow Twankey. Mrs Halliday, on paper and now here in the flesh, looks like the very sort of woman you would want to look after children – but I have heard enough from Mary to realise that her looks will be deceiving.

I step into their very perfect house. I am so impressed how people with children manage to live like this. I see a wicker basket in the corner of the open plan living space that looks like it may have a few play-things for Jacob, or any other visiting child. Mary steps out from the kitchen area drinking a cup of coffee. Behind her is the kitchen island which has hardly anything on it. I'm amazed and impressed once more. In my house any horizontal surface soon becomes storage for the children's or Lloyd's stuff. I've forgotten what some of the worktops look like. I smile at Mary.

'Hello Louise, good to see you. And great that you have now met Sue.'

Mary is far more welcoming and friendly than our host. I'm not sure that I am going to be able to easily manage 'Sue' – not with that unfriendly haircut and these immaculate surroundings. I also can't help but wonder where Jacob is.

Sue eventually smiles and asks if I would like a coffee.

'Yes, lovely thank you. You have a beautiful home.'

She accepts the compliment with a small inclination of her head. I look past Mary – who watches me with a smile – through to the bi-folding doors into the garden. Even as a child I was always more interested in exploring people's gardens than their houses. This garden looks like the house, very neat and tidy. The shrubs are in lines and hairdresser skills have been applied in the pruning and shaping of the lollipop buxus plants. There is hardly a flower in sight though – which is a good indication of "easy maintenance". I try hard not to be judgemental and love shrubs – but looking round the house and garden I see a whole lifestyle constructed around a sort of stylish ease. I am reminded again of the holiday home feel – perhaps they enjoy going away.

While Sue busies herself with a sleek coffee machine I turn back to the interior of the house and notice a few items that reflect an interest in travel. An African mask is placed neatly on the cream wall. I smile and think about the hundreds of masks and heads from various places in Africa that are dotted around my own house in chaotic technicolour. A Moroccan tagine pot sits unused on its own shelf in the kitchen. I suspect that they like – or once liked – their holidays. Holidays, I have to say, just don't happen like they used to once you are a foster carer. I toy with the idea that perhaps they manage to foster short-term then have a break. Wow. What a fantastic idea. How lovely it would be. I just can't imagine pulling it off.

As Mary and Sue chat away I am still curious to know where Jacob is. I'm desperate to meet him. I am only half listening to their conversation when suddenly my eye is pulled to the open door of another room off the main hall. I see a figure lying on the floor. I guess it must be Jacob.

'Do you mind if I go and say hello?' I ask Sue, but it isn't really a question. Before she has a chance to say anything in reply I am off. It doesn't feel right standing around chatting about a child that I haven't yet met – who is only a few feet away from me. I am sure that Mary would agree – I know already that I am her kind of foster carer.

I walk slowly up to Jacob. He might be asleep and I certainly don't want to scare him. He's lying on a gym mat with blankets swathed around him.

His face is turned towards the big window above what looks to me like a G-Plan style long cabinet with the most perfect display of apples. How they manage to live in a space that resembles a show home is beyond me.

'Hello Jacob,' I whisper gently.

Not a thing.

I carefully walk round his body to crouch down and say 'Hello Jacob' again. This time I put two fingers on his arm and gently stroke across his jumper saying the words, so that he can sense me if not hear and see me. His eyes are closed – as I am soon to learn they are closed most of the time – but he is not sleeping.

I'm just about to greet him again when I see a few creases appear around his eyes and mouth. He's smiling!

I'm totally sentimental and utterly smitten when it comes to children. I famously never cry – unless it's about a child. I almost feel as though I want to cry now. My heart leaps and that is it: I'm hooked. I have fallen in love with this amazing boy and his little smile tells me that he and I are going to embark on the journey of a lifetime.

I sit down on the floor next to him and look out of the window in the direction that his face was turned when I first came in. I wonder what he was looking at. I get right down to his level and try to position myself at the same angle. There isn't much to look at. All I can really see in my frame of vision are the tops of a few shrubs, the top of the garage roof and the sky. I wonder if Jacob notices the changes in the colours and movements of the clouds. I go for walks up on the hills most evenings just to see the clouds. I chat away to Jacob, telling him about the shapes I can see in the sky. There is a rabbit and a sort of egg cup shape and one that could be the top of a tree. I shift position so that I am half lying on the floor with him, half trying to read his reactions and take him in.

I am struck by the ease with which Jacob smiles. His smile looks totally natural: joyful. I bet he hasn't spent any time – like other children – gazing at themselves in a mirror learning what expressions they can make, seeing themselves as others might. I wonder if he has ever actually seen himself. There is something so charmingly innocent about his face that I feel that giving him a mirror might change that. I also know that giving him a mirror might seriously transform his world, enabling him to feel connected to it in new ways.

I love the unusual. I love it when life offers me difference. I love the children that others don't 'get'. Jacob is all of these things. We are going to get along just fine.

I move my head to see Mary in the door frame. She has an expression of delight on her face, and we exchange a knowing nod. This is in marked contrast to the reaction of Mrs Halliday – Sue – who in fact looks rather horrified that I am lying on her floor next to Jacob. Perhaps she is worried that she hasn't vacuumed the carpet in at least the last hour or so. It's cleaner than many of the surfaces in my own house, but by the look of her face it's as if I'm rolling around in mud. But I'm enjoying myself, and bonding with this dear little boy.

I know already that this is going to be the most unconventional placement in my fostering career so far – and actually that gives me a strange feeling of excitement. My stomach is churning and jumping with a healthy anxiety about what lies ahead, but mostly with a desire to get going.

Mary enters the room and kneels down next to Jacob, on the other side from me. She smiles and greets him with a 'Hello there, young man.' I notice that the cut-glass consonants and rounded vowels – that can sound a little harsh and intimidating sometimes – soften to a gentler sound. Sue opens the blinds a little wider by adjusting something on her mobile. I am fascinated by all the gadgets in this household and wonder what would happen if they lost their phones.

I lift up a soft toy that I have pulled from my bag: a little furry rabbit. I hold it very close to his hand, I want to see if he can open his hand to take it from me. I don't know yet what motor skills control he has. His eyes are still half-closed, but he sees it and knocks it with his hand. There is a slightly mischievous smile on his face. He is playing with me, and it seems as if he is watching to see how I will react. I love that!

Mary is carefully watching our interaction the whole time and seems to be enjoying it. I look at her and her eyes light up – it as though we have both just discovered gold in these hills. I can tell that this young fellow is going to make me work and I can't wait. I reach down to put the rabbit near his hand, along with a fabric book that I have brought with me, carefully selected for the crunchy sounds it makes. It is a story about a sheep that was Jackson's when he was a baby. He was fascinated by it and played with it beyond the toddler stage, until he was about four. He kept it on his bed along with his teddies – so I know that it has tried and tested appeal. I move my face past his face. He opens his mouth to respond and it could have been a beautiful moment. Instead I am nearly knocked out by the stench of his breath when he opens his mouth. His teeth are thick with plaque, and his tongue has a layer of white across it. I wonder if Sue or her husband have bothered cleaning his teeth; it doesn't look much like it.

I have a list of signs of physical neglect that many children who come into care display: poor eyesight, wax in their ears resulting in poor hearing, dehydration (manifested in wee that is like treacle), the start of tooth decay or worse: entirely rotten teeth, and weight or height issues due to poor diet and lack of exercise. While I am momentarily taken aback by Jacob's breath, I know that I have smelt worse. I once looked after a little girl who, when she opened her mouth, released the pungent reek of an open grave. She had problems with her digestion and stomach that had been previously left unnoticed.

Mary, with her own years of experience beyond mine, has clocked my face.

'Is it bad?' she mouths.

I don't know if Jacob can hear me – or understand if he does – but I am not prepared to make him feel bad because of my carelessness in responding. I turn my face towards her and manage to communicate a 'yes' with my eyes. There is something deep inside me that just wants to gather Jacob up to take him home straight away, but I know that I can't do this. I have to wait to go through all the proper channels. But blimey am I having a zillion ideas of how to get him going with his milestones when he does move in with us.

'Does Jacob like music?' I ask, turning towards Sue who is still fiddling with something on her mobile.

She shrugs her shoulders.

'What about programmes or films to watch? What are his favourites?

'The cartoon channel. That's mostly what he likes.'

I wonder if that is selected just to occupy him rather than because he has indicated a preference. For some reason Pingu pops into my head – the children's claymation animation series about a cheeky penguin who slides around in the snow and ice of the South Pole getting into various comical scrapes. My children loved it. Part of the appeal, I think, is that there is no actual dialogue, just noises that sound like words. When my sons were young I asked a male colleague, Matt, and his husband if they could babysit for me for a few hours. When they arrived the boys were avidly watching a Pingu DVD. When I got back all four of them had watched the entire series.

Matt, who is American and therefore hadn't been exposed to the same catalogue of children's programmes growing up, was in his element. 'I have never seen this before but it's amazing. I have had the best time. This Pingu dude has made me feel so chilled'.

I wonder if that Pingu dude might do the same for Jacob. 'What about animals?' I ask Sue. 'Does Jacob like animals?

She looks slightly puzzled.

'Do you have any pets?' I follow up, only realising as the words are out of my mouth what a ridiculous question that is – cat or dog hair has no place in this world.

'No, no pets,' she confirms. Of course not. I make the rather harsh judgement that not only are pets messy, responsibility for animals would also mess up the Hallidays' travel plans. Did I mention that I try to avoid being judgmental? Sometimes I fail at that.

I turn my attention back to Jacob. The pull towards him is huge. He is quite magnetic. This young man is drawing me into his world, I think. He seems as if he wants to have some fun and I am most certainly up for that. If what I have read on his file about him is true – that he has been more or less ignored for five years and left to entertain himself for much of the time – then this boy has a lot of lost time to make up for. There are going to be some long days ahead. After an hour or so, I fear I might be outstaying my welcome.

I suppose, much as I don't want to part from Jacob, I must leave and get on with the day. I kneel down next to Jacob to say goodbye to him directly and notice his warm little pencil-drawing of a smile appear as I fall into his line of vision. I see that Mary notices it too.

'I'll see you very soon, Jacob. I've loved meeting you today.' My words are gentle on the air; I don't want to alarm or upset him. I notice that I am subconsciously smoothing his arm that is closest to me, encased in a soft sweatshirt. I like to think that I'm not a frequent crier by nature and hardly ever leak tears. But all of a sudden I'm overwhelmed by the wave of powerful emotions I am experiencing and reach for a tissue.

Jacob's eyes are still half closed but the smile remains. He seems to be sniffing. I am momentarily concerned. He hasn't seemed as though he has a cold. Then it strikes me: he is smelling my perfume and learning who I am.

'Thank you,' I say, and brush imaginary flecks from my shirt as I stand up to try and draw attention from the dabs I am also having to make at my eyes.

Mary's phone rings and she draws away back into the hall, dealing with some other situation that can't wait – as is the life of a social worker.

I wave goodbye and mouth a thank you to her. Sue sees me to the door. She gives a supportive smile. She too has evidently tuned into the emotional charge of the moment. The rigid features fall away for a second or two and she seems nicer than when I first arrived. I wonder if my snap judgements of her have been too harsh, then she suddenly reverts back to a model of efficiency, ushering me out so that I almost trip out of the front door. 'Naaaa,' I say in my head. I am not a fan of anyone involved with working with vulnerable children unless they do it for the right reasons and put the children first. I don't believe she does that.

Back at my car I dump my bag on the passenger's seat. I am just about to turn on the engine when my text message alert beeps. I look at the phone and see *Mary Social Worker* flash on my screen. She has sent me a text asking if she can buy me a coffee. *Can meet in ten minutes at the cafe at the big Sainsbury's on the way out of town?* How she has managed to do that while simultaneously speaking on the phone I have no idea, but I'm not one to turn down a free lunch or coffee. Though I am well aware that there is no such thing.

I drive off, park at the supermarket and have just made my way from the cafe toilets (I didn't dare ask Sue to use hers) to find a table when Mary walks past me, peering in that way people have when they are scanning the room. I call to her.

She beams back at me. 'Where do you want to sit?' I head towards a free seat by the window, always my preferred choice and one I inherited from my adoptive mum. She refused to sit anywhere but by a window and it had to be in a position where she was able to see the exits and fire exits. I prefer to people-watch, so her habit suited me and I have continued it.

My latte arrives and with it a tea cake that I haven't asked for but which looks delicious. I do like Mary: she's a little bit rebellious in tiny ways and these sorts of people always appeal to me.

'So, now that we can talk a little more freely, what do you think?' she asks.

'I adore him. I want to bring him home with me now.'

'Good. I thought so.'

I don't know if she is just buttering me up but she adds, 'He really connected with you, didn't he? I saw that.'

I don't really know what to say. I have never looked after a child with this level of disability before, and though I think I felt a connection with Jacob, perhaps I have just wished for it and made myself think it. I am pleased that she has acknowledged it, buttering me up or not.

'Delay – it's just delay isn't it? Global delay?' I say, emphasising as I repeat. 'That means he can still meet some milestones?'

She looks directly at me. 'What you need to know is that Jacob is my last case before I retire. I am absolutely determined that this child gets everything he needs. I know the system and I know how to get it – so don't worry about that side of things. From you he just needs to be noticed and loved.'

We make a pact over our shared tea cake ('Oh, go on then, just a bite, I shouldn't really') that between us we will do the very best we can for Jacob.

As we are getting up to leave, Mary says with a wry smile, 'And that may just mean that I have to bend a few rules along the way.'

Chapter Three

A slight change of plan to my day. Dara, my supervising social worker that I live in fear of losing because she is a locum and therefore temporary, calls to ask if she can pop round a bit early, before Jacob arrives.

I am never worried about Dara visiting unexpectedly. Having worked in tandem with her previously, I know I have nothing to 'fear' from her. I should qualify that statement: if another social worker had called to say that they wanted to 'pop by' I might have been slightly alarmed. It's a little bit like when I am driving and catch sight of a police car in my rear view mirror: I suddenly start feeling and behaving like a felon, or as though I am the innocent child at school who feels inexplicably guilty when the headteacher warns of bad behaviour in another year group. I don't know if it's to do with my own childhood trauma – or if everyone feels and behaves like this. I need to know precisely why anyone official is calling me or wanting to see me. I hate being left in a place of not knowing. I had an accountant when I was younger who would leave the same message on my answer machine, 'Hello Louise, Anthony Doo Da here, can you call me back as soon as you can please?' That message, left in his authoritative cadences, would send me into a spin every single time. I would think I was going to jail for tax avoidance. When I did call back, fingers quaking, it was never anything to worry about.

Dara is soon at the door. The sun is shining behind her and she seems to bring it through the door with her.

'You are going to have to cut that wisteria back soon,' she smiles. She is carrying a large bag which she struggles past me with, its bulk taking up the hallway. I am intrigued: what appears to be a feather boa trails purple feathers from the top of the bag.

'Now, Louise. I know how creative you are and I just wonder if you can find a use for all these – how do you call it? Bits and bobs. Well, perhaps not you, so much, as Jacob.'

She begins pulling out scarves and streamers and feathers and lord knows what else, like a magician. I am captivated by the colour and promise that has already filled my house. I hope that Jacob will be too. He isn't even here yet and already we all love him. Not only that, but Dara hasn't even met him yet. Though that state of affairs won't last much longer: Mary is bringing him here at midday today.

'That's very thoughtful of you, Dara. You have clearly been doing your homework.'

'This is nothing, just things I found at home. But you

are right, I have been doing some homework, and I am putting together a little list of things that might be fun for him to play with. There are plenty of good websites with specialist toys.'

'All good, Dara, but I still haven't even decided what bed arrangement is best for him yet.'

Dara registers the wobble in my voice that reflects the internal wobble I'm having. I swing between 'I've got this' and 'who do I think I am?' I'm so worried about letting Jacob down that I am beginning to wonder if this is the right move for him. The boy has been through so much already and, as with so many children with disabilities, he is never going to be most foster carers' first choice. I just hope I'm good enough. Yesterday and last night I thought I was. Today I am not so sure.

'What's the worst that could happen?' she shrugs, conversation over. 'Now, are we having a cup of coffee?' she asks next.

'I might hurt him – inadvertently. Or make him feel unloved somehow.' I know her first question was rhetorical, but voicing my fears helps.

Dara knows me well enough to spot when I'm worried.

'Louise, Louise. I have watched you care for all these children. You can only do your best, and you always do better than that.'

'I don't think you can do *better* than your best,' I begin to explain, but then realise that this isn't a grammatical

107

misunderstanding.

'And even the weather...' I don't know how to explain that I feel somehow responsible that the beautiful blue skies from earlier have been replaced by the very familiar English grey – and worried that it means Jacob will get wet and cold.

As if she can read my mind, Dara looks directly at me to say, 'He's more robust than we know, you know.'

I hear her, but there is a part of me that just wants to be able to nurture and protect him and make everything perfect.

She pulls a feather boa from the bag with a flourish and begins waving it in the air while taking some rhythmic steps forward like she is performing in some bizarre (clothed) burlesque show.

I laugh and grab another boa, throw it round my neck and do my best impersonation of Liza Minnelli in *Cabaret*.

Dara laughs too. 'And zat, my friend, is why Jacob needs to come *here*: he needs to have some fun and this is where he will get it!' She sounds more Polish when she is being emphatic.

I know I am good for that, at least. I look at the scarves and handkerchiefs and all their colours and decide that Jacob *will* be fine. I may not be perfect, the house may not be perfect, but it is a warm and caring home.

In a fairer world he would be at school running around and having fun at his age, but he is still stuck at the crawling stage. I need to think of him and his progress in terms of milestones rather than in age related terms. My job is to bring him on, not worry that he isn't where he 'should be'.

'Am I putting this coffee machine on myself, Louise?' Dara interrupts my thoughts, but the magic spell she has cast with her colourful gift has done its work.

My phone pings as we drink our coffee. It's Lloyd, away once more overnight, but remembering what is happening back here: *Hope day one goes well and I look forward to meeting Jacob tomorrow.*

That is sweet of him and nicely timed – our new foster child will be here very soon. Lloyd is not the only one looking forward to meeting Jacob. Lily is already enchanted with the idea of him and, unbeknownst to me, stayed up last night long after she should have been asleep, making paper bunting with stars and moons and the letters of his name. She presented her handiwork at breakfast before she left for school this morning.

Jackson and Vincent, by contrast, have done nothing – other than shrug their shoulders in acceptance of Jacob's arrival. It seems to wash over them. I'm not sure if it's the basic difference between the way males and females are programmed to respond at this age or not, but the girls have always been the ones to organise cards, presents and anything thoughtful. But maybe that is my influence too. Back in the days of having boyfriends I know that I always ended up sorting out their Christmas cards, remembering

birthdays for their family, buying and wrapping presents –
all of it, in fact. I stopped before I met Lloyd. I decided that
it was, in fact, not in the best interests of my future partner.
I was not helping them advance their skills – and I certainly
wasn't doing anything for feminism. These days, if the men
haven't got their acts together for gifts and cards, they can
deal with it.

I am draping Dara's gorgeous bunting and streamers
around the kitchen when the doorbell rings.

I look across at Dara. She makes a funny face, scrunches
up her hands into fists and performs a little dance – and that,
in a nutshell, is why I like Dara: for her visceral, emotional
reaction to any situation rather than the textbook one. I
rush to the door.

Mary is standing behind the tiniest of wheelchairs. In it
sits Jacob, safely strapped in and, somewhat unexpectedly,
sporting a baseball cap.

'Wow, love the hat!'

Mary laughs. 'It was in my car, left over from an outing
to the new adventure park. *Someone* discovered it!'

I have heard about the new park. Perhaps Jacob has
heard about it too – which is why he grabbed the hat. But
then I remember that he can't read. How would he know?
I wonder if he has seen it advertised on TV. Who knows?
Why am I overthinking everything?

In they come. Thankfully the hallway is wide, and today
I have made sure that it is clear of the shoes and bags and

coats and debris of the school day that somehow manage to clutter it regularly. I realise that a new regime may have to be introduced to prevent that happening so that we can readily accommodate his wheelchair.

I look at Mary and realise that I am terrified. 'Right. So – what happens now?' Uncharacteristically, I am at a loss. I am usually good at welcoming people into my home, but there is so much at stake today that I hardly know where to begin.

It is Jacob who saves the day. The same little pencil line of a smile I saw the other day appears, and my heart lifts. Then he raises his arms, ever so slightly.

Mary, who is much smaller than me, moves to lift him out. I interrupt, and summoning my Amazonian strength from years of swimming and gardening, I offer to take Jacob out of the wheelchair. He's undernourished, but still much bigger than any baby or toddler I've carried.

'Over to you, Louise.'

I lean in to him. 'Master Jacob, may I escort you to your play area?'

Though his eyes remain in that half-closed position there is a tiny increase in that little flat smile, and I can't help but smile in return.

As I go to lift him I notice that he smells of baby milk and the sweetness of Farley's rusks. We'll soon have you eating something a little more grown up than that, I think. I wonder how long it will be before he's tucking into a coconut curry or a spicy fajita. Or even a Big Mac. We are a family – or group of blended people, if you prefer (an equally valid description to me) – who love food and everything about it. Culinary exploration of food traditions from around the world are high on our list of priorities, and a milky rusk isn't going to sit comfortably in that mix. He really has been 'babied' and I reason that this must influence some of the global delay he exhibits.

He is also not quite as light as I imagined he would be. I ease him out of the chair and carry him into the sitting room where I have made a play mat area for him. I have dug out the boys' baby activity arch for Jacob to play with and surrounded it with lots of different items from around the house. There is a wooden spoon and spatula from the kitchen, as well as water bottles and Tupperware filled with rice or pebbles to make sounds. There are some wine corks in a basket for counting and building with and for making shapes. There are little fluffy toys, a rainmaker toy and a tambourine. The whole area is draped with Dana's magical finds. I almost want to climb in there and play myself.

I place Jacob carefully down on the mat and take time to introduce him to the different toys.

'Shall I make the coffee?' Mary offers. She is as direct as Dara is, but I know that she is being helpful. We have a proper machine that grinds the beans and makes wonderful coffee. It has developed something of a reputation in local circles. All the social workers who have been here love it and comment on how nice it is to have proper coffee.

I can't be bothered to explain how to use it to Mary – it is quicker to do it myself, so I leave them all in the sitting room while I make coffee for everyone and a drink for Jacob. I have been told that he has baby bottles full of milk, but even though I have placed him underneath a 'baby' activity arch I am not keen on him being treated like a baby in other ways. Given his age it doesn't seem appropriate and I think it may just be laziness on the part of the Hallidays. I half fill a sports bottle with cold milk. It has a straw-like tube inside it that will be a step up from the teat of a baby bottle. I wonder if perhaps the milk has been filling him up and that's why he isn't yet eating solids. It may be that no one has so far bothered to introduce them. We shall see.

I have another momentary crisis of confidence before I pick up the tray. I really don't know what I'm doing here. I have some intuitive thoughts but they aren't really backed up in any systematic, researched way. All I know is that somehow, in the short time I have known him, Jacob has activated a wealth of maternal, almost primal, instincts in me. *Trust them, Louise*, I tell myself. And I echo Dana's earlier reassurance. *What's the worst that could happen*? I want to do the right things for him, but how do I know what those right things are?

I take a deep breath and march through to the play area carrying all the drinks and plenty of biscuits. I have bought pink wafers because Jacob might enjoy sucking on them even if he doesn't want to eat them. Who knows? I'm guessing, firing arrows into the dark. This will all be a case of hit and miss but I will keep going.

So sucking on the biscuits isn't such a good idea of mine, I quickly discover. The pink sludge slides everywhere. Within seconds it is on his chin and most of his face, and the mat – well, oh my, I won't do that again. But it does give me the chance to see two things: firstly that Jacob is keen on food and sweet things just as most children are. I knew from my visit to the Hallidays that his fingers can hold items if I put them in his hand, and now I know that he has enough coordination to move them towards his face. We have made progress, even if it doesn't look that way right at this moment.

I grab a packet of wipes that I keep under the kitchen sink. These days I occasionally use them for cleaning the furniture, no longer sticky faces and hands. I will need to put them back on the shopping list.

Ever practical, Mary says, 'I'll take Jacob's bags up to his room.'

'Good idea. I'll give you a hand.'

As I go to move, Dara is straight down onto the floor next to Jacob, chatting and holding up objects. Jacob has a way with women, that's for sure. He's got three of us running around after him today.

Mary helps me to unpack Jacob's clothes. They are

a miserable collection of hand me downs from friends of the foster carers, a sight I see too often and one that frequently makes me cross. The young people who go into care deserve new items just as well as the next child, and Jacob is no exception. I think that new things are an act of kindness that suggest the worth of a child. Our allowances, small though they are, allow for the odd new shiny item of clothing that will give so much pleasure to a child. I can't stand watching looked-after-children in clothes that are out of date and ill-fitting. It adds to the narrative that they are not valued. Too long, too tight, too loose, too old – it's all too bad.

I would ask anyone who looks after vulnerable children if they would be happy to put themselves into such an ad hoc selection of clothes then go out to work and be marvellous all day. It wouldn't happen. Self-esteem and dignity don't simply 'happen' by themselves. They require nurture and support. I can remember my own experience of weird ensembles that my adopted mother put me in. I can vividly recall dreading a non-uniform day when I had absolutely nothing cool or new to wear. We live in different times from our parents and are the victims of our own success in the global economy. It became the norm to have expensive trainers in the 1980s, so why in the 2000s would we think it's okay to put our already traumatised children into rank clothes? I say some of this to Mary.

'Nappies.'

I don't quite register this as other thoughts rush through my head about equity and rights for children.

Mary says, slightly louder this time, 'Nappies.'

I look at the half pack that Sue Halliday has packed and make a mental note to put them on the shopping list. It's growing, this list.

As we survey the paltry possessions that amount to the record of Jacob's existence so far, Mary tells me that she has made an appointment 'out of county' for Jacob to see another paediatrician.

'So this sounds like an interesting adventure,' I laugh.

She smiles. 'Oh yes.' She is refolding every item of clothing and doing it quite beautifully. I feel a little inadequate as I admire her skilful folding.

'Where did you learn to do that?' I ask.

'Convent school.' She shrugs nonchalantly.

I am slightly surprised and I'm not sure why. I'm still learning the middle-class adult life skill of not being nosey and I haven't completed my study. 'Did you enjoy it?' I press.

Mary smiles enigmatically and continues to shake out and fold clothes. 'No, actually. I hated it. I was a boarder, I hardly ever saw my family and because I was a scholarship child I was treated far more harshly than the fee paying girls.'

I am surprised. I hadn't expected her to open up like that. 'But you sound so...' I stop myself before I say something that might be considered insulting. 'Wouldn't there have been ways to pay your fees? What did your father do?'

She looks away from me, fixating on something out of the window. 'He was a diplomat. But it was the fifties, and he was still engaged in machinations from the second world war. My father died, in what I suppose one might call mysterious circumstances. My mother was forced to return to her childhood home in Cornwall, to live with her parents. We were sent away to boarding school.'

She tells it all very matter of factly, but I can see the sadness that clouds her eyes. I am desperate to ask more questions – I mean, the mysterious circumstances of her father's death is a thing in its own right – but I check myself. A shared car journey to an out of county hospital may be a good opportunity to have that chat. I can't just leave it there though.

'That's harsh. Were you at least able to be with your siblings at boarding school?'

She sighs. 'It all seems such a long time ago now. I was with my older sister who largely ignored me most of the time. But I think I probably ended up as a social worker because I think boarding schools, especially religious ones like a convent, can be abusive places.'

Wowzah. Now I am absolutely desperate to keep talking, but my new, beautiful young man Jacob needs – and deserves – all my attention today.

As we are walking back down the stairs, Mary suddenly

stops short. 'Where are the little doggies?'

I laugh. 'They are with my neighbour. I didn't want to freak Jacob out. I'm still not sure about his feelings and reactions to animals.'

'To be fair, he was found in a dog basket on a farm,' Mary reminds me.

'Maybe,' I smile. 'But I'm talking about Douglas and Dotty here. They are quite full on. I know that they will want to sit on him and lick him.'

'Let them, I should. He may find it very amusing – and enjoy it as much as Douglas and Dotty will.'

'Okay, you win. I'll get the dogs back when we're all done here.'

I don't want to get rid of either Dara or Mary, but I wonder if they will actually ever go. Jacob has an electromagnetic attraction for caring women; we all just want to look after him. As I'm officially his foster carer now I shall have to encourage them to go at some point, but not just yet: I think Master Jacob is rather enjoying all the attention – and why not? He deserves to know that people think he's rather wonderful.

The clock hands edge towards 2pm. Finally my lovely social workers begin to make leaving noises. Of course, I know that they both have lots to do and I very much appreciate their support in welcoming Jacob into our home. Both have gone above and beyond the call of duty in this instance – but I suspect that is Jacob's influence rather than mine. He is a little charmer.

We make the necessary practical arrangements. Mary will drive here and then we can go in my car to the out of county doctor. Dara is a willing participant in our conspiracy and thinks it's a great idea to get a second opinion. None of us want anything but the very best for Jacob.

Those arrangements made and then departures done, I sit back down on the floor next to Jacob. I chat about this and that and ask what he would like for dinner. I pick up his hand as I talk. I tell him about the dogs, and how naughty Dotty can be. 'She is a funny old thing. I think you are going to like her.'

I notice a squeeze on my hand. I look at those eyes, half-covered by their lids as ever. 'Do you want to meet them?' There is no discernible nod, but I notice another little squeeze. He is communicating with me, for sure. I stand up and look for my phone. It always greatly amuses my family that I have a mobile phone. They call it my 'static' phone because it's the very last thing I think about and is the thing least likely to be found about my person or in the place where I am. I regularly remind those mockers that people used to manage just fine without them. The children call me a loser in response.

That reminds me. The other children will be home just after 3.15pm so I need to get their snacks ready before they raid the kitchen. Every week I load their food account up with money to buy lunch and snacks and an extra drink but they complain that there isn't anything to eat. After all Jamie Oliver's efforts to get pupils to eat better food in schools there seems to have been a return to cheap, mass catering. I chuckle to myself, remembering footage of dear Jamie and his school dinner ladies dishing up wholesome good food – while the children's mums were outside posting chicken nuggets through the fence. I would be with them, except that I would be one of those mothers posting carrot sticks and hummus through the fence to my darling starving children.

I finally locate my phone, tracking it down to the hallway; I must have left it there when Dara or Mary arrived. I text Jean, my kind neighbour over the road who loves the dogs almost as much as I do and is more than happy to have them to help me out on occasions like this. Within just a few minutes the doorbell goes and I can hear Dotty's high pitched yap outside. She too is communicating; this is the pitch she uses when she knows that there is a new child here.

'Here they come, I won't be long,' I tell Jacob, and dart to the door. Jean is standing there laughing.

'That was like being towed by huskies,' she laughs. 'They pulled me here at speed. I'm surprised you can't see the trail in the road behind me!'

'They know exactly what's going on,' I tell her. 'They're just keen to meet the new arrival.'

After closing the door I take their leads off and deposit

them in the usual place − wrapping them over the neck of the 'standing man' in the hall − a statue who holds out a tray that we put our keys on. No sooner than I have draped them the dogs are away, racing into the sitting room. By the time I arrive behind them they are already on top of Jacob. Oh, no − he can't get himself out of their way; I enter disaster mode again. It soon becomes clear that my panic is needless: Jacob's face is an absolute picture. He is all smiles and making a gurgling sound that I choose to interpret as laughter.

There is nothing to do but stand over this chaotic scene and watch the dogs jump all over him wagging their tails. Now Jacob is gurgling − laughing − his head off. This is the most beautiful sight to behold and I'm almost annoyed at myself for thinking way too much about risk. Mary was right; he's basically grown up around dogs and lived in a dog basket most of his life. What on earth was I worried about? I thought he would find the dogs traumatic but he seems so happy and familiar around them. It doesn't take long for the dogs to settle down and lay in tightly next to him.

It occurs to me that there is something of a smell in the air, and I wonder briefly whether Jean has let Dotty and Douglas out to roll around in unspeakables − then I remember that Jacob is in nappies. I lean in towards him once more and, with a smile ask, 'Jacob? Is there a little something we need to do?'

He gives me a deadpan expression in return. I am

almost certain he has understood. Oh, this boy is a little monkey. I love it!

I just about manage to get Jacob back on the mat, clean and happy with the dogs when the children start appearing at the door. Because I largely work from home I haven't given any of them a key. I have memories of a children's TV series called *The Latchkey Children* where the children got up to mischief whilst their parents were out at work (or wherever they were, we were never quite sure). My half-birth-siblings – who are younger than me – told me about how they were left alone while our birth mother was out. The oldest one would collect the youngest one from school and when they got home they would find a can opener and tin of beans on the side. They watched TV and waited for a long time every day for the adults to come home. There is a great sadness about this scene which I think continues to affect me.

Before moving here to work from home and foster children, I remember the days when I was teaching and lecturing and used to half kill myself rushing from work to nursery and school to collect the boys so that they didn't have to do after school clubs. Of course I had to rely on clubs and other people from time to time, but Vincent and Jackson always seemed happier when we went home.

Sometimes I recall those days with regret, lamenting that I didn't have more time with them – but what are modern working parents meant to do? Hardly anyone I know can afford the luxury of one partner not having to work enabling them to be at home, and what does 'being at home' mean anyway?' The child care system in this country has always seemed to me to be prohibitively expensive. I do remember explaining to a colleague who worked in human resources at my old university (where I taught in the art department) that it cost nearly my entire salary every month to put both my children in nursery while I worked. Because one was a baby and the other was a toddler they were both too young for me to receive the free childcare hours then offered by the government. My children went to a regular mainstream nursery: nothing fancy or progressive. My colleague in HR simply did not believe me when I told him. He only finally accepted it when I brought in the monthly invoice from the nursery.

'How on earth do you manage?' he asked, genuinely horrified by the costs.

'With great difficulty,' I returned. 'And I'm a well paid university lecturer. If I struggle to meet my bills how would a woman with lower pay cope?'

It was one of those occasions when the ridiculousness of the situation was plainly apparent to all parties – but there was nothing anyone could do about it. Things don't seem to have changed a great deal in the intervening years. If anything, perhaps it continues to get harder.

Thankfully, these days I am lucky enough to be able to be here – and it remains important to me. I leap up to let the children in. Each one has a different knock on the door. Jackson has a bailiff's knock, urgent and demanding: bang bang bang. Vincent has a persistent, fast knock that manages to suggest his time is very important. Lily has a polite little tap-tap-tap. It is so gentle that it has been known for me not to hear her, especially if I'm working on a painting and have some uptempo Jackson Browne playing very loudly. My studio is at the front of the house facing onto the street. Sometimes I have been working and singing away and I will look up to see the sad, dejected little face of Lily looking at me – like the abandoned orphan Annie. Happily, she soon recovers, and sometimes reminds me that if needs must she can do the big eyes and sad face to get my sympathy and attention whenever she wants it. It can be a hard one with foster children: in some cases they want the attention from the adult who is now looking after them back-dated to cover what they may have missed out on, but they also need to move on from that behaviour to avoid becoming a difficult friend for others in the future.

Once they are all in and huddled in the kitchen, I ask them to come and meet Jacob. They are well-used to meeting new foster children, but this time their reaction is different. Lily would ordinarily be first in sussing out a new arrival to determine whether she has a suitable new play mate or not, and she is superb with younger children. She loves being the provider of wise words gleaned from her undisputed role as the experienced foster child in the house – but today she seems reluctant, offering a half-hearted shrug. Vincent and Jackson are similarly reticent and engage in various delay tactics.

'Yeah, in a bit, Mum.'

'I might make a start on homework first.'

Voluntary homework concerns within a few minutes of arriving home are definitely not the norm. It occurs to me that they are scared, and I don't blame them. After all, I too have spent the hours until his arrival wondering if I am qualified for this. I sense that they don't know how to 'be' around him and his disabilities – it is outside their range of experience. I try to reassure them. In the last few days I have taken time to explain everything to them – or as much as I have been able to. I thought I had prepared them for him and persuaded them that we can meet his needs.

'Remember all the stuff we talked about?'

There are more shrugs. And now I experience another little crisis of confidence, as the whole thing starts to feel a bit awkward. I don't want Jacob to feel bad or unwelcome – especially not on his first day.

'Come on guys, he's looking forward to meeting you.' I don't know this, exactly, but he seems delighted to see new people. That doesn't work either. There is more foot-shifting and avoiding eye-contact. It goes on for a little while until I feel my own frustration build up and start to become a little cross with them. They are usually very dependable and right now they are letting me down. I have never seen them like this before. I throw my hands in the air and do a dramatic and slightly sardonic, 'Well, thank you *very* much!' and flounce from the kitchen angrily.

I return to see Jacob. I guess, much to my despair, that he has probably heard all of it. I don't really know what to do or say, or how to make it better.

'Would you like to watch some children's TV?' I ask, rather desperately.

He makes no response to indicate yes or no.

'Shall we try something and see?' I say, thinking that he has been lying on that mat now for a long time.

Just then, Vincent comes in and offers a rather gruff, 'Alright, Jacob?' but doesn't really look at him.

He marches over to the tech bit of the room where leads, wires and devices are kept. I think I might be about to get even crosser, when he turns to Jacob with a controller in his hand and says, 'Do you want to game with me?'

Don't be daft, Vincent, I think, before I suddenly notice that Jacob is lifting his hand to wave it at Vincent.

Jackson appears next at the door and says cheerfully, 'Hello there, Jacob. You alright, my friend?'

Jackson helps me to turn the mat round to face the TV. Vincent gets himself a floor cushion and sits down right next to where Jacob is lying. He grabs a couple more cushions and arranges them behind Jacob, so he is propped up a bit more. I can feel the energy and excitement beginning to pulse through Jacob. I am learning fast that this is going to be an unpredictable and crazy time.

I step back to watch the ease with which Vincent chats to him. Jackson also sits down on the floor with a pack of Cheesy Doritos. He offers the open bag to Jacob to try. To my utter amazement Jacob lifts his hand while Jackson is looking in the other direction trying to find another controller for him. He puts his little fingers in the bag and pulls out a perfect orange triangle, directing it straight into his mouth. He makes the most primitive 'mmmmmm' sound. I stand by the door and reevaluate. We are going to need to do this our way, the Allen way. Jacob needs to feel like a regular child and have access to all the normal stuff that children do. My children are the ones to help this happen. They can do it all so much more instinctively than I can.

Lily still hasn't appeared. A few minutes later I see why. She has evidently been busy changing out of her school uniform. She is now wearing her trendiest clothes: she has evidently dressed up for Jacob. I don't know if he is aware – he has, after all, never met Lily before, but I certainly appreciate it. It's never the wrong occasion for a child to put on an outfit to show a new friend in my book. I go back into the kitchen and tip three small packets of Doritos into a bowl, placing it low down near Jacob and the others. He is quickly one of the gang.

The house is in a bit of a state. I look round the kitchen and beyond into the hall at the semi chaos that Jacob's arrival has brought. There are a multitude of things to do. In spite of having few possessions of his own, Jacob's needs entail a lot of 'stuff' and things already seem to have found their way all over the place in the space of just a few hours.

'Aww well, it's a home,' I reason. Instead of clearing up I choose to go and hang out near the children to learn their magic.

'Pass the Doritos!'

Chapter Four

Mary has explained to me that because of the lack of men on the farm where Jacob has come from, he may be a bit wary of Lloyd. It may well be worth introducing them slowly to each other, and in a calm and gentle manner.

In our house I hope I can pull this off!

Before Lloyd returns from his business trip I show Jacob pictures of Lloyd and help him get used to the idea of a man about the house, in order to, hopefully, feel safe. I am mindful that he has come from a house of only women and I don't want him to be frightened. I also talk it through at length with Lloyd over the phone. It's tricky to have to come home to that. In the event, it goes without a hitch. I think it is helped by the fact that Jacob has already become accustomed to Jackson and Vincent.

Jacob struggles with the first consonant, as he does with my name. He is beginning to sound out a few words now, but the novelty is such that for a short time we all call Lloyd 'Oyd' – until Lily points out that it might not be helping with Jacob's speech development.

By Monday morning Jacob looks more than a little wistful as he watches his new buddies file out to school. I made sure that he was up and about at the same time as the others: I think he needs to be as much like them as he can be but I realise that in order to make that happen I will need to get going at least an hour earlier in the morning than I usually do. I had no idea how long everything takes. It has been so long since we have had someone with so little independence in the house. I am loath to say that it has been a long time since we have looked after babies. I am determined to shift mindsets and not consider Jacob in those terms. He is five years old.

Never mind that it happens 190 times a year on all the school days, for some reason the preparations for departure are never entirely smooth. After all the practice, you'd think we'd have it down to a fine art between us, but each morning the house is filled with the inevitable cries of 'Where are my trainers?' (Where you left them.) 'Who's seen my PE bag?' (All of us, we've tripped over it in the hall.) 'I can't find a pair of socks!' (Not true, there are plenty in your drawer; you just have your mind set on a particular pair that are currently in the wash.) 'Someone's moved my homework!' (No, it's still on the kitchen table; it never made it to your bag in spite of repeated reminders last night.)

The children are reasonably uncomplaining as the litany of 'Where's this?' and 'Where's that?' goes largely ignored by me for once. I am preoccupied with trying to search for a suitable chair that will work at the table for Jacob. Last night we all had a picnic in the sitting room but we can't do that all the time and Jacob needs to sit up and be part of the family. I also have some art projects in mind for him that will require him to be at the table. Online searches have located a few but none of them are cheap and most are more than double his weekly allowance. This is something I will have to talk to Mary about. If this is going to work then Jacob needs equipment.

Only Lily is grumpy. 'Stop fussing over him and his chair and think about us for five minutes. He's fine.'

'If you had Jacob's needs, Lily, you'd want me to be sorting out equipment for you, too!'

'We all have needs!' she says and huffs off to school.

After the children have gone, Jean takes the dogs out for me – she's a good neighbour and I'm mindful that I shouldn't take advantage – but I'm not ready to take Jacob in his chair *and* the dogs yet, I need to build up to that. Jean gets it. She is a widow and a retired primary school teacher so she totally understands my work and is very supportive of anything that helps children. She has told me plenty of stories of days when she had to report her concerns about children in her classes to social workers.

Sometimes I think there are so many people connected to this sector who can still find it within them to be good people for no discernible reward. Jean refuses all gifts and offers of payment for looking after my dogs, and I have tried a number of creative methods. She says simply that she enjoys their company and the exercise is good for her. She is also honest. She would like to have dogs of her own, but she is more than happy to borrow mine because she doesn't want the responsibility of a pet when she holidays with her friends. To give you an idea about Jean, she really made me laugh one day when I was standing with her in her kitchen. Her husband had died the year before from cancer. Jean was furiously cursing her daughter-in-law who had put on Facebook that she thought Jean should get a dog. It had set off quite a number of comments from her friends and family: It would be good for you. Dogs are therapeutic and could help you heal. It would give you something else to focus on.

Jean's response to the Facebook feed, delivered while she was nearly purple in the face was, 'Why can't they understand that I don't want a bloody dog? I want to go out and have a good time because after nursing David for two years I want a break – not something else to keep me here because it needs looking after. Honestly, what's wrong with people? Just because I'm retired and widowed doesn't mean I'm a lost cause!'

After hearing her passionate outburst I developed a huge amount of respect for Jean – and remember never to tell anyone that they 'should' be doing anything. This morning I am just grateful that she is there for me. I shouldn't feel guilty. She wouldn't do it if she didn't want to.

I am thinking about this, and Jacob's chair, and where I can get nappies in the right size, and a million other things that have floated into my mind this morning when Mary drives up. I see her from the window. She parks up and gives me a cheerful wave, before walking up to the house. She has done so well to organise this appointment for him at short notice.

'Door's open,' I call, but Mary's so polite she doesn't enter. I suspect that she would only ever stand at the front door until I invited her in. I can imagine knowing Mary for ten years and still she would never assume it's okay to step into our house uninvited. She seems to be the very model of manners. I wonder how she got on with the statuary unannounced visits that social workers have to do. I may ask her when we're driving.

Jacob is on his mat surrounded by strange inventions that Lily and I made yesterday evening while the boys were gaming. The feather boas and scarves that Dara brought round have made their way onto a makeshift washing line that we fashioned from tying garden twine from the chair arm next to Jacob and pulling it to tie round the leg of a kitchen chair. It's a little bit Heath Robinson, but it looks quite jolly. We have tied and pegged Dara's bits along with ribbons and a dream catcher and some toys on string. A small plastic giraffe looks as though it is being half-strangled as it dangles there, but Lily has decided on an animal theme and who am I to interfere? To add to the fun Lily has plugged in a fan on mixed settings so that it goes from low to fast, blowing everything around it crazily in its wake, all to amuse Jacob. He loves it.

I make sure that the fan is switched off before lifting him up to carry to the car seat. I grab a couple of small scatter cushions to offer Jacob more support. It takes a good few minutes to get ourselves organised and into the car. I dash back with my bag of snacks and treats and 'just in case' items that I have standing ready.

'Right, that's the lot, I think.' I announce, shuffling into position, bag safely stowed.

'Good stuff,' says Mary.

'Now, we need a budget, Jacob needs a budget,' I begin. Somehow I know that I can go straight in with Mary. There is no need for small talk. She has a manner that invites you to cut to the chase. I explain all the items I think Jacob needs, almost without pausing for breath. I almost go on to say, 'I can pass everything on to whoever looks after Jacob next,' but catch myself in time to avoid saying it. I don't really know why. I suddenly feel sad at the thought of Jacob moving on and who might be next in line to look after him. These are most certainly conversations to have when he isn't able to hear. This poor child was ignored for years, and in the last few months has sat in rooms and at meetings while everyone has likely continued to ignore him and his thoughts. I will not do that EVER, I promise myself.

We begin our long drive. The children's favourite

station, Kiss FM is on. The stereo in the car is permanently tuned to this. Jacob is unmoved. Mary, who I know is wise beyond belief, raises her eyebrows, lifts up her bag and pulls out *Abbey Road* by the Beatles – so clearly her generation of music, and I suspect that Mary was a bit of a hippy.

'Jacob enjoyed *Yellow Submarine* when we were on our way back from the hospital last time,' she explains, as she inserts it into the player. 'My grandson claimed that CD but I spotted this on sale cheaply.'

I turn up the volume as CDs seem to play more quietly than the radio. 'Try track five. *Octopus's Garden*,' she suggests.

How does she do it? Jacob transforms straight away. He makes some jerky movements that I think are dancing. I put it on again – then realise that *Here Comes The Sun* is track seven.

'That was my favourite song for a while when I was a child,' I tell them both. Mary nods her approval and we sing and laugh along to the song. Jacob seems to be joining in with odd sounds here and there. I don't know what he can understand of the lyrics but he certainly seems to be enjoying the music. He hits the back of my seat with his foot when it has finished, I assume to make me put it on again. I love the fact that a band such as the Beatles and an album that is more than fifty years old can have this effect on a little boy, in the here and now today.

As we drive to the hospital I manage to take three wrong turnings in classic Louise style – which makes me a little stressed because I don't want to be late for Jacob's appointment.

We circle the car park a few times, round and round looking for a space. It seems a lost cause.

'The hospital should warn us that we need to allow extra hours just to find somewhere to park,' I moan.

I keep singing along to Beatles tracks to avoid plunging into a pit of frustration, when suddenly a car to my right pulls out in front of us creating a marvellous, good-sized space. I reverse in, and I'm still looking over my right shoulder to check the distance between mine and the next car when there is a little knock at my window. A lady stands there waving a car park ticket.

'It has a couple of hours left on it, so it's yours if you would like it.'

She hands over the little card which I immediately place on the front dash. These little things make me happy. Not only has it saved us a few pounds, it has also saved us precious minutes. We manoeuvre Jacob – who smells like he may need a nappy change already – into his wheelchair that Mary has expertly unfolded from the boot. That lady's kindness and the fortuitousness of finding a good spot near to the main building means that we have time to take Jacob to the toilet and change him so that he is fresh to see the doctor. Jacob is in a good mood – he seems to respond well to any change of scenery, which is perhaps unsurprising given what we know of his restricted experiences before this. We manage to make the lift an adventure and he is delighted by the 'surprise' of the lift doors opening up to a new place.

'How come he hasn't done all this before – the medicals, the hospitals?' I can't help but ask.

Mary keeps her eyes straight ahead and mutters, 'neglect' with a shake of her head, choosing not to say anymore on the subject.

Jacob is so stimulated by his new environment that his eyes seem more open than usual. We walk along the corridor to our appointment and I watch him try to take everything in as though his eyes are greedy for sights.

We pass through a set of double doors and wheel him into the reception area. A big teddy sits on the desk, welcoming children in and helping them feel more at ease. This space looks less clinical and hospital-ish and more like a giant play area. I park Jacob opposite me so he can see us. He is more alert than I have seen him so far. It is as if he knows that something important is going on; he manages to look both wary and excited at the same time – excited by the hospital and all its 'business'.

'How did he get on at the last hospital appointment?' I ask Mary. I haven't entirely got to the bottom of why we are doing all this out of county business.

'Oh, alright.'

I'm learning that Mary's 'alright' means anything but.

'Mary?'

'Let's just say that his last foster carer wasn't that supportive. He didn't have your energy to thrive on back then.'

It is a lovely thing for her to say, and I appreciate it. Energy is something I have in abundance, and always have had. There is more than enough for Jacob and me. All three of us if needs be.

A nurse comes out with a clipboard and calls Jacob's name. We all troop along behind to see the doctor. As we walk into his consulting room, I see a small, slim grey-haired man. On his lanyard is his name – Babak Jahandar.

He is wearing a pale blue shirt and tie, and doesn't introduce himself to Mary or me. Instead, he looks straight at Jacob, then beams at him as he gets down to his level. His eyes crinkle at the corners in a way that makes him seem kindly; even as he peers through glasses, assessing every reaction. 'So, Jacob shall we see what you can really do?'

We are surplus to requirements here – which is as it should be. It is Jacob's consultation after all. Dr Jahandar is a natural with children, and within a few minutes I am quite star-struck. He is a slight man, but there is something elegant about every movement he makes. He has a carefully-shaped beard that I actually like; not an unruly bush on his face but a sculpted thing that accentuates the cheekbones and gentle lines of his face. Stop it Louise! I caution myself. Concentrate!

Dr Jahandar invites us to help Jacob up onto the examination bed. We lay him down and I notice that he is scared, in spite of the doctor's comforting bedside manner. I am desperate to hold his hand and reassure him further, but the wonderful Dr Jahandar is already there and on it. He too has clocked Jacob's anxiety, and the doctor's voice is like honey as he introduces a narrative about something called the Amen bird.

'Have you heard about the mythical Amen bird, Jacob? He is a bird that never stops flying and he makes people's wishes come true. Do you like to hear stories, Jacob? This is a story that my mother told to me when I was a little boy back in Iran, a land far away from here.'

Jacob's half closed eyes open slightly more as the doctor begins to tell him the story. 'Amen is what we say in English, but it is really 'Morge Ameen' and in my culture this is the name of the angel bird who flies and flies and flies – soaring above the earth. It would be hard to fly continuously and never rest. You would think this bird would be very tired. And it is only a small bird, but it is brightly coloured like a jewel and has a long tail which must help with all that flying!'

Jacob's eyes open a little wider.

'This bird keeps flying because it has such an important job to do. If anybody needs something in their life and they say that wish out loud, it will come true if the Amen bird is passing overhead. Isn't that rather wonderful?'

I may be imagining it, but I feel that there is almost a nod from Jacob.

'The Amen bird is called the Amen bird because he says 'Amen' over and over again while he is flying on his never ending journey of accomplishing dreams. He says 'Amen' because that is the name of a star in the sky that shines down, and gives the Amen bird his power.'

All the while that he is speaking, the doctor is moving his hands gently over Jacob's head and face and neck. Jacob tilts his head a little further back on the examination bed – searching for a star in the sky perhaps, but he is forming the position that the doctor needs to conduct his examination.

'Do you know what the most marvellous thing about the Amen bird is, Jacob? Sometimes you don't even have to say that wish out loud. Sometimes the Amen bird just knows what you are thinking, so you don't have to speak the words. Isn't that fantastic? The Amen bird just keeps on flying and flying and saying 'Amen' when he makes those little dreams come true.'

His eyes flicker towards the window. I think he is looking for this magical bird. Mary and I are like little children, as captivated as Jacob is. Somehow we both find ourselves murmuring 'Amen, Amen' to Jacob.

The doctor indicates to us to hold Jacob up so that he can feel along his spine. He does this without breaking his narrative. So easy and assured is Dr Jahandar's manner that Jacob barely notices he is being 'examined'.

Now he moves to looking at his eyes and ears and mouth. 'Can you see an Amen bird out of the window, Jacob?' Again, Jacob's eyes move in the direction of the window. We all join him in looking out of the row of municipal square panes to the sky. Miraculously, some starlings happen to be flying across at exactly that moment.

'Do you think one of those is the Amen bird?'

The doctor's gentle fingers continue to move across Jacob's head, feeling through his hair to his skull and down through his body. It is like watching a sculptor carefully mould the clay. His actions are as mesmerising as his storytelling.

We sit Jacob up on the side of the bed while Dr Jahandar lifts his legs and arms, then inspects his fingers and toes. Nothing is left unexamined.

'I have to say, Doctor, Jacob never got an examination as thorough as this when I took him to see the other doctor,' Mary gushes. Mary gushing is quite an 'unMary' thing to do. She is as much under Dr Jahandar's spell as I am, as Jacob is. The doctor only smiles, perhaps modestly masking his professional pride.

Even if he has a view on the other doctor's practice – and how could you not? – he doesn't share it and doesn't falter in his study of Jacob. Mary and I continue to hold onto Jacob, keeping him upright on the side of the bed for the final checks.

The doctor moves to his desk and I expect him to begin

tapping his notes into the computer. Instead, he opens the desk drawer and pulls out a picture of the Amen bird. I am glad because I want that little bit of magic to carry on for a few moments more.

Next he reaches into his pocket – I wonder if he will pull out another instrument but no, it is his iPhone. He presses a few things then shows Jacob a YouTube animated film of a dancing Amen bird. It is a real bird, animated to move its mouth in time with the Persian drumming.

Jacob makes a kind of chuckle sound, then stretches his leg out in a small kicking motion again, just as when he kicked the back of my chair in the car to replay the song.

'Ok, so would you like to sit down? Dr Jahandar asks, retrieving his phone.

I pick up Jacob and sit him on my lap. I don't know how he's feeling, but I'm yearning for a cuddle. He has been so brave and well behaved, and I want to tell him that. I might swing by the 'Costalottee' down by the entrance and get him a smoothie and cake. He deserves a treat.

The doctor sounds as though he is about to launch into the feedback from his assessment. Before he can begin, Mary cuts in. She has armed herself with the scariest version of that Received Pronunciation accent, I notice. She takes him to one side as I am making Jacob comfortable, so that Jacob is out of earshot.

'The last doctor said we were just to give him milk and keep him warm because he would not amount to anything.

I'm hoping that you have a more heartening prognosis for us.'

Dr Jahandar's face does not give away what he thinks about the comments of a fellow practitioner. He nods his head to show that he has understood and invites Mary to take a seat.

'Jacob certainly hasn't had the easiest start in life. The extent of his neglect has caused a global developmental delay. As far as I can see and based on all I know, there is no reason that Jacob can't catch up at some stage and meet his milestones. It's continued neglect that has delayed them, and I can see from the combined determination of the two of you two that certainly isn't going to continue.'

He hands me a leaflet and directs me to a list of websites. 'You can find more information here. Essentially, it's important that you know that things like temper tantrums, if he were to begin to have those, we would perceive as a good sign of development. If you look at the kind of milestones that might be expected in an eighteen month to two-year-old, say, that's just about where we are. If he begins to be suspicious and less trusting of strangers, that would be another example of good development. Pointing and gesturing for what he wants. The more demanding the better! Any kind of imaginative, pretend play. It is those sort of things we are looking for.'

He stares into my face in a searching way that means I can't help but listen. 'Mrs Allen.'

I smile; no one really calls me that these days.

'You have a very important job. I'm sure I don't need to tell you this. You are Jacob's support and it's largely up to you to deliver a daily programme of joy, colour and excitement to Jacob to stimulate and energise him.'

He does make it sound rather as if I am about to begin a crazy adventure, perhaps with Bilbo Baggins and a giant dragon at the end of it.

'Jacob has been left on his own for so long,' he continues, 'that he is bored, plain and simple. I am sure he wants to catch-up and play with friends. There is no magic wand here. There is no magic tablet. My prescription cannot be written on one of these.' He holds up his prescription pad. 'He needs love and care and fun.'

'Oh, he will get plenty of that at Louise's house,' Mary pipes up. 'You need have no fear on that account, Dr Jahandar.' The icy cut-glass tones have been replaced by softer syllables now. But it's not just the way she says it, it is what she says. It is another rather lovely way to define someone – and after all my doubts about my capabilities in looking after Jacob, I know that this is true. She's right. Fun I can definitely do.

'Now, there are some formalities and practicalities,' Dr Jahandar says, his voice becoming more serious. 'I would like to arrange an MRI scan for Jacob so that I can examine his back more fully – I want to confirm that everything is in order there.'

Mary and I nod in unison.

'I will also make an appointment with audiology to get grommets put into his ears.'

More nodding.

'And I would suggest a sensory diet.'

'I haven't seen that particular cookbook, but I'm more than happy to give it a go. What is it?' I ask.

Now it is his turn to smile. 'A sensory diet has nothing to do with food,' he says, 'though it is very nourishing. No, a sensory diet is, I suppose, a kind of treatment that encourages development in children like Jacob, who have sensory processing issues.'

I am all ears.

'It comprises a programme of physical activities that Jacob can undertake at home, a kind of sensory routine. We can also set you up with an occupational therapist who can design the programme so that it is unique to Jacob and meets his needs exactly.'

He taps again into his computer to make this magic happen.

'I rather like the sound of that,' I say. 'It sounds fun – and is right up my alley, so to speak'.

'An excellent idea,' confirms Mary. 'I shall submit a bid to my manager to fund sensory play therapy as well.'

I am genuinely excited by all of this support, and by the thought that Jacob will get to experience the most wonderful things. I don't say it aloud, but I am also quietly thinking that no matter what we all decide to call it, to me this seems to be about experiencing all the things a 'normal' childhood would offer, condensed into a more intense space of time. I have something of a problem with the word 'normal', but perhaps that is partly because people would be very unlikely to apply the word to me. I also like to remind myself that normal is just a setting on my tumble dryer.

And, if I'm honest, I have to confess that I miss all the fun crazy things I used to make and do with the boys and Lily when they were younger – so this is also a self-serving endeavour.

'So,' concludes the good doctor, 'I have made an appointment for another examination in a few months' time and I am confident of observing positive things.'

Then he turns to Jacob as we are saying our goodbyes and strapping him back into his wheelchair. 'Jacob, you are a lucky boy!' and finally, as Dr Jahandar opens the door for us, he says to me, 'Mrs Allen, you are a lucky woman.'

I know exactly what he means.

As we traverse the maze of corridors back to the car park, Mary is talking through the corner of her mouth – as though she doesn't want anyone but me to hear. Or perhaps not even me. I catch the gist of it, though. She is talking about the other doctor and says something along the lines of, 'We'll show you, you old bag'.

It makes me chuckle; it seems especially potent when delivered in Mary's rich, plummy tones.

Once outside I notice that Jacob has his head turned upwards as though he is looking at something up in the sky. As we near the car I hear, distinctly, 'Amen', on the air – a word formed in the sweetest, quietest voice.

I do everything I can to hold back the tear that forms, but fail.

It spills from my eye onto my sleeve. Mary looks at me, puts her hand on my arm and says, 'It's okay.'

'Did you hear what Jacob just said?'

She wrinkles up her brow and shakes her head.

'He said "Amen", clear as a bell. I heard him,' I insist.

On cue Jacob looks up at the sky once more. This time it comes out loud and clear. 'Amen'.

'Amen to that,' says Mary, her mouth contorting a little.

When I look back at her, she too is dabbing away something from the corner of her eye.

Chapter Five

We drive out of the city and I have to navigate some unfamiliar roads. I am a little way away from my driving comfort zone and have to concentrate to make sure that we don't miss the turnings we need. It may be another hour or so before we are back on the familiar roads that lead to home. Once I am on the dual carriageway I risk asking Mary a little about her experience of boarding school. We don't know each other very well, so it could seem impertinent, but she opened up to me a little the other day.

I had a boyfriend who went to a very well-known boarding school. All the time we were together I had the notion that the experience had troubled him, and I share this with her now.

I tell Mary about his description of watching his parents drive away for the first time after leaving him alone with a trunk that was nearly the size of him outside the school front door. He was six at the time and ran after the car. In his fanciful retelling, even managing to hold onto the bumper – but they kept going nonetheless. The feeling of abandonment was profound. He remembered the cigarette smoke pouring out from their windows and their heads set straight ahead.

'He told me that he hated his time at boarding school but also couldn't ignore that he had made life-long friends there. He sometimes joked about how they were bonded by trauma,' I explain. 'I think that because us mere mortals associate private education with privilege we can somehow forget that these are just children, missing their home and family and trying to survive the best they can.'

Mary slowly nods her understanding. 'Oh yes: the damage that 'being left' can do,' she agrees. 'I know all about that.'

She glances over her shoulder into the back seat, and I follow her glance in the rear view mirror. Those regularly half-closed eyelids are fully shut: Jacob has dropped off with the rhythm of the engine, exhausted from all the stimulus he has had already today. Mary relaxes a little further back into the passenger's seat, settling in to tell her story. 'My father was killed. A few years after the war.'

I can't help but notice the way she puts it. 'You say "was killed"?'

'Who knows? There was a thick cloud of mystery over precisely what happened to him. Certainly some suspicion over how he died – which side was responsible. A suggestion that perhaps, like several other intelligence agents working for the government during the war, he had become a threat once the war was over – as a result of knowing too much.'

It sounds crazy, like the premise for a TV drama or a film, but I remember my birth mother telling me something equally bizarre about her own father – my grandfather – who had something to do with developing the technology used in recording devices during the war. He supposedly disappeared, then reappeared in Southampton living under a different name.

'After he was killed – or murdered – me, my mother and three siblings were swiftly removed to the grandparents in Cornwall. From there we were all sent to separate boarding schools. For my sins I won a place on a scholarship to the convent school where my older sister was already studying.'

'A scholarship? That's impressive.'

'Not that we particularly needed it; there was never any financial strain for our household. While he was alive, my father was paid handsomely for whatever it was he did. So, with this scholarship I was sent to a convent school where...' she pauses. I can hear from the timbre of her voice that it had been a difficult time for her. I check on Jacob again in the mirror. He remains firmly asleep. His head has flopped to one side and a trail of dribble dangles precariously from his chin. I hope he is dreaming of the Amen bird.

'Let's just say that I never got on with the nuns,' she continues, having composed herself. 'There was one nice one called Sister Fidelma. She was the art teacher, and was just very cool, different from the others. I never really understood what she was doing there: she must have been hiding from something.'

I laugh. 'Only the one nice nun?'

'Yes, only her. The others were terrible. Sister Angela didn't like me because I was a scholarship girl and she was a snob. And as for Sister Padraig – she was a bitch.' There is a venom to her words and I am slightly shocked by Mary's use of bad language, but I like her all the better for it. Sometimes only certain words will do the job.

'Why was she a bitch?' I ask.

Mary pauses again. I think she is deciding how much into her confidence I am to be taken.

She sighs. 'I will be retiring soon and I don't think you will be talking to my manager,' she says, giving me a sideways glance that I can't return as I am trying to keep my eyes on the road.

'I won't,' I promise her. I do another quick, instinctive check on Jacob in the back. He is still snoozing away happily and dribbling heavily, drool beginning to soak into his clothes. I can wash his t-shirt later, I figure. Then a thought flashes into my mind that perhaps I should have put on a bib on him. I quickly talk myself out of this mindset, reminding myself yet again that he is five years old. Until this morning's appointment I had not heard the previous doctor's terrible words – that he should be kept warm and given milk because he will never amount to anything. A bib is on a par with the baby milk bottle. Where I can I will endeavour to treat him as I would any five-year-old boy.

Mary collects herself again. 'Sister Padraig was nasty. She made me clean and polish thirteen pairs of shoes every night, every single night. The other girls didn't have to take their turn; it was my responsibility. I also had to administer thirteen doses of malt every morning to the girls – even though, as a scholarship girl, I wasn't entitled to a spoonful of malt myself.'

I laugh once more. 'Well that was a blessing, I should say. Malt is disgusting.'

Mary shares my laughter. 'But get this, then: I only had one pair of socks – that was my 'ration'. And I was only allowed one pair of knickers – a single pair! The other girls got five pairs. Imagine that? I washed them every night and rolled them in my towel to help dry them for the morning.'

'But that's awful,' I say.

'And when I started my period I was only given one sanitary towel.'

'Did scholarship girls bleed less?' I quip.

'No, they didn't,' she laughs.

'Blimey, Mary. It sounds pretty bloody horrible.' (I feel I can afford a 'bloody' after her comments about Sister Padraig.) 'Abusive, even.' I am wary of saying things like that because sometimes one person's abuse can be another person's 'normal' – until they realise.

'You say that. There was an incident with Sister Padraig

that took me years to fathom out. One evening, my dorm pal Emma was in bed and I was sitting on the end of her bed chatting to her, quite innocently, when Sister suddenly burst in. I jumped up and got into my bed.'

I wait. There is clearly more to come.

'She shouted at us, "You disgusting, filthy girls". I was only twelve, too young to have the foggiest idea what she meant – why we were disgusting. I only understood later that what she was suggesting was that we had been intimate with each other.'

I give another glance in the rear view mirror. Jacob has moved his head to the other side of his chest and is still asleep. I shake my head. So many people have had tough childhoods – and we come from all walks of life. There is this daft idea that children who are abused and neglected inevitably come from financially poor backgrounds – and that is simply not the case. I know it to be untrue, as does Mary.

I feel this huge wave of compassion towards Mary – who, after all that (and I know that what she has disclosed to me will only be the tip of the iceberg) had gone on to become a social worker. I suspect part of her motive for choosing this line of work was to help children who have experienced the trauma that she herself had. I have often wondered what drives any of us towards children's social care. Of course, there will always be an element of individuals in the field who are corrupt, devious or hugely ambitious – but on the whole, I think that most of us have silently, or sometimes not so silently, experienced the dark side of adults' behaviour when we were children. Adults who took opportunities to be nasty simply because they could.

By now we are driving on the country roads away from the motorway much closer towards home. I put the question to Mary. 'Why *did* you become a social worker?'

She sighs again. 'I know what it's like to be on the receiving end of abuse. But I'm afraid that I also know that I have had enough. My health isn't what it was and it's hard, hard work. Times have changed quite unrecognisably from when I first entered the profession. When you believe in the rights of the child, when you believe above all else that they should come first, you can come across quite a lot of opposition. So Jacob will be my last – and, oh boy, am I going to make sure he's okay!'

She delivers this announcement with such vehemence that I can't help but be inspired once again by her commitment to the cause. I don't doubt her for a second, and say my own silent 'amen' even though I'm not religious in the slightest. The doctor's story is still working its magic on me. Jacob is a lucky boy to have Mary fighting his corner.

I park up outside the front of the house. Mary and I get out of the car and I open the door by Jacob. He is still fast asleep. I unplug the car seat – which I want changed for a seat that is more suitable for his age and needs. 'Making do with cushions to prop up his head in the car is not good enough,' I complain.

Mary is compiling a list and she gets out her notebook to add this to it. We both know that her manager will say 'no' to most of it, but this remarkable woman is optimistic about getting everything Jacob needs and I already know that she is a formidable force.

'By the time our requests hit the finance person's desk, Jacob will be at secondary school,' I joke, nevertheless. 'And I, and whoever else looks after him, will be broke.'

'We'll see.'

There is a grim determination to her tone. I wouldn't like to be in opposition to her, I know that much. For perhaps the first time in my dealings with the financial side of social services, I'm quietly confident that she will be successful.

As I lift Jacob out he snuffles into my shoulder and it makes my heart melt. I carefully carry him through to the sitting room to lay him on the sofa and let him continue his sleep. I open the door to the dog's cage, which now has curtains, matching cushions and soft toys – thanks to Lily's interior design work.

Dotty and Doug come out gently, doing their 'yoga' stretches as they go. It is a sight which never fails to make me laugh. They both move towards Jacob wagging their tails.

'Away for the moment! Come on, leave him alone,' I command, in a slightly deranged whisper. I stop myself from making a wall of cushions to keep him on the sofa safe and still, as I might have done to the boys when they were babies. I let him spread out, knowing that I have to start believing in him and trusting his ability to grow and take care of himself. He will have a sense of self-preservation and protection, even in sleep. In fact, there's no reason to suppose that he doesn't have a heightened awareness of these things, given the environment in which he has spent his formative years.

Mary, as always, does not interfere. She stands back, rolling her shoulders to stretch, before returning to her upright, perfect posture. I wonder if she is perhaps in a little pain. It was quite a long journey. She just observes, communicating kindness and support as she does so.

'Would you like a cuppa?' I ask.

'Better not,' she says. 'Tempting an offer though it is. No, I must get back to the office and get cracking on the list of essentials for Jacob. I also have other children to sort, complete paperwork and write reports about.'

Her phone goes on cue, as if confirming her workload. She walks out of the room to take the call, with her hand in the air indicating an apology. I stand away from Jacob and watch his smooth, kind face in its gentle, resting pose. It's a privilege to see. And it's such an important time. I have always imagined that the children – birth, step or fostered – literally grow while they are sleeping. I picture tiny bones stretching and creaking as they increase their size.

If he is still sleeping when Mary has gone, I will draw him, I decide. I draw and paint portraits of all the children. I like to do a large portrait every two years or so to capture their changes. Jacob will have his portrait, too. I do it for all the children who are with me for any length of time because I want them all to know when they are older that they were worth the effort of a portrait. Photographs are fantastic, but a portrait is a very special thing. It is important that they have pictures of themselves but a painting is in a different league.

Mary comes back in and whispers, 'Sorry about that. One of my teenagers is in a bit of trouble.'

'What's happened?'

'Well, since you've asked, a girl is being sectioned after she was placed in a residential unit and tried to smash her way out of it.'

Wow, and I thought I was having a full-on day.

'Poor thing. Why is she in the residential unit in the first place?'

'Oh, because she was raped by the adult who was supposed to be looking after her.'

Everything she has just said makes me want to scream and cry and shake my fist at the world.

I repeat Mary's words back to her to make sure I have properly got the gist of this horror story. 'So, a girl who was raped is placed in a secure unit and when she tries to escape she is sectioned?'

'Yes,' says Mary. 'That's the long and the short of it. I'm going to see her now and try and get her out. She can stay with me if needs be. I have three spare bedrooms.

I turn back to look at Jacob, still peacefully asleep, and feel a little bit sick. I know that unpleasant things have doubtless happened to him, and now this poor girl who was raped. I feel as though the injustice of the whole thing will consume me. 'But these things have happened *to* her, and she is being punished? Isn't something a little bit round the wrong way?'

'Isn't it? The system is toxic when it punishes children for the evils that happen to them and that is why I am retiring. Retiring from the system, but not from caring. That I could never do.'

She pops the phone back into her handbag. 'I can't save them all, I know that. But I will do all I can from the wings to help the children I have worked with. I have stayed in touch with some of the carers and adopters, and make sure that I am available in an advisory capacity.'

She winks at me. 'All that experience can't go to waste, now, can it? I know a few little circumnavigating tricks – and I like to share. That's only fair.'

I do like Mary. I admire her indefatigable optimism. She really does care.

'Any system has inputs which go through certain processes to produce certain outputs. I find those *certain processes* inefficient at times, so I simply find ways to make them work better.' She shrugs her shoulders as if butter wouldn't melt in her mouth, but I somehow feel that she is promising me that Jacob, not to mention this other poor girl she is working with, will get what they need to survive.

And more than that, to thrive.

Chapter Six

After Mary leaves and I have made some preliminary sketches of a sleeping Jacob, I begin to worry that actually, Jacob has been sleeping for a long time. Far longer than usual. He has been here for a few days now, so maybe he is beginning to feel safe. I know from experience that when children from trauma come to stay and begin to settle and relax they sleep. It's no mystery, I am not the keeper of any magic. The formula is very simple: they get regular good food, warmth and security and the realisation that I care and will be doing everything I can to support them. Maybe that's all any of us need.

The fact that children are still going hungry in the 21st century is a disgrace. It is such a basic right, and we are a 'wealthy' nation. But greed prevents fairness. That a Premier League footballer has to embark on a one-man mission to ensure those who cannot afford food get fed properly, forcing those in power to make a U-turn on the government's meal voucher scheme, is magnificent – but also a sad indictment of a system that fails its most vulnerable. I reflect on the money that the foster carers and agency have received – for not looking after Jacob well or doing right by him so far, or not enough to change his life. I suspect there will be battles ahead to ensure that he gets what he needs. But we have Mary in our corner, and for that I am immensely grateful. I suspect she doesn't care for greed too much either.

I begin picking up cushions from the floor and plump them up to scatter on the other sofa. This a piece of furniture that is now resting on two bits of wood – after Jackson, who is now as big as his dad – threw himself on it yesterday in order to make Jacob laugh. It worked. We got that lovely gurgling giggle, but we also got four wooden legs giving way. Jackson and the middle of the sofa ended up on the floor. That's another few hundred quid down the pan. Jackson has always been a bit of a Tigger and over the years has cost us a fortune in broken furniture, garden pots, broken plates and taps. But I couldn't be cross: Jacob's mirth at Jackson's misfortune was priceless. Ah, well. I put the cushions meant for Jacob's sofa in a pile on a chair. Where did all these cushions come from? I wonder. They must breed. In fact, why do we keep so many cushions when the children just end up throwing them at each other? Maybe there should just be two per sofa, I decide. But which two? They're all so pretty. As I drift off into more meaningless thoughts I hear a sound that instantly makes me turn.

'Oo-weeze.' The sibilant syllables come from little Jacob. I am amazed at how much he has learned to do in such a short space of time. I beam at his sleepy-headed features. 'Well, Master Jacob, how are you? Did you enjoy that rest?'

He looks so perfect. Dark hair curling against pale skin, full lips and long eyelashes. He is beautiful. The moment I met him I think I knew he was waiting to have his time to shine. I bend down to the sofa where he is lying and put my fingers across his fringe to sweep it away from his eyes. I wonder if I have enough authority delegated to me to cut his fringe. I doubt it. Hair is hanging in his eyes and making him blink in what looks like an uncomfortable way.

I text Mary to ask where the delegated authority for haircutting lies and finish the message with *Can I have it soon? The boy needs a haircut!* It sounds simple but it can be anything but. 'Delegated authority' is the name given to the process that enables foster carers to make those common sense, everyday decisions about the children and young people in their care – ordinary things such as allowing them to go to friends' houses for sleepovers, or signing the consent forms for school trips and, as is the case right now, arranging haircuts. Authority can be delegated to foster carers by whoever the holder of parental responsibility is, so that they can make these sorts of decisions and arrangements. Foster carers never have parental responsibility for a fostered child, so they can only make decisions about the fostered child where that authority has been delegated to them by the local authority or the parents.

My local hairdressers have cut the hair of all my foster children. I have been impressed with their discreet whispers, well away from a child new to my care, when they have told me in the past about head lice and trapped sweets at the roots of self-created dreadlocks. I have watched their tenderness as they carefully comb through deep tangles of neglect. Many of them have their own children and, like the rest of us, struggle to bear witness to the mistreatment that some of these children have experienced.

Within seconds my phone pings. It is Mary, back with a quick reply in the affirmative. *You have full delegated authority. Go get him coiffured!* I love her no-nonsense responses that get things done fast.

I look into Jacob's face and wonder about what life he will have. Then I feel incredibly motivated to play my part to make that life as good as possible. I mean it in a philosophical way, but there are important practicalities to see to as part of that process. All children need the loo when they wake up – and I have already decided that treating Jacob like a baby is not going to help him – or us – at all.

'Can I check your nappy?' I ask.

Asking him about his body, rather than making assumptions, is how I am going to help Jacob understand that his body is his – and that, eventually, he will need to take responsibility for it. With his half open eyes and half hearing ears my meaning is obviously not clear to him straight away. I repeat, in a sing-song voice, 'I need to check your nappy, my darling boy.' I gently pull down his shorts and, without having to look on the inside, I can smell and see from the lack of plumpness in the nappy that he is dry. Good. Perfect opportunity then. I pull his shorts back up. 'How about you try the toilet?'

I ease him up and as I do so remind myself that he needs to build his strength up to be able to sit himself up. That will be the first stage to eventually being able to walk up the stairs to the bathroom independently. But we are a long, long way from that. Today I carry him straddled on my hip as if he is a koala. His head leans into my neck and I melt away – it is such an affectionate little gesture. This child is drawing out of me every emotion imaginable, all good ones, and emotions that keep me wanting to do my very best for him. We eventually get to the little loo at the top of the stairs, and it is no mean feat, I can tell you. Today's workout is underway!

I stand him up so he rests on me next to the toilet. I pull down his shorts and nappy and lift him onto the loo. I can tell he has never done this before. I wonder if he has even seen a toilet before. It must feel very strange. I bend down next to him and hear my knees creak. I tell Jacob that I need some oil. I wonder how much of this he understands. How much does he really know about the world he has been in? It is impossible to tell. I sit him right back and apologise profusely as I direct his 'you know what' to face the bottom of the toilet. I put one flat hand behind his back and steady his shoulder with the other. To both of our delights he does a big wee. Wow. I wasn't expecting such sudden success. This is quite a big moment. I have no desire to push an already challenged child to perform but the sense of accomplishment triumph brings is undeniable. In this important aspect of self-care it will make an enormous difference to his level of self-esteem, I'm sure. I don't flush straight away; I need to see what colour it is, and if it smells. That's been hard to determine from a nappy.

After I stop cheering and telling him how clever and amazing and grown-up he is, I pull back up the nappy and shorts. I hold onto a now standing Jacob and look into the toilet behind him. He definitely needs to drink more fluids. His urine is too thick and too dark. I wonder how many children and adults are dehydrated. I'm sure it can affect people's moods.

On my list of required items is a large potty – but after this accomplishment I am wondering if that might drag him back. I decide to scrap the potty and get him on the loo as often as I can. I remember with the other children waking them up in the night to get them to go to the loo and get them out of nappies. Potty training can be quite a job if it's not done early. I know that some reception class teachers in primary schools have recently complained that some parents haven't bothered potty training their children before starting school. Pull-ups are far easier in the meantime, and some have deliberately waited until the child starts nursery or school so that it is another thing for the teachers to sort out. Some nurseries and schools refuse to take children until they are toilet ready.

I know that all children develop at different rates. I have in my arms the perfect example of this. But I think parenting in recent years has focussed a great deal on the emotional side of things, in some cases at the expense of children learning the practical skills for life. I decide that one of my goals is to get Jacob on the loo by himself before he moves on – and my big ambition is to get him walking. Dr Jahandar didn't think that there was any reason for Jacob not to be up and walking and running around with friends – though he doesn't yet have any beyond our family. This global delay is caused by nothing other than neglect. I would love to see Jacob playing football or running along the beach. Blimey, I think, has he ever even been to a beach? I may have found my next project.

I carry Jacob back downstairs, trying not to let him see the puffing and panting this causes, and sit him at the kitchen table. I strap him into his seat. It is one of our old ones, from when the boys were younger. He needs a new, proper seat that is age-appropriate and serves his needs. Or does he? I'm beginning to wonder if maybe I need to think about all this differently. I decide to make do until he has had his MRI scan to see how his spine is. If all is good I will relinquish 'special' items in pursuit of Jacob using regular furniture.

I get the felt tips, crayons and paints from the cupboard in the garden room. As I enter that space I have a flashback to when little Eden was here, another foster child who stayed with us some months ago. She used to sit on the bean bag with the dogs to do her drawings. I wonder how she is. I haven't heard about her in a while. I will ask Dara to see if she can find out. I collect lots of pieces of paper and place them on the table in front of Jacob. I put the Beatles on the CD player once more which immediately encourages his smile. I start singing along enthusiastically, and thankfully he is either too polite or – for now – unable to say, 'Please stop! You're destroying my ear drums'

I also open a bag of chocolate buttons and put them in a bowl not too far away from Jacob. I hope that the smell and anticipation of the taste might tempt him into wanting to reach out and pick them up. I sit down next to him and give both of us a piece of paper. I start by showing him, as I have shown every child I have known, how to draw a cat and dog out of circles. I draw two circles side by side. I add two semi-circles onto them to become the eyes. I add another bigger circle round the two little circles and make a head. Next I draw lines for whiskers onto the two little circles that are cheeks. I draw the eyes in and stick ears on the sides. I attach a neck. I don't know why but this works every time. Children love it. I was taught to do this by Sean, an Irish Navvy who lived in the blue caravan in the orchard next to where I grew-up. He was the sweetness during an otherwise very sour time and I remember him fondly. I also remember feeling proud of learning a new drawing technique that I still know how to do today.

Children love learning new skills. Jacob has watched the entire demonstration. I hold out the clear felt tip pack. 'What colour would you like to use?'

He points at red. I take the red one out, then stop myself from taking the top off. I wait to see if Jacob will try and do it. He hesitates and puts it down. I get another pen out as if I am going to use it. I watch him watch me take the top off and begin colouring in the dog's head. Those half-closed eyes are taking note. Jacob leans forward, puts his hand out and reaches to pick up the red pen once more. I carry on colouring in my dog as I watch him, pretending that I'm not.

He does it!

I am doing triple flip flaps on the inside. I stay calm outwardly, I hope. With his left hand – interesting, I think to myself, he's left handed, good to know – he moves the pen backwards and forwards across the paper, leaving a stain of red lines. I begin to colour with more gusto to see if he will follow, and he does. He suddenly screeches with joy. I look at him. His tongue is hanging out of the corner of his mouth with the effort of his focus and concentration. I try not to smile directly at this wonderful sight.

Making an exaggerated 'mmmm' sound, I reach across and take a chocolate button. He frowns, wanting some of that. He is totally transparent and I love it. With the other hand he reaches out to the bowl and takes three buttons. He puts them into his mouth and makes a 'mmmm' sound too. I can smell the chocolate as he sucks it into his mouth. I watch the brown dribbles fall down his chin. I turn around and pull off a piece of kitchen roll from the roll that sits on the butchers block behind me. I don't wipe his face. Instead I hand it to him making sure to direct it towards his empty, chocolatey hand.

'Wipe your chops, Jacob.'

With all the intensity of a surgeon performing brain surgery he raises the kitchen roll to his mouth and sort of wipes it. It doesn't matter about chocolate on clothes or anywhere today because today Jacob grew up and, judging by his smile and demeanour, he loves it.

I watch Jacob make marks on his piece of paper, and know that this is good. But I wish I didn't feel so much like a phoney therapist. I'm not an art therapist – though I am an artist and ex-teacher and have worked with so many people in different settings from schools and hospitals to prisons. Yet I find that I feel 'held back' from working with Jacob in a way that my artistic nature suggests to me, in case I do something wrong. Because nearly every aspect of looking after children in the care system has become 'professionalised' it can seriously undermine the confidence of those working with children. I think about this for a few minutes. I have so little experience of looking after a child like Jacob that I feel self-conscious about what I am doing here. I look at my phone and see two texts: one from Mary, the other from Dara. I read Mary's first. She is asking me if I have received the delegated authority forms to sign that she has sent by email. She is on it, that woman. I read Dara's, who asks me if I have had a chance to read her report for our annual review, an event that happened weeks ago.

I know administration isn't my first, second or even third love. If I'm entirely honest I would say that I loathe it. Nevertheless I am efficient, mainly because I don't like deadlines and outstanding paper tasks hanging over my head and spoiling my day. I make a dash into my studio, grab my laptop and bring it back to the table. I notice that Jacob has eaten a few more chocolate buttons. I'm pleased about that. At first. But there is another little voice, on my other shoulder, saying that he shouldn't have the chocolate, and he shouldn't have it at this time of the day. Where does this voice come from? I think it comes from the various training I have undergone in my role as a foster carer. I am wary of the professionals who train foster carers but rarely meet our children. And I am also scared because of Jacob's prominent 'difference' to children I have looked after before. *He is just a child*, I say to myself. *I can only do my best here*. I've looked after many children. Dozens and dozens over the years. He is just another one in a long line. I am not going to allow his global delay to scare me – or at least I'm not going to allow my fears to interrupt my instincts and practice. There are expectations I put upon myself and there are those that I feel are imposed upon me. It is important to try to separate these out.

I look at the chocolate dribble and the happy little face of Jacob. This is a good thing. How can it not be? I remind myself that I am more than capable of looking after Jacob. This contented, absorbed little face – that's what we want. That's exactly how I am going to do this. I must let go of feeling that because I haven't got the 'relevant' qualification for the specificity of his need I am not good enough. It's a form of imposter syndrome. But I have plenty of other skills and experience that I can transfer to Jacob. I can only do it my way and I have to believe in myself. I know Mary and Dara believe in my capabilities. That should be enough.

I open my laptop and check my emails. Nothing obvious as yet relating to delegating authority or annual review. I go into the search box and type in both Mary's and Dara's names – nothing. There is an email about a coffee morning for foster carers. I delete it without entertaining the thought of attending even for a second. Before anyone starts to judge me for this, let it be known that I have been to plenty of these events but there are generally more staff from the local authority than foster carers – who are probably too busy to go along – and we never get to actually talk. Instead we form our own networks, away from the formality of the Social Services offices and personnel. I have several WhatsApp groups for foster carers that ping periodically, and I chat on the phone to foster carer friends when I want to and need to. Foster carers don't want to talk about their experiences of fostering in front of staff – it's an entirely artificial scenario. There is little trust these days, and we feel self-conscious talking openly and honestly in front of some social workers and managers. Not Dara or Mary, thankfully. I feel as if I could tell either of them pretty much anything, which is surprising in the case of Mary, who I have known for such a relatively short space of time.

A few years ago, I was standing in a car park chatting to a fellow foster carer. We got along and were busy swapping phone numbers when, out of nowhere, a social worker appeared.

'What are you doing?' she asked, as though we had been caught in the middle of some criminal activity. Sometimes fostering can feel like a funny business.

I text Mary and Dara and tell them that I haven't got their emails yet, and get back to Jacob's rather interesting and increasingly energetic drawing.

After a while he stops what appear to me to be random markings on the page and begins to draw the circles to make the dog. I think he needed to see what his felt tip could do before he launched into something more structured – fair enough. I watch him, and see how awkwardly he holds the pen, straight upright, bunched in his fist. Should I interfere, or let him experiment? Ordinarily, I would support the development of a child directly. The art teacher in me can't help it. If I would do it ordinarily, I should do it for Jacob. Why is this so difficult to get through to myself?

In an airily confident voice I say, 'Here, let me show you how to hold the pen to make it work better.'

As if by magic his drawing suddenly looks much more controlled. Good. It is another tiny confidence boost that I really need. I *will* do this my way.

We don't get as far as completing an actual dog, but single circles, and then concentric and overlapping circles gradually fill one page, then another, and another. He is nothing if not determined, this boy.

We break for a drink and snack, but he points to the paper again afterwards and is back to it. Changing colours, occasionally getting frustrated. I remember what Dr Jahandar said and embrace the frustrated moments as important signs of progress.

I notice the time and realise that the other children will be home in less than an hour. I am not quite sure where today has gone. The hours seem to have been sucked away. I am aware that a lot of my attention is going to Jacob and knowing my children – well, all children, in fact – I need to address this balance or we will all feel the consequences.

My children seem to love the rather traditional, old-fashioned idea of a mother being at home with hands covered in flour preparing glorious cakes and biscuits and wonderful meals for their delectation. Part of me would like to say that I am that woman, but I'm really not. Baking is something I have had to learn on the job, and it really began only in the early days of having children, partly so that I could at least say that I had tried to fulfil this picture and thereby avoid inadvertently ruining their childhoods.

For some reason, inexplicable to me, I have mastered the art of making tablet fudge. It takes a bit of time and patience, and my inspiration came after a visit to Edinburgh with my friend Lynette, who happens to be one of the best bakers I know. Next to our hotel was a fudge shop. The owner gave me his recipe and I did master it. The children love it. But I would have to dedicate an entire afternoon to do that. And this afternoon has got away from me. I grab my laptop and search for 'quick biscuit recipes'. I know that when the children see biscuits or cakes resting on the cooling rack they feel that life is all good. Even if my biscuits are slightly burnt or taste bad they still eat them. It's the thought that counts. Mary Berry's quick fork biscuits! There are three main ingredients, four short recipe instructions, and the webpage marks them as 'easy'. I feel victorious and I haven't even baked them yet! I busy myself lightly buttering a couple of baking trays, just as Mary tells me too, humming as I go. Another Mary in my life, helping me along the way.

Checking the cupboard it seems that I have the flour

and butter but no vanilla. It should be a store cupboard staple but Lily and Jackson have taken to cooking recently, which is great, but has two major downsides: I end up having to wash up everything because they seem to use every receptacle and device in the kitchen, and I am often 'caught short' because when they use up ingredients they never write it on the shopping list. I have lost count of the number of late-night dashes to the supermarket when I discover they have cookery at school in the morning. (They generally don't tell me that either, but I sometimes find a timetable or discarded note from school by an act of serendipity.)

Butter, sugar and flour come together quite miraculously to form a dough, but they do look like rather 'plain' biscuits. I double the quantity, figuring that we might go for quantity over quality today. I have no doubt that they will all be eaten. Some people live by the motto 'Fake it till you make it'; I'm a bit more 'Fake it till you bake it'. Soon I have thirty odd little dough balls. They look more impressive once I have embarked on the wet-forking phase of the recipe. Quite biscuity now, in fact. The little light is yet to come on telling me that the temperature has reached 180 degrees on the oven. We have a few minutes.

Jacob continues with his serene circle-drawing. He is quite taken with the whole thing, and we are getting closer to something resembling a dog, which is giving him a great deal of pleasure.

'I wonder. Do you need the loo?' I ask.

He returns my look – more wide-eyed to accompany a big grin, and makes a kind of 'ess' sound. Everything is soft and sibilant with him.

Okay. We are in business. Let's see if we can repeat our earlier success. I undo his straps and carry him to the bottom of the stairs. Just the thought of koala-ing him back up there makes me feel exhausted. I go to hoist him back into position and then think, 'I wonder if he can climb up?' It's worth a try. We are on a roll today.

'Jacob, I have an idea. Would you like to try walking up?'

Almost before the words are out of my mouth and I have had a chance to blink, his hands are heading straight for the bottom step. Blimey, I think, someone is keen. I quickly move to put my hands on his lower back as he wrestles with the steps. I don't fancy a trip to casualty on top of everything else. He looks a bit like he is trying to swim up the stairs as he hauls and flaps his arms, head lolling all over the place, but he is developing a 'technique' of sorts and is absolutely determined to do it. Unlike with the pen-holding, I don't know that I have any helpful advice here. It takes nearly fifteen minutes. More time for that oven to heat up, I tell myself. Against the odds, he gets there, finishing his marathon climb by landing at the top of the stairs and flopping down onto his side, with every appearance of a long distance runner who falls to the ground just after the finish line.

He holds out his hands in front of his face and smiles. But, of course, this is only the first phase in his mission. Next is the toilet itself. I sit him down and hold his shoulder, knowing already that we are too late. He has already been. Part of the straining on the stairs is there to see in his pull up. We go through the process anyway. I take off his nappy while he sits on the throne, surveying new kingdoms. I watch his eyes move across the tiny toilet room, taking in every picture. I forget, because I live in this house, that to other people it must feel like a visual explosion. There is colour everywhere in the art and objects that adorn the walls and shelves. It's years and years of collecting things that we like. To some people I guess it could look a bit weird or over the top, but not to Jacob: he loves it. He is fascinated by it all. I am reminded again of the lack of stimulus he has had in his life so far.

Prior planning and all that; I have kept a packet of pull ups in each loo for exactly this eventuality. I pull on Jacob's clean pull ups and chat away about this and that to distract him. He is touching my dress as we talk. He likes to feel things. Ah, the next sensory project will be touch. I have so many things he can play with. We can build on all the bits and bobs that Dara brought with her. I am very conscious of the time as we finish up and make the decision to carry Jacob downstairs. Going down might be more daunting, and I don't have another fifteen minutes if I am ever going to get these biscuits baked.

The children soon file in, throwing bags down and kicking off shoes across the hall. The boys' feet have gotten so big that kicking off their school shoes is a different kettle of fish these days. Not only do they take up so much space, they can be lethal missiles if misdirected.

As I predicted, the children pile into the kitchen led by the fresh-baked smells, straight to the cooling rack of biscuits. Clearly Mary Berry did not bake these, but they love them anyway. I have achieved small miracles this afternoon!

Vincent turns to Jacob. 'Would you like one, mate?'

We see an enthusiastic nod. I wonder how much the children will inspire Jacob to try new things. I note that he watches everything they do, not always an unadulterated good thing, especially when Jackson drops some biscuit on the floor and calls out 'Where are the four-legged hoovers?' (This is of course why Dotty leans towards being tubby.)

Jacob has perked up from his early calm. He seems to enjoy the chaos and energy that this lot bring with them, feeding off it himself. Cupboard doors open and close in a flurry of syncopated rhythms, Diet Coke appears from out of the cupboard and fizzes up in glasses. I make a face that is as disapproving as I can. I try and keep sweets and fizzy drinks for the weekend, but that would mean 'hiding' it – and this lot would be able to track down anything.

I notice Jacob's face beam as he watches Vincent pour cola into a glass. Jacob is almost salivating. I look at Vincent and direct him with my eyes towards Jacob. 'Oh mate, you want some of this, too?'

I still have a beaker with a lid. In spite of all our progress we are nowhere close to a glass yet. I dash out to the overflow cupboard in the garden room. Vincent pours half a beaker full and I make sure the lid is on tight. I ask Vincent to pass it to Jacob – who has not taken his eyes off the drink – it is as if he has responsibility for guarding the crown jewels. Vincent plonks it unceremoniously in front of Jacob and gets back to eating the biscuits.

Not to be outdone in the 'caring for our latest arrival' stakes, Lily notices that Jacob hasn't got a biscuit; she selects a nicely golden one for him, leaving the ones with burnt edges for the rest. I am proud that they have learnt the social rule of 'family stand back' which roughly translates as leaving the best of everything for the guests. Not that Jacob is behaving a guest – he has settled in well and already managed to make himself very much part of our family.

It has been a really, really good day. After all my anxieties about not being able to look after Jacob properly we have made huge leaps. Well, not actual leaps, but after seeing him climb those stairs, leaps might not be too far away.

I've got this.

Chapter Seven

I have begun to set the alarm clock on my phone for 5.30am. I need to get so much done in the mornings before I begin working with Jacob. Once he is up and about he takes so much of my time. Three weeks into our placement he is doing so much in the daytime, managing the interaction with the other children, visiting new places, developing new skills. His eyes are soaking up so many new things and with toilet training and climbing up the stairs and all the art activities – not to mention the time he likes to spend laying on the mat with Dotty and Douglas, he ends each day absolutely spent. He is asleep each night almost before his head hits the pillow. This is great on so many levels. Night times can be difficult even for well-adjusted adults when they are staying somewhere new – let alone traumatised children trying to settle. Another bonus is that I am letting him sleep in for longer, only getting him up now when he wakes naturally.

This morning it feels like much longer.

The others have all gone to school. The last one out was

Lily, moaning that she hates PE and it's not fair that they make her run in the heat. I refrained from pointing out that it's late October and heat isn't generally a problem. Lily, like many children in care, seems to become an echo of anything problematic in early life experience. Lily's family were not into activity. When she was in Year 4 and they had their compulsory run around in the morning before class (which I thought was a brilliant idea to wake them up and get their brains going) she used to start limping half way to school. By the time we arrived she was in tears and very angry as I reminded her that the limping only began when she remembered she had to run around the playground before classes. She would do all she could to wriggle out of exercise, but her teacher and I had already discussed this and Mrs Phillips was not having any of it. She managed Lily brilliantly and just scooped her in with all the other children, somehow managing to ignore her vociferous protests. Lily became fitter and had more energy as a result.

'Energy makes energy, don't forget!' I call as she is eventually persuaded to leave the house.

She gives me a murderous look. 'Enjoy your day with HIM!' she shouts.

She's in a right old strop this morning. I think she will always have issues around health, and by that I mean in terms of looking after her health, but as I keep saying, I can only do my best. When she arrived here all those years ago she was dehydrated – as so many children coming into care are. I guess if you're hurting or neglecting your child in some way you're probably not going to ensure they have plenty of water. She was given liquid though: cans of those hideous energy drinks which, when she was a small child, may have harmed her heart and certainly her teeth. Luckily they were her first teeth, but they had to be removed because they were so rotten.

Jacob hasn't had any of that, thank goodness. The tell-tale sign is the breath, and that day that I went to meet Jacob at the Hallidays' house was a big concern. His mouth had the whiff of an open grave – but his teeth have not experienced too much sugar thus far (though I seem to be making up for that!). I don't know much about his life at the farm – but I'm not sure anyone has been looking after his teeth. That's another issue I'm determined to crack, and another milestone I'm determined to meet.

When the boys were little I used to clean their teeth for them until they were old enough and tall enough to learn how to do it effectively themselves, and then I would stand by and inspect. It wasn't always a popular strategy, but it worked. It's one of the issues with looked-after children that I find so depressing – that their teeth have been allowed to rot and decay due to their adults being negligent.

I looked after a teenage boy for a while whose parents had never mentioned cleaning his teeth. Of course it's not only the immediate healthcare issue. I have to explain that it's not pleasant for all those living around them, and unfair at school for the children sitting next to them. The teenage boy had all his second teeth removed when he was 15 due to years of neglect, and acquired a set of false teeth. Not a desirable prize, and a sight that will always stay with me. It is a stark reminder that no matter how tired I am the children must clean their teeth, and do so properly.

I rush about conducting the general business of the morning: screwing the tops back on the marmalade and honey jars, wiping down the cutting board and table with antibacterial spray, collecting the breakfast debris and gathering discarded socks along with anything else that stands in my way. I put the first load of washing into the very big tumble dryer which lives in the garden room. It always makes the whole space smell of fabric conditioner which remains one of my favourite and most comforting scents. I load another pile of school uniforms and towels into the washing machine. There was a time in the era before children, those halcyon 'BC' days, when I would have separated out the towels to wash without fabric conditioner to rough the cotton up for better drying. How I laugh now. Those days have well and truly gone. These days I scoop it all up into a big load and use the technique of 'hope'. Hope that nothing is ruined, or that I haven't inadvertently included a sleeping cat in the wash. Thankfully neither has happened thus far.

I check on Jacob once more. He is still fast asleep. I take the opportunity of precious extra minutes to head to the studio to check my emails. I sent Dara and Mary an update last night on Jacob's drawing and toilet progress. Nothing back and still nothing from Mary with the official delegated authority, which I am expecting any time now. Perhaps the social workers have a meeting or training session, or perhaps Mary is just too taken up with her poor teenage girl at the moment. I sometimes wonder how they manage to do it all. They are wonderful women in the workplace, with their own complex lives too. I shall endeavour to be patient.

I message my editor and let her know that my corrections will be with her tomorrow morning. It buys me a few more hours, but means the laptop will accompany me to bed tonight. Lloyd's still away so it doesn't matter, I will get away with it. I don't feel at ease about working in bed with the light on when he wants to sleep, but equally he doesn't like it when I stay up and work in the studio. Sometimes I wait for him to fall asleep and then go down to the studio and work for hours into the night. Come the morning, like a naughty child, I'll pretend that I haven't, and find various strategies to hide the fact that I'm tired. We're such strange creatures, us adults.

Next I do a little more research into the 'sensory diet' prescribed by Dr Jahandar. I know already that children use their senses to explore, understand and make sense of the world around them, and that they do this by engaging all of the senses. I know, too, how evocative some of those senses can be. I have been caught, occasionally by smell, but often by music, in a way that transports me back vividly to a certain time in my life. The power of sense is such that the brain triggers a flashback memory to those crucial moments and formative times. My instinct about music has been well-researched: a quick internet trawl leads me into a warren of ideas about music as an alternative therapy. I think about Jacob's reaction, just in the car, to certain tunes – how he lit up at the sound of the Beatles. We can do more of that, and in a more structured way.

A further search tells me that providing opportunities and constructing situations for children to actively use their senses is crucial to brain development because it helps to build nerve connections in the brain's pathways. This, in turn, will support a child's development towards more complex learning, more sophisticated tasks and encourage cognitive growth, alongside the other key areas of language development, gross motor skills, social interaction and problem solving. Okay, not much I don't know so far.

However, there are two others that are commonly missed, apparently. There is something I have never heard of called 'proprioception'. Right, I'm all ears, or eyes, or one of the senses. Proprioception is a fancy name for 'body awareness' and comes from the feedback to the brain from 'stretch receptors' in the muscles and 'pressure receptors' in the joints. I didn't realise I was in for a human biology lesson this morning, but there are diagrams that are all too reminiscent of science exams from long ago. These receptors give a sense of where our bodies are in space. Okay, yes. Jacob could probably do with more of this. The other 'sense' that is missed is balance. There are more big words here. This is something to do with 'stimulation of the vestibular system' which controls the signals that tell the brain about our body position in relation to gravity. Sensory play is play that stimulates the five 'ordinary' senses, but also these spatial and balance ones. The website lists multiple reasons why sensory play is beneficial, most of which involve building positive neural connections, but I am interested in some of the examples they give, of the way that this kind of activity can develop different skills, particularly around sound, but also touch. There is then a long list of practical ways that all this can be achieved: salt painting, play dough, sponge painting, sand art, finger painting, frozen paint.

Okay, well this I can do.

Before Jacob stirs from his slumber I quickly knock up some play dough. More store cupboard ingredients: flour, salt, cooking oil and food colouring. Even after yesterday's fork biscuits there is enough flour left over for this. I mix the ingredients together, and find an unexpected pleasure while I am busy kneading in the food colouring. It is another one of those simple sensory moments that I was just describing, and it hits me from nowhere: I love this smell, the smell of homemade play dough. There is something so reassuring about it. I think it's to do with happy childhood memories of making it at primary school and my wonderful, understanding teacher who let me create all day long. I wish the school curriculum was that sensible these days. Sometimes children just need to make things and go at their own pace, rather than conforming to sets of generalised criteria. I wrap the dough in cling film and put it in the fridge for later. It will be ready when we need it and it's at its best when cold.

I search through the kitchen cupboards and drawers looking for anything else that can be included in Jacob's sensory diet.

I'm really enjoying myself and begin to remember so much more from my experiences of school. I tip out macaroni and pasta into two plastic cereal bowls, finding both the sound and their shapes interesting, acknowledging them for the first time in years. I am transported back to my own childhood again, recall knowing what pasta, macaroni and rice were as a child, because I had seen them at school in the craft corner, but I had never eaten them.

My adopted family had deeply simplistic ideas about food. Everything was as plain as possible and bought from frozen food shops. The menu consisted mainly of pies and peas and I remember them being stored in a white chest freezer in the shed. They put a big lock on it to keep me and my hungry adopted brother, William, out of it. We were left to sort through the bird food from the white enamel bread bin. I have kept the bread bin now in my shed, full of bird seed. My own children have no idea of its significance.

I run upstairs to check, but Jacob is still blissfully sleeping. I head back to the studio to check on the internet for other ideas. Shaving cream painting, now, that looks like fun. I watch some YouTube videos to make sure I have a good idea about what is involved. More food colouring and 'popsicle sticks' – well, I can improvise with those. I manage to find a new unused can of shaving foam from the bathroom cupboard: perfect! Back down in the kitchen I get the kitchen table set up with all our activities for the day. I am going to have as much fun with this as he is, and I may even have found an idea for my own Christmas cards this year. I ignore the nagging voice about how much mess will be made in the process. Mess is necessary for creativity as I know only too well, and this, I am sure, will be worth it.

I walk past the front door on one of my trips – I seem to have done quite a lot of running around already this morning – and scoop up the post that has been pushed through the letterbox. As always, nearly everything is for Lloyd. I sort through and put his envelopes to one side. There is one addressed to 'The parent or guardian of Jacob Tillyard'. Right, that's me. I open it up and read that Dr Jahanda has sorted out the MRI scan for Jacob. Someone else working fast. This is good news. We can work out if there is any damage to his spine from being left for years to lie in a dog basket. I check the appointment date. That too is quick, in fact it's in two days' time. I had better let Mary know. I pick my phone up from the table and notice that Mary has already called a few times and left a couple of messages and a text. How did I miss that? I must have been absorbed in play dough and shaving foam.

I listen to the voicemail. I like Mary, but sometimes she can come across as abrupt. It's that cut glass English accent, exaggerated in her 'phone voice'. I think it feels ill-fitting and incongruous for her. She is so clearly a delightful woman and I know that she is still connected to her 'hippy' roots. It's a strange juxtaposition. She wants to sort out the arrangements for contact. I am surprised by this because I thought Jacob was on a full care order – but parents have legal rights too and maybe his mother wants to see how he is. Fair enough. I listen to the next message.

'Ignore all previous emails. Contact has been cancelled. Jacob's mother has decided to not see Jacob, having expressed concern that it would unsettle him.'

One less thing to worry about. That's a mature and sensible approach but they may also be feeling the benefits of not having a disabled child under their feet. I am torn, and feel a shudder of annoyance, even though it makes life easier for me. That soon passes but I am beginning to feel a bit grumpy about the lack of response to emails. In truth, I can't accuse my social work colleagues of not being on board enough with Jacob. I know they have other children in their caseload and I am but one among many. They've done so much already, especially Mary. I work hard to contain my frustrations until the phone goes again. It's Mary, and I turn back into a small child, scared of authority, defensive as if she could hear my thoughts of a moment ago. I answer, waiting to be told off.

Mary asks if I have received any of her emails.

'No, not yet,' I say. 'I've checked a few times this morning.'

'Bloody privatisation!' she exclaims.

I'm confused and ask what she means.

'All business support has been commissioned out to a private company and it's causing havoc. I've sent all sorts of things your way.'

I haven't had the opportunity to share my personal views on the privatisation of children's social care with Mary, and I tend to deliberately avoid it because it's one of my main bugbears. I usually start with 'Privatisation, don't get me started' and then go on for quite some time, but in this instance I don't have to. Mary is off and running. She launches into a rant about how the social workers are having to go back and do things all over again when paperwork doesn't go through.

'Everything is taking even longer and costing more,' she fumes.

It's not like me to change this subject, but I feel like I need to for the sake of her blood pressure. I ask what happened about the contact.

'Ah, yes, that's another debacle. Would you be so kind

as to explain to Jacob that he won't see his mum this week. I'll come by when I get the chance and explain the rest to him, because that's my job, not yours.'

'Thank you. I appreciate that.'

I do admire this attitude to social work. I have been left by some social workers to deal with all sorts of issues that shouldn't really have been mine to handle and have left me in very awkward positions, blamed for things that are out of my control, especially in relation to contact visits, which can be an absolute minefield.

I tell Mary about the MRI appointment.

'Well, that's fantastic that it has come through so quickly. Sadly, I'm not going to be able to be there with you. My colleagues and I are on a three-line whip to clear up the administrative mess left by the private company. Get this – we're not even sure where their offices are.'

It sounds awful. I assume that if it's a local authority initiative then it must be the same for Dara. I'd better give her a call later.

'No worries. I'm starting to feel more confident getting out and about with him – especially after yesterday's successes with the stairs and toilet.'

'Oh yes, marvellous breakthroughs. Well done to both of you. Let me know as and when there are more developments.'

I like that she hasn't said 'if' there are more developments.

We hang up and I ready myself for the next stage of the day, wondering what new breakfast Sleeping Beauty up there could try today. I turn the oven on in preparation of warming up some croissants. I can't hang around for him to wake up any longer. I head upstairs, for the fourth or so time this morning, to his room. I quietly put my head round the door – not wanting to startle him whether he is awake or asleep. I am greeted by the sight of him peacefully staring at his hands. He is lying on his back, holding them in the air above his face, almost as if seeing them for the first time.

He notices me after a moment and gives me the most gorgeous smile I might ever have seen on a human face. I well remember the morning faces of the boys when they were small, so full of wonder and excitement for the day ahead, that I couldn't help but be enthused by it too, even in the early days when I was sleep deprived and not ready for the day ahead at all.

Jacob has this innocent exuberance that is full of that same zest and love for life. I feel the prick of those hot salty tears trying to escape again, overwhelmed as I am by this simple expression. But no, they need to stay inside my eyes or Jacob will be confused, I need to introduce emotions slowly. I know that global delay thrives on lack of adult attention, and I don't want to overwhelm him or scare him back into his shell. I shall just endeavour to enjoy the moment.

I can't resist opening the blind with an exaggerated, 'Wow, Jacob, the sun is shining for you today'.

As I get closer I find myself reaching out to tickle his tummy. Again I have a momentary hesitation. What am I doing? I should know that this is a terrible thing to do. I don't know if tickling was used as a way of accessing him for abuse, or if he has been hurt in the past, but, luckily for me, my need to tickle him is rewarded with the most wonderful giggles. He is adorable.

'Now, how do you fancy croissants for breakfast?'

He rewards me with another smile, even though he can have absolutely no idea what a croissant is, and repeats, 'cusssssa'. Well, perhaps French lessons can wait until another day. I might be getting ahead of myself here.

I help Jacob out of bed, looking forward to the day when he can do this for himself. I can't wait for him to jump out on his own accord, to run freely down the stairs and ask for his breakfast. One day, I tell myself. I pull back his duvet and help him to sit up. The MRI scan – that is so soon now – will reveal how well his back is and if there is permanent damage to his spine. Then we will really know where we are. Mary has told me a little more about how he was found in a dog basket coiled up like a snake. That image has never left me. His poor tangled body. I hope he will straighten out.

I remember all the stories I have heard over time about how humans defy medical prognosis. I read a newspaper article a while ago about a woman who had been diagnosed with sickle cell disease as a child. She suffered from horrendous pain in her wrists and ankles and her future would undoubtedly have been in a wheelchair had she not been so determined to do sports. In fact, she has never been in a wheelchair and is now an active, although in pain, mother of five. I hope that Jacob has that type of determination.

He'll need it.

Children in care will always have to work harder in our society than other children.

No matter how enlightened and informed the adults are around the child, they are a bubble, unrepresentative of the rest of the world; a world that will not have the insight into the system to understand that it's not actually the child's fault they are in care and that they are as valid and important as every other child.

I think I need to get on, get Jacob dressed and get his breakfast in order to break away from my thoughts on injustice – or I will be on the phone to the Prime Minister by lunch time. Not that a phone call from Louise Allen would do any good, more's the pity.

As I hold Jacob's hand and put one hand on his shoulder to steady his shaky walk, I am reminded of Bambi trying to stand up for the first time. Those bendy limbs are capable, they just don't yet know what to do properly. I talk us along to the bathroom, gently coaxing all the way. This is the recently-decorated children's bathroom, a different space from the toilet we visited yesterday. Once again there is so much to see in this room, and this time everything in there is themed. Almost over-themed, if I'm honest. I had a friend who once made the mistake of telling everyone that she liked frogs. Every Christmas and birthday she received multiple frogs in one form or another. In the end she dedicated her downstairs loo to housing the frog collection. It's a bit like that with the children's bathroom, except that everything in here is water or sea influenced. The bath and wood panels are a deep ocean blue. There are shells and fish and model yachts, bits of ship and boatyard signs and anchors, boaty-looking roped things. We have had to put in extra shelves to house it all. I almost feel that we need to put it up as a status on Facebook: *No more sea-related items for the children's bathroom are required.* We have enough.

Each child has their own flannel hanging up in there. It's old fashioned I suppose, and if I'm honest I don't think the children use them for anything much other than to wipe out toothpaste or dried soap from the sink. I am the last generation to have grown up with the face flannel. My adopted mother used to say to me, 'The three Fs': Face, feet and fanny. It sounds decidedly un-Victorian, though that's what her child rearing methods were. I remember thinking, 'what about under the arms?'

I encourage Jacob onto the blue plastic child step so he can see himself in the mirror.

There are little boats at the bottom of the mirror and, as Jacob stares at them, it occurs to me that he may never have seen a boat or even the sea. I decide that tomorrow, when I've spent today clearing the admin and doing all the jobs that need doing, we need to go to the beach. While leaning Jacob against my side I take his flannel off the hook. His is the only damp one. I run it under the hot tap and begin to wipe his face, removing all traces of sleeping dust and dried dribble from his radiant features. It is a labour of love: there is something absolutely magnetic about this boy. He has something indescribable within him that is like pure energy, the seed of his potential beginning to take hold. Perhaps this is charisma.

I put a little soap on to the flannel and quickly wipe down his body while holding him with one hand. He remains ever so slightly unstable, so that I have the perpetual feeling that he is about to fall. When all is done I smile and pronounce him 'clean as a whistle'. I mean his whole self, not any 'male' areas. Oh boy, being a foster carer in a time of accusation culture can be a little bit like tripping over yourself. I have a pathological fear of accidentally saying anything that might be interpreted as sexualised. I grew-up watching *Carry On* films and *Are You Being Served?* – so many sayings and the tendency towards innuendo are hardwired. I don't know how foster carers who are a generation above me manage to cope with the changing lines of what's acceptable. Maybe they just give up and carry on as normal. It's funny to me how the most recent understanding of words count. Lily nearly bit my head off when I said, 'How is she?' asking after a friend of hers who has recently come out and now prefers the pronoun 'they'. Later on Lily herself referred to the same friend as 'her' and was forced to acknowledge how hard it is to shift old words and habits.

I accidentally drop the soapy flannel on to the floor. As I bend down to get it, leaving him less supported for a second, Jacob puts both hands on the sink and stands up straight and tall. I see a good straight back. I know that perhaps I am seeing what I want and desperately hope to see, but I have not seen him do this before and it fills me with encouragement ahead of his appointment. I wonder how much more inside Jacob there is to be revealed: a hell of a lot if the last few days are anything to go by.

I wrap a towel round him like a sari and take the opportunity to clean around the sink as he sits down on the floor. His back is getting stronger. It must be: he can bring himself up into a half-sitting position. He does it now.

He smiles – oh that sunshine smile. It does for me every time.

I walk him back to his bedroom where together we choose some clothes for the day. I lean him against me once more as we open the top drawer and find some pants and socks. We are getting quite a knack going with this leaning business. He chooses pants with ninjas. Why not? I open the next drawer and he reaches in to pull out a t-shirt. I am impressed with his reach and coordination, not to mention his choice: it's a 'Surfer Dude' t-shirt that I bought new the day after he came. I remember quietly thinking 'this boy needs fashion, not these ugly hand-me-downs that he arrived with from his previous foster carer'. I chose it because it reminds me of a favourite t-shirt that Vincent had when he was about the same age. It had originally been Jackson's, and was mainly red with tiny black skulls printed all over the fabric. Vincent wore it as often as he could for the best part of five years until he was ten. By that stage it literally would not go over his head anymore. I tried to find another version but couldn't. This top has the same colours and I am pleased that Jacob likes it. I know I talk about the clothes of children in care a great deal, but their importance can't be underestimated. The horror mish-mash of garments he arrived with has no place in a twenty-first century wardrobe.

In my momentary reminiscing I haven't noticed that Jacob has pulled himself off me and is standing up right of his own accord, holding onto the top of the chest of drawers. Now that I see it I am thrilled and excited by every tiny piece of evidence of his growing independence, but a bit of me feels rejected by it at the same time. We are funny creatures.

He turns his head. 'Look.' Both the first and last consonants are sounded clearly, this little monkey has plenty of words inside him. And it really is a 'Look Mum no hands' moment, as he lifts both sets of fingers away from the top of the drawer.

He has a devilish little streak in him that actually makes my heart sing – it's so full of hope. Somehow he knows what power he has to affect those he comes into contact with. It is just as when the boys were younger and would jump off a wall or look like they were going to fall: my thighs go tight and cold. I think it must be some primal instinct. I feel this with all children, not just my own. I wonder sometimes if foster carers and adopters can do what they do because they have this primal reaction for all children.

Jacob stands up straight and tall without any assistance.

I turn my head and shriek with delight. 'Look at you, Master Jacob. What a clever and strong boy you are.'

His face lights up. I don't know how much his mother and grandmother talked to him or looked at him but I know that he understands what I have just said, and I sense that he has been absorbing everything from under that table. He probably understands more than we all realise. It's so difficult to know, but he already seems like such a different boy from the helpless child splayed on the floor in the Halliday household.

After he's fully dressed – and, significantly, has clocked himself in the mirror (that Lloyd deliberately positioned at small child height so that they can see themselves), we hold hands and begin to walk along the passageway to the top of the stairs. His little hand goes to the Victorian curved handrail and we both walk in unison down to the bottom where two happy little dogs and Mabel, Lily's cat (who thinks she's a dog) are waiting for us. Jacob loves the animals and I'm not sure who makes who more excited: the dogs or him. Before I know it, he has pulled me down to the floor by tugging my hand and is playing with the dogs. I feel that today may be one of those days when not a lot gets done officially, but loads will be done with Jacob and his development.

Eventually I prise him away from the pets with a promise of new adventures. Today I think I would like to make a 'sand art' picture with Jacob. It's the next recipe in his sensory diet – or at least the diet I am constructing until we get the appointment with a therapist. Overnight I have put together materials, having taken inspiration from Cornish artist Alfred Wallis' work on the marvellous Tate website.

Before we begin today's session, I am mindful that I don't want to make this arduous in any way. At the same time there is a part of me that wants to introduce the idea of school to Jacob – because that's where he should be. Every primary school I have been into offers sensory play. And, as children ourselves we all did it, I think, before it was given any such name. I know that he may enjoy the bits of activity around the actual exercise as much as doing the work.

Of course, prior to art-attack extraordinaire, this little fella needs to eat.

I pour out some orange juice to go with the croissants, and, while I'm in this conquering mood, put it in a small coloured glass and wonder how he will manage without his Tommee Tippee sippy cup. I needn't have worried. As with everything else so far today – and it's not much past 9am – he reaches down, picks it up and drinks from the glass with only a dribble spilled. I can't wait to tell Mary.

Actually, I make the decision to call Mary right now, in the moment. I can't resist. Before she has time to answer I have her on speaker phone so I can clean up and get on with the creativity.

Mary answers the phone with her smart, precise way of talking. She seems to eject words and cut them off more quickly than the rest of us. 'Hello there.' If the BBC are in search of an actor to replicate a broadcaster from the 1950s, they need look no further.

Jacob recognises her distinctive voice and smiles. 'Mary!'

He looks confused, because of course he can hear the voice but she is not in the room.

'Good morning Jacob, how are you?'

He looks bashful but I can see the glint in his eye as he repeats, 'Mary.'

She is thrilled and continues to talk to him but he is now distracted as I turn the breakfast table into an art table and it is a rather one-sided conversation.

'I'm afraid his interest has already moved on,' I tell her. She laughs 'Quite right. Don't worry, I'm used to it.'

I explain to Mary that she is on speaker phone if she hadn't already guessed, and that the dogs and Jacob are the only ones listening. 'And to be honest, they're not actually listening, I'm afraid.'

A confession: I have loved the advent of speaker phone. If I am on the phone I tend to walk about and do things anyway, it's just the way I am. I was recently involved in some research into people types where they were categorised as predominantly kinaesthetic or auditory. Unsurprisingly, I fell into the former category. Kinaesthetic people are touchy people, to put it simply. They value hugging, holding hands and cuddling – things I embrace one hundred percent. (Pun fully intended.)

I share this with Mary before I start telling her about some of my revelations relating to the sensory diet and what I have so far researched and discovered. 'If we didn't have the restrictions of the early learning curriculum, I don't think he is very far away from being able to function in school.

'Oh I know, bloody auditory wankers.'

As ever, the contrast between Mary's plummy tones and her fluent Dockyard are incongruous and slightly shocking. I also wholeheartedly enjoy it!

Most social workers I encounter, and over the years there have been very many of them, tend to conduct themselves utterly professionally and would not use this kind of language in any working context – perhaps always striving to hide their real feelings. In Mary's case, it just serves to make her seem more human, approachable and real. I shouldn't condone it, but it cheers me immensely. I have always been drawn to rebels and rule-breakers – so much more fun!

'You're quite right,' she goes on. 'And it's not just the curriculum. Technology is designed by auditory people and we, the rest of the world who are kinaesthetic, have to try and understand their logic and if we don't they have the nerve to call us stupid.'

She's off on one again. I love her passion and hear echoes of my 'Don't get me started' self as she continues her rant. I think she knows she has found a kindred spirit. 'Frankly it boils down to utter stupidity, arrogance and misguided assumptions that everyone is like them.'

'People who design curriculums are people who like sitting behind a desk and moving a mouse around all day. That doesn't suit all of us.' I glance at Jacob, who has already lifted a piece of A4 paper off the pile I intended for Lloyd's printer. He will be back later today – I'll dash to the supermarket to get more before he returns. Jacob has also picked up a pen and is drawing a version of a dog.

'Oh, Mary. You should see this,' I say and explain all Jacob has remembered from yesterday and our circle drawings. 'I love that he has done this unprompted.' Not only is it unprompted, Jacob seems inspired enough to keep going independently.

I tell Mary all of Jacob's behaviour breakthroughs: about Jacob standing up by himself, drinking from a glass, speaking a growing number of words, climbing the stairs, albeit in a truly original 'Jacob' way. All the wonderful things he is doing.

I say it out loud, not minding that he hears, because I am proud of this beautiful little person.

She congratulates him enthusiastically. Then checks, 'Have you had a copy of the care plan through?'

'No,' I laugh.

Mary is furious and begins another rant on a previously visited topic: why the devil have they privatised the administrative services. 'The commissioning manager is personal friends with the guy who set up the local authority business support and...'

'Mary, it's the creep of neoliberalism and it's all over the public sector.'

Sometimes, since leaving teaching at a university, I can still feel my brain harden up when it comes to matters of social justice. Jacob seems oblivious to our rantings and I have no fears that he will repeat this negatively back to a manager: I suspect that young Jacob would be on the side of equality and justice on these matters since the money that is earmarked for vulnerable children in care frequently seems to be redirected to profit for private companies. But these are not his battles to fight. They are ours – on his behalf. He has begun to stick his tongue out while working and concentrating. It is the sweetest thing ever, and reminds me of exactly what I am fighting for.

Mary is still raging about the culture of her organisation when I see a text message flit across the top of my phone. It's from Dara.

'Mary, I'm going to have to go now, but when are you next due to come back to us?'

'I need to schedule the statutory visit shortly.'

'Right you are.' I know all about these and all things statutory because I have a copy of the government's Fostering Services: 'National Minimum Standards' document: more than 60 pages and 31 different minimum standards that are required to be met. I keep it on a shelf just in case we experience some non-statutory ideas or behaviours towards the children in our care. I am ever-confused by its title though. Why would organisations aspire to 'minimum' standards?

Mary ends the conversation by telling me that she will call in tomorrow – the day before the MRI scan. 'I am ignoring the times for statutory visits,' she explains. 'Instead I'll come to see Jacob when I can. If that's alright with you, Louise.'

'Just text and I'll put the kettle on.'

'I don't want it to seem over the top, but Jacob is my last child before retirement,' Mary reminds me. 'And I want to make sure he has everything he needs. And, well, he needs a lot!'

'I'm starting to think that some of what he needs can't really be bought. Love and support and to be with creative people who are prepared to roll their sleeves up and get stuck in.'

I say goodbye to Mary and, to keep Jacob on his creative roll while I call Dara, I supply a bowl of green grapes. A delicacy that Vincent introduced to him – although I suspect it was Vincent, too, who got Jacob onto the less-healthy Nutella.

As always, Dara answers straight away and, as nearly always, is on her hands-free set in the car. 'I may disappear soon as I go through a tunnel.'

I know exactly where this tunnel is and have been amused by several social workers losing connection when they are saying something important. The miles social workers must cover is amazing. Dara is always driving, it seems.

I noticed in a recent job advert for a post as a social worker that, in the essentials for the job, 'own car' was high up on the list. I hope that they are compensated for the wear and tear of their vehicles, but then it occurs to me that foster carers don't get any support other than a paltry mileage claim allowance.

I return from my travelling thoughts and tell Dara that she is on speaker phone this end too, which she is used to.

'Hello Jacob, how are you today?' she calls, in her alluring Polish accent.

He lifts his head, disconnects his tongue from his top lip and waves at the phone. He has made the connection with the voice and device.

I love the fact that both social workers understand the importance of affirmation and talk to him directly. This hasn't always been the case in the past.

'It is time for our statutory supervision,' Dara reminds me. It is a monthly requirement, but to have a supervision meeting with Dara is always a delight.

'This week is probably out,' I tell her. 'Lloyd's been working away again. He gets back this evening for a few days and will need to catch-up on emails and stuff. He also wants his mum closer to us so he's preoccupied with sorting that.'

Dara already knows a bit about the situation with Lloyd's mother. She lives nearly three hours away and we both see a future of more and more driving to help with the house and garden and to sort out medical appointments. 'Also, it is Jacob's MRI this week, so we have that going on too.'

Dara is her understanding self, and we schedule our catch up for a few days' time. I've now spoken about the MRI twice this morning, and it has shaken me up somewhat. I don't know why, and I haven't really voiced it yet (Lloyd hasn't been here to talk to and Jacob is generally around when I speak with Mary or Dara) but I don't have a good feeling about the MRI.

I don't say this out loud, of course, as I do not want to alarm Jacob.

I had to have several MRI scans myself last year. After looking after a lively and somewhat violent child, I pulled a muscle in my side while lifting him to carry him away from a dangerous situation. Apart from an overzealous social worker trying to make an allegation against me for hurting him (That's another 'Don't get me started….' rich seam of ranting) I was hurt myself. After months of pain not going away I eventually went to see the doctor – who said the pain could be my liver or kidney, or something else. I didn't much like the sound of any of those options.

I went for an ultrasound that revealed a dark patch on my liver. I remember thinking, I don't drink that much, or do I? I certainly enjoy a glass of wine at the weekend, and I'm sure I'm as guilty as the next person in underestimating my alcohol consumption, but I usually don't drink during the week unless there is a special reason. From the ultrasound, things escalated quickly. I was assigned a cancer nurse and a whole load of worry as I went for blood tests and more and more scans.

In my head, I had confronted and worked through the idea of the worst happening and had begun to think practically about what would happen to the children. Adding to the concern was that I had 'inconveniently' seen the doctor at a time when we were in the business of switching our life insurance policies. It was not a conversation I particularly wanted to have with the doctor's receptionist, but I needed to ensure that if I died Lloyd would not be in a financially insecure position.

Thankfully it all turned out well. The relief when the consultant at the cancer unit said, 'These shadows are benign,' was immeasurable.

But the eventual diagnosis led to something else. As I sat looking at the X-ray, trying to find the explanation for the shadows, it occurred to me that on the last night of living in my adopted home just before I ran away, something happened. In fact, it was the very reason that I ran away: the oldest male child in the house had beaten me up and kicked me in the side after he knocked me to the floor. There was scarring on one of my ribs. The consultant said it looked as though it had been broken and repaired a long time ago. I felt like crying. I knew damn well what this was. It took a cancer scare to reveal how severe those old beatings were. The consultant asked me if I was alright. 'Yes, sorry. It just all makes sense now,' I said. I know that the emotional injuries of child abuse stay long into adulthood, but I had forgotten that sometimes the physical ones remain too. I was too sad to tell him more.

I know very little about what has happened to Jacob in his past, beyond that he was neglected and spent his time curled up in a dog basket. I know how unresponsive he was when I first met him and I fear that the magnitude of his global delay might have more sinister causes linked to the lack of stimulation as well as the extreme physical confinement. I want the MRI to prove me wrong, but I am terrified that it won't.

Time to get back to Jacob. The sun is shining and I ask if he wants to ride the tricycle. He nods his head enthusiastically. It's an old one of Jackson's, from when he was a toddler, before he had his first bike, but Lloyd has raised the seat up as high as it will go and that makes it perfect for Jacob. I lead him out into the garden and hold the handle bars steady as he steps onto the seat. My own legs feel weak as I watch him wave his legs about, struggling to gain purchase on anything. I place his feet carefully on the pedals and then jump ends to put my open hand behind his back, support him and help him pedal forwards.

He is ecstatic – laughing, burbling, repeatedly waving his arms around. So much so that it's hard trying to get him to keep his hands on the handlebars at all – but he's having a great time. There can't be anything really wrong with him, can there?

Chapter Eight

Last night I was awake for hours thinking more about the MRI scan. Magnetic resonance imaging doesn't sound too terrible as a technology, but I know that many find it a frightening, traumatic experience to go through. There is still another day to go but it is really playing on mind. After my own experience I can see how it could be terrifying for a child. I have to admit I fell into the category that the radiologist described as 'Busy Mum', meaning that I actually fell asleep throughout the entire event and had to be woken up several times to hold my breath and breathe out on command. I suppose it felt peaceful lying on my back in a tiny space with weird noises around me. Others have described it as like a womb and, with no one else to think about for once, I nodded off in my safe space within about a minute. The fact that the radiologist had a name for women like me is, I suppose, testament to the crowded lives that many of us lead.

But I'm fairly certain that Jacob has not had many life experiences outside his dog bed and Five Stones Farm. I fear he won't understand what is happening to him and may be scared. I don't want to unravel the great work that has taken place over the last few days to counteract some of that global delay.

I think about that farm a great deal, too. I would love to know where it is so that I could take a look. This notion tips over into the unacceptable and 'none of your business, Louise' territory but, in defence of curiosity I also see this as part of my understanding of his history. I think it is a natural human instinct. My adopted mother, who operated beneath the radar of the local authority, found out where my birth family lived. She stalked them until she created a plan. She drove me to my birth grandparents' house and dropped me off with a note and carrier bag of clean clothes before driving off – so I, of all people, know that boundaries need to be kept intact here.

Mary is due to be here today. Having not slept very well I am up before the alarm and downstairs to let the dogs out, who – after their gentle morning dog-stretch yoga session – approach the back door as though they are ferocious attack dogs, almost beating it down with their paws in their haste to get out.

I turn on the oven for those who want warm croissants and pull out some bowls, plates and cutlery. This makes sure that I have (nearly) every base covered. For those mums out there that manage to run their houses like clockwork, decide each day what their children will eat and have it prepared before they get down each morning, I salute you. I think perhaps I occasionally had that level of control before we began fostering but now I have let it go. Well and truly. After incidents of children spitting food across the room, or flat refusal to eat anything that was not a Pop Tart, or upturned cereal bowls, or cold chicken nuggets as the only acceptable breakfast food, after major rows and fights at the table between fostered and birth children, I tend to take a more laidback approach to – well, nearly everything – but especially mealtimes. There are more important things in life and I choose my battles carefully.

While the rest of the household continues to slumber I snatch the opportunity to unload the dishwasher, put on a load of washing and feed all the animals who, after nourishment at breakfast time, have just about enough energy to go back to bed for another little nap. Oh to be a pet round here.

Then, with the help of Mabel, I walk to all the children's rooms to finally wake them at the latest possible hour while still ensuring that they will be in plenty of time for school.

First I check on Jacob who is still asleep, lying flat on his back, mouth slightly open, snoring away with his obligatory dribble sliding down one side of his mouth towards his chin. He sleeps like a log thanks to all the stimulation and fresh air. I hope it isn't too much. I have a slight concern about the sleep, a little nagging worry. I push it away.

I wanted to take him to the beach today but, what with

Mary and my concerns about the MRI scan, and the fact that he is sleeping in again, I think I may have to move that and hope the weather holds until Friday.

Along the corridor I knock on Jackson's door who growls out, 'I'm awake' which, roughly translated in teenager, means 'back off and leave me alone'. This state usually lasts for about fifteen minutes, until I will hear an elongated, 'Muuum,' accompanied by some request or other which suddenly renders me no longer surplus to requirements. 'Where's my PE kit?' being a typical follow-up.

Lily is her usual cheerful self in the morning 'Mmmmmh, yes thanks, I know it's the morning.' Such a bundle of joy, but it is just her way. She generally brightens up once she has got dressed.

Last, but not least, I climb up the stairs to Vincent's room. He lives in the eaves and has, in my opinion, the best room in the house. None of the others wanted it when we did a decorating change – and he called dibs. Vincent is certainly the most decisive of all the children and loves the fact that because he's up there I sometimes forget him for jobs and homework questions. But he would be annoyed if I forgot to call him for dinner.

'Morning, Vince,' I sing out, knowing that from him is the best chance of a civilised response. He replies, from somewhere beneath his Mexican skull duvet, something approximating 'Ello Mother'.

'Your breakfast will be ready soon,' I tell him, and bend

to pick up some stray clothes from the floor. More will appear when he is finished in the shower. I spend half my life foraging for dirty washing – which is frequently mixed in with the piles of recently neatly-folded clean laundry on the floor.

They are all at different but crucial stages in their development. I have to make sure that my sons know how to not be a pain in the butt for any future partner or housemate by not cleaning up after themselves or not understanding that there are no housework fairies – it's down to them. Equally, I need to live in a functioning household. I sometimes think women have been conned. We have jobs to help pay the horrendous cost of living these days, and when we are home we start all over again, cleaning and sorting and organising. I recently read somewhere that 70% of women's labour is unpaid. Here I go again. Another unhealthy train of thought especially at this time of the day.

I head down to the kitchen to find my pooches have trotted back in – but not to see me with effusive affection, merely to check if any spare food is going yet.

For a while Jackson kept giving the dogs extra treats, and also removing some of their actual food. He loved them, and thought he was doing them a favour. Dotty began to get quite tubby as a result. In fact, she looked like a loaf of bread with a head. I'm strict these days about their food intake as I don't want any unnecessary vet bills – ever since

I saw my old vet drive off in a gold Rolls-Royce. I have a view on vet bills, like I do on most things, and my view on vet bills is simply that I don't want them. Gradually I hear the pitter-patter, or perhaps stomp-stamp, of young teenage feet on the stairs.

Once the chaos has faded and the older children have headed off to the same school but in different directions (due to top site and bottom site logistics of the school entrances), I turn the radio up and move round the kitchen, clearing and cleaning as I go. All this activity doubles up as thinking time. When I eventually stop, I have decided on a plan – and also decide to start the enquiries before Mary arrives. I hold the MRI appointment letter in my hand and call the number. When I get through to the right person, I explain my worries for Jacob under his particular set of circumstances, and how I am concerned about quite how he will react. The warm, reassuring voice on the other end of the telephone invites us up that evening, when it will be quiet.

'Come along with Jacob so that he can see the equipment, try it out, get to meet some of the staff. Then nothing will be unfamiliar when he comes back the following day for his actual appointment.'

She offers this as though it is no problem whatsoever, an ordinary part of the service. What a wonderful response, and so far above and beyond the call of duty that I am quite overwhelmed. I'm full of admiration for the hospital.

A good start to the day, after all that lying awake anxiously last night. I feel so much happier. She's put my mind quite at rest.

It's time to collect his Lordship from his slumbers. But, yet again Jacob has outsmarted me and exceeded expectation. As I walk up the stairs I see him lying across the landing pushing a toy car and making 'brrrm brrrm' sounds. Such a small thing. Such enormous implications. What a difference a day makes. And here I go again, I'm fighting back the tears. They are never very far away at the moment.

'Good morning,' I say to Jacob, as though this is perfectly normal and not some magical feat. He ignores me more or less, so busy is he with his toy car, squinting through its windows.

I loathe to interrupt his play, but there is a day to get on with. 'Do you fancy getting dressed and coming down for breakfast?'

He doesn't answer directly but rolls onto his back and does a starfish with his arms and legs, accompanied by one of his infectious giggles. He rolls again, back onto his front, and I discover the method by which he got out of bed and made his way into the hall. It's quite a neat little technique.

He rolls back into his room, then pulls on the headboard to stand up. He manages all this in a very accomplished way, but it is all done with a mischievous little grin. He knows the progress he is making and he is delighted with himself. It is writ large in every millimetre of his smile. I sit on the bed next to where he is standing. He is seeking approval and acknowledgement, and I dish it out in spades.

'Well, oh my. And haven't we been busy this morning. Is there no end to these talents? You really are the most amazing young man, Jacob, you know that, don't you? You are smashing it and I absolutely love it. And you. I love you.'

There. I said it. Out loud. I have made my declaration. I can't hold it in any longer. And it is true. This little boy has moved me almost more than anything else until now ever has. I want him to understand the impact he has on people. On me. I put my hand across his.

'Do you know what love is?'

He looks at me, and I am sure his eyes are more 'open' than they have been until now. He gives me another delicious smile, lifts his hand away from mine and says, 'You are love.'

Oh, my.

Okay, so he doesn't understand, quite, but my goodness me, it is astounding. It is also his first sentence. First we had sounds, yesterday we had some words and names. But 'you are love.' I've never been called that before. Whatever it means in his version of a world order, it is a beautiful thing to say, and, yes, I feel prickly behind the eyes again.

Right. Onwards. I am winning at life today. I am embracing my chance to be with a child full of energy and zest for life. It is infectious, and he is a delight to be near.

Yesterday I dreamed that he might pull back the covers and get himself out of bed. He's done that. So he's not quite jumping out of bed and running down the stairs, but this is already way beyond expectations.

Next I help Jacob dress.

I pull his pants up, today without a nappy. I am taking the view that he needs to potty train and tell me when he feels like going to the toilet. I strongly believe that being independent, away from the nappies, at least in the day time, will help him feel that he is growing up and demonstrate that he is more like the other children. I am well aware that this is going to create a lot of extra work. Not to mention more cycles of the washing machine.

No matter.

That's why, I think, the last foster carers hadn't helped to move Jacob on: because they couldn't be bothered. And that just isn't fair. I don't think anyone should foster if they're not going to put the work in. I feel sick in the stomach if I learn of foster carers taking the allowance and not doing the work. There are so many people out there who would be fantastic foster carers but just haven't thought they could or should.

I do wonder if the old-fashioned model of a foster family – husband, wife and a few birth children, then foster children following on – is missing the opportunity of a much broader range of foster carers. I think single people, partnerships, gay, straight, LGBTQ+, black, white, all walks of life, all ages, whatever, absolutely none of that should matter. I have met people with the biggest hearts and wonderful spirits that could look after other people's children but local authorities and agencies struggle to send out this message. It's a shame. There are many versions of family these days and, whatever the model, as long as the love and care is there, and the goal is to do the best for the children, it should not matter. As an aside, last week one of my foster friends told me her local authority were in trouble for recruiting gang members as foster carers, who were simply recruiting the children into the gangs. How do they get it so wrong? The fostering world is a skewed place.

I am distracted from my thoughts by red marks on Jacob's lower back. I have noticed them before, but I wonder now if they are part of the residue from the previous neglect in that foster placement. Could he have fallen, or hurt himself somehow? It's another possibility. But these marks look pretty persistent. They don't seem to want to go away. Mary has spoken about trusting instinct. Could the marks be older than that? Some accident, or action, from the farm? I look at Jacob and wonder. It doesn't take much for a paedophile to access a child – especially if there is absolutely no threat or resistance. I know Mary has told me that there were no men, but I wonder. There must have been farmhands, workers. The other adults may have never known. I sincerely hope not. I wonder if Dr Jahandar saw them. He didn't comment if he did.

Once Jacob is dressed – he selects a superhero t-shirt today that feels entirely appropriate given all his achievements – I hold his hand and we walk out the door. Unsteadily, sure, but he is taking steps and managing his own weight rather than me supporting him. I glance back towards his unmade bed and untidy room and think to myself that I will straighten it out when I get a chance later. Right now I want to spend time with Jacob and return to his sensory diet. Who knew that such a strange phrase could become such a natural part of one's vocabulary? The inverted commas that were around it in my head originally when I heard it from Dr Jahandar, and the little pause I have been giving before I say those words out loud, have disappeared.

Jacob holds my hand more tightly. No doubt this is for his security, but it is an overwhelming sensation for me. I can't believe how, as they say in the profession, 'attached' we have become in such a short space of time. I always try to bond with the children in my care, but I don't know that it has ever happened quite so fast or so naturally before. The social scientists and psychologists like John Bowlby, who anyone associated with foster care or adoption is likely to be familiar with, accord great importance to attachment. In young children, and actually these days amongst adults, attachment is classified into four different styles or patterns. Put simply these are strategies for responding to a caregiver: 'secure' which is as it sounds and is distinguished by autonomy; 'anxious-resistance' which comes across as preoccupied and might manifest as punishing a caregiver for absence; 'avoidant' which again, does what it says on the tin and can look dismissive or uncaring; and 'disorganised' which is very unpredictable and reflects unresolved attachment issues.

Nowhere in that description does the word 'love' appear. I wonder if social scientists have a problem with using the term 'love'. Maybe it is avoided because it can't be measured.

I have seen children, and indeed experienced it myself, where many feelings that could be described as 'attachment' seem to surge through the heart and mind and behaviour. I'm surprised by the feelings I have for Jacob, but I do wonder if children in the care system are given too many labels. I found Lily sitting in the kitchen a few months ago looking awful. I asked her what was wrong. She said she had 'extreme anxiety'. When I asked her how she had arrived at this conclusion she showed me a questionnaire from a website about young people's mental health. If you say to anyone now 'well it didn't have a name and we just got on with it' you would be shot down. But, after talking to Lily – who was convinced she was suicidal – I do wonder if having so many labels actually conspires to make people feel worse about themselves. I don't know. I'm reflecting on my old life as a young person growing up in care and experiencing abuse. My determination to not be in that situation outweighed the feeling of recognising it and suffering. Maybe it goes back to those kinaesthetic and auditory differences. But because Lily was looking at those websites, and that must have stemmed from how she was feeling, I have kept a close eye on her ever since, and all the children for that matter. I'm not convinced that talking therapies for children and young people is the best answer. As ever, I don't have all the answers. I know that I need to be aware and have information and support ready if anything else happens for Lily.

Though he isn't quite ready for the London Marathon, Jacob does brilliantly as we walk down the stairs and into the kitchen. I do support him in the precarious moment in between each step downwards as his weight shifts, but he is getting the hang of things. This doesn't even look like the same child who undertook yesterday's 'stair-swimming'.

The dogs, as always, greet him as though they have never previously met. Full introductions accompanied by wagging and licking and jumping and fuss. I let go of his hand when he pulls hand away to react to the dogs. I find this hard as I naturally want to protect him, but he wants to grow, and it is my job to let him.

He shuffles towards the chair, unaided now. It is an awkward movement with its own, strange momentum, but I look at his posture and his back and shoulders. I'm not an expert, obviously, but he seems to have a good straight back. I am wishing for that so much for him.

He manoeuvres himself towards the chair he sits in, the one with the straps. He pushes the straps away and drags himself awkwardly onto the red-painted bentwood chair next to it. I found the chair in a junk shop over twenty years ago and it is a feature of our mismatched kitchen collection. I am worried that it isn't sturdy enough for him. My heart is beating fast, my weird thigh thing is happening, everything is on full alert as I watch him haul himself up onto the seat of the chair. I can't just watch though, and find myself standing holding the back of the chair to steady it, in perfect position to grab him if he wobbles.

Again, my protective instincts are unrequired.

He does it!

It makes my morning. How my days have changed since Jacob arrived, and in what new, small ways I derive pleasure and joy around his progress.

I move his seat forward until he is sitting safely at the table with his legs in and no straps. I am not entirely comfortable with this new arrangement but he has selected this chair and it will therefore have to do. 'What would you like for breakfast today?' I ask him, just as I do all the children. I don't really expect a reply yet. He is still on catch-up. It is early days. He doesn't know what the possible options are, nor his own tastes as yet. But I want him to feel that we are all waiting for him to ease in when he's ready. I start listing the choices: toast, cereal, croissants and so on. I am still not sure how much he is distinguishing between the words, and what associations he can make. I am just about to get the items out to show him to help with the decision-making.

'Toast.'

Inside I am dancing but I am conscious that I can't keep over-praising him and overwhelming him with my joy. I beam right back at him and say, 'My Lord Master Jacob Tillyard, we are in business!' I make these silly titles up and I always call the children by their whole names, Mr Benjamin Green or Miss Zoe Collins, and so on. It is important to me that they hear their names. It's an important part of the creation of their identity and it reminds them that we have not assumed ownership over their pasts and lives.

'And what might you like on your toast?'

As I head to the fridge to find the jam and marmalade, I watch him begin to look deeply unimpressed. In fact, I see a frown of disappointment and disapproval. I'm a bit confused by his reaction. I move towards the pullout door of my (overpriced) handmade kitchen units. (I limited the planned number of units when I saw the cost). At the point of the door opening his face lights up. What skullduggery is afoot here, I wonder. Ah, chocolate spread, that's what!

I am a mum who grew up in care, and early life experiences that were filled with trauma and cruelty. But alongside the abuse, there were many gaps in my childhood experiences, some of which might seem trivial – like not going to see the film *Grease*. All my friends went, but my adoptive mother thought it would corrupt me to see it – an age-appropriate film that everyone else in the world was talking about. Small things: I never had peanut butter until I had tea round a friend's house. No frivolous expensive extras for me, which is why, I'm sure, that my children and all those who stay here are offered almost everything. So Nutella it is for our young friend. I wonder which of the other children has already manage to corrupt Jacob with chocolate on toast, because blimey, they're swift. It must have been last night when I was upstairs. I thought I caught a whiff of toast but ignored it, assuming it was a teenage munchie attack.

I have stood on the doorstep after a sleepover while mothers collect their offspring and inform me that they had managed to keep their children away from chocolate spread until they came here – where they had it on their breakfast pancakes, thank you very much. I cut the toast up into triangles and place it on a side plate in front of Jacob.

Once breakfast is over, Jacob claps his hands together, as if to say, 'Come on then, what's next?' It's become a bit of a habit for Jacob to have a few nibbles whilst he works, so even though he has only just eaten, I go to the fridge to get the grapes. I discover the empty plastic container with a few grape twigs in the bottom. Delightful. Thank you, everyone. I say 'everyone' but I bet that was Vincent. Oh well. I head over to the microwave area knowing that I have a new packet of Ritz biscuits in the cupboard. I look and look and wonder if I have gone mad but then the realisation hits me. I'm living with locusts! The biscuits have gone too.

I break all my own rules and end up slicing up a Milky Way into small pieces and putting them in a little bowl near Jacob – who looks delighted. I replaced Lloyd's printer paper yesterday so I feel no guilt about raiding it again. I take the felt tip pens from the arsenic-green antique in the corner. (My kitchen is the same colour as Doc Martin's surgery and definitely the same colour as the chemist where the dotty lady with the neck brace works.) I put them down and wonder if a fourth coffee of the day would bring on a headache. I'm an ex-post-punk rebel. Of course I will have another coffee – and blow the headache. I turn on the coffee maker and watch Jacob take the top off two felt tips and use them together, one in each hand. Ambidextrous now, are we? I think.

I hear the phone. It's Mary and she's outside – here sooner than expected.

'I didn't like to just knock. I wanted to see if it was okay to come earlier. Or I could wait in the coffee shop at the local garden centre?'

It's a lovely level of politeness. 'Come now. You're in luck. I'm just making coffee.'

'Am I on speakerphone again?' she asks.

'Not this time,' I laugh. She already has the measure of me.

Mary's visit is more than social. She has news of a potential adopter who has expressed interest in Jacob.

'But don't get too excited, and no breath-holding. My manager is already kicking up a fuss because of the cost. This person actually comes from another county and via a national charity, so I will have my work cut out making it happen. You and I both know how tight funding is, so let's not count chickens, and obviously not a word to Jacob. I don't need to tell you that.'

By the time Mary reaches the front door, Jacob has wriggled his way out of the chair at the table and shuffled himself along the stone kitchen floor into the hallway. He has clocked what is happening and is coming to greet her too. Or that's my reading of it. The dogs stand guard as he pulls himself up on the hall furniture – as though ready to catch him if he were to fall. Mary stands at the open doorway with a big smile on her face, 'Oh good morning Jacob, what a clever way to get around!'.

I notice something moving in Mary's car behind her. I look a little harder and am surprised to see a small boy.

Mary turns around to follow my gaze. 'Jacob, and Louise, I'd like you to meet my grandson, Ben.'

I feel slightly out of kilter and can't quite work out what is going on here. I wasn't expecting to see another child and it throws me.

Mary beams. 'It's actually my day off and I thought you needed a break. The boys can play together.'

My face must betray my confusion because Mary looks stern, briefly. 'We're going to the beach.'

'But I...'

'You don't need to do anything other than get yourselves into my car. I have a picnic and all else that we might possibly need.'

I am stunned. I am definitely someone who likes spontaneity, but I realise in that moment that I only like it when I have arranged it. Oh the irony – and I so like to characterise myself as a free spirit.

I grab Jacob's shoes and start rummaging around in the hall cupboard for suntan lotion. Mary rocks back on her heels. 'Did you not hear what I said? I have it all. Suntan lotion aplenty.'

How did she know what I was looking for just then? I shrug my shoulders, resigned to the fact that this woman has the better of me. In a good way. I adjust to my new plan for the day and surrender to the idea of not being in control for once. Mary is a bloody marvel. And she is doing this with her day off. I run off to lock the back door and put the dogs away. *Okay, Louise. Release that free spirit*, I tell myself. We are about to have a wonderful, impromptu adventure.

Chapter Nine

By the time I have fussed around with the necessary arrangements to leave the house so unexpectedly, Mary has already put Jacob in the car. I notice that she has a new child seat. I look at it wondering why she would have such a seat. Perhaps she has a disabled grandchild. She hasn't said, but then I already know that she is full of hidden depths and experiences and nothing much would surprise me. Jacob looks like a king sitting tall on his mighty throne in the back.

'It's good, isn't it? Jacob's new seat. I managed to get my manager to cough up. Jacob can give it a spin today and we can transfer it to your car when we get back.'

Sometimes, when you know proficient people like Mary, life can start to feel like a Christmas Day, full of happy revelations. I check that I have my bag and purse, clamber into the car and within a few minutes of Mary's arrival we are on our way to the beach.

It's a school day, which is a great time to take preschool children out for the day. We park as close as we can to the beach for Jacob's sake, though I am beginning to think that at his current rate of progress a walk with Jacob would not faze us.

'I didn't bring his wheelchair,' I say, feeling a sense of rising panic.

Mary shrugs. I am enjoying being in the company of a social worker who shrugs, and doesn't write everything down. Sometimes as a foster carer you can begin to feel like a robot who must process every little detail of the care you give to a child. Mary is allowing some of that responsibility to fall away from me and it is a liberating feeling.

Mary gets Ben out of the car first. He is four years old, so very close to Jacob in age, and a darling. The boys have already managed to strike up quite a friendship in the back of the car. I clocked a mischievous look on Jacob's face en route. I love that face. He deserves some mischief. It strikes me that he probably has tragically little experience of boys his own age, so it must be wonderful to encounter one – perhaps for the first time. Mary and I decide that we will hold a hand each with Jacob and walk both boys down to the sandy beach. Mary has Ben on the other side of her, while I have one of Mary's rather large rag bags across my shoulder. It's heavy, but I'm hardly in a position to complain, and I know that Jacob's burden is far bigger. He is struggling to walk, each step seems to make the next one harder as he performs an action that his body isn't used to. He refuses to give in. It's as if he has decided that he will not allow his body to slow him down and he gets the fillip he needs when he takes in the sea. His face is a picture. In fact he stops us, stands upright with his arms outstretched, and shakes his hands at the ocean, windmilling with pleasure.

I suddenly feel emotional again. His reaction makes me sure this is the first time he has seen the sea.

I begin to prop Jacob against me, worried about him standing independently on this uneven ground.

Mary pulls my arm back. 'See if he can do it himself. It doesn't matter if he falls,' she whispers. 'It's safe.'

So I stand nearby, my arm positioned by his shoulder. We stare out to sea, and I tell him all about it. I point out the huge seagulls that have already begun circling in their predatory way. I guess they see a small human and think 'food opportunities' having learned that children usually drop crumbs or are easy prey for a snatched morsel. Years ago, when I lived in Portsmouth I became a governor at a middle school. I had been working as an artist in residence. I would work with a handful of different children each day and we would paint the walls with their designs. I remember sitting outside at lunchtime with a group of children while I ate my sandwiches and feeling terrified as these huge white gulls bombed the children for their food. Sometimes we had to run inside to escape.

Jacob quickly loses his strength and slides down onto the blanket that Mary has laid on the shingle. I resist the urge to pick him back up, guessing that Mary is watching and willing his independence. But she is preoccupied with Ben, who cannot get out of his day clothes fast enough. In the blink of an eye he's in his swimmers and off to the sea. He is wearing his crocs to protect his little feet from the pebbles. I take in Mary, who follows barefoot and walks down to the sea without a flinch. Some people seem to be able to cope with walking on pebbles. I don't belong to that species. I don't know how something that looks smooth can cause me such problems, but walking across a beach I seem to perform a kind of frenzied dance that might suggest to an onlooker that I have been shot by a sniper at regular intervals. I hate it!

Watching his new friend race down to the ocean gives Jacob another little spur, so we gather ourselves once more and I hold his hand as we make our way slowly and far less gracefully down to the water's edge. I show Jacob the sparkly twinkles of white light dancing over water. I marvel at his open face as he drinks it all in, his eyes big and round with delight. Again, I feel an overwhelming maternal instinct. It reminds me of when I took our boys to the beach in Southsea when they were tiny. They ran about and played, and I remember this feeling of holding one hand as they cautiously tried their toes in the water for the first time with a mixture of fear and exhilaration. Jacob is cautious, too. The shock of the cold and the sensation of the shingle sucking away as the waves pull back is like nothing else. We stand and giggle together as the water washes over his feet, but I feel his laughter rather than hear it. The chatter of gulls and the sea breeze with the rushing of the water carries our sounds away into the distance.

As with everything he does, Jacob soon becomes a little more daring. After a few minutes he begins to make little jumps over the tiny waves as if he can beat them. He looks so happy in this elemental moment.

I don't know quite what it is about sea air, but blimey does it bring on an appetite. I know that Mary said she had everything but I wonder if that meant snacks and lunch. I hope so, and if the weight of my bag was anything to go by then we might be in luck. I'll know soon enough.

Jacob tires again quickly and I wrap a towel around his shoulders as we edge back to our spot.

I am reminded of other days and other adventures – all the foster children I have brought here over the years. I know once that I was sitting on a blanket just like this talking on the telephone to a social worker about one of the children who was playing in the sea, just as Jacob is now. It was a little girl whose older brother had been living in a children's home when he had got involved in joyriding. He and two other lads were out in a stolen car which crashed, killing all three boys. The social worker was planning to come round that evening to tell the girl. I remember staring at the child while we talked about how to tell her. Fostering is not an easy activity; it takes such an emotional toll.

I push that unhappy memory aside. I am grateful for

the release that today has brought, and Jacob is thriving on the experience.

Mary comes out of the sea. She has rolled her jeans up to her knees and looks carefree, though I know she is not. The sea air is working for us all. Ben, beside her, is having a wonderful time darting in and out of the water. I sit down on the blanket and pull out a bucket and spade from one of Mary's large rag bags. The bags are brightly coloured and eye-catching and I wonder if they are her own creation. They have a Peruvian or Guatemalan-inspired look about them.

'Did you make these, Mary? They're gorgeous,' I call out as she walks towards the blankets.

She gives a little laugh. 'No, not my work, I'm afraid. My husband brought them back from Peru. He was working there for a bit on an education project. We've had them for years and years actually – they have always been the beach bags, even when my own children were little. They've done well over the decades. Definitely well made – the benefits of local craft work!'

I nod. They have reminded me of when I was a student and became friendly with some humanities undergraduates who branched off and did social work. I recall just how 'different' social work students seemed back then. They were usually quite radically left wing and made sure they wore that on their sleeve. Not just on their sleeve but all over. They had a certain 'look': Palestinian scarves, ripped jeans, badges with political slogans pinned ironically on their army bags, and the distinctive waft of patchouli oil emanating from them. I have a vivid memory of sitting in a courtyard with a bunch of them earnestly discussing *Das Kapital* by Karl Marx. There was a real passion for doing good work. Some of their ideas were a bit mad and 'out there', but on the whole they believed they could agent change for the greater good. Mary would have fitted right in with that group. I wonder what they are all doing now and whether they have remained true to their ideals, or have even stayed in social work. Maybe they are managers, or maybe, like Mary, they have fallen by the wayside in the cut and thrust of the profession. I have met many managers in children's social care who seem to basically say 'no' to the foster carers, social workers and children. It seems difficult to imagine that they once held beliefs like this. I wonder if they remember?

Mary breaks off that train of thought by turning to Jacob and asking, 'Are you hungry?'

I hope he understands and says yes, because I know I am!

Mary doesn't wait for an answer but brings out a white Tupperware container.

Jacob nods enthusiastically.

Oh good, I think, and wait for the rest of the picnic to come out and join us. Sadly, it doesn't. That is it, a few meagre sandwiches and a banana each. I try very hard not to register my disappointment by smiling merrily and being grateful – after all, I have brought nothing to this party. I watch Jacob and I'm sure I don't imagine that he looks a bit disappointed too. It is already clear to me that he has days where he just does not stop eating. I let him eat as he obviously needs it and may be making up for lost time, not to mention all the additional calories he is burning through the greatly increased movement and effort that each day brings. I do think that children – and adults, come to that – end up self-regulating their eating. I surreptitiously eye up the fish 'n' chip restaurants and ice-cream parlours along the sea front and think we may call in on the way back to the car. That can be my treat and my contribution to the day. I went hungry for much of my own childhood and I know only too well how it can affect your mood and enthusiasm.

The boys soon make light work of their lunch, then resume play with the bucket and spade and cups that were also in the bag. It is a gentle, pleasant way to while away the afternoon; made more so by the fact that Mary and I are able to sit a few feet apart from the children and I get to ask what I have been dying to know: what happened to her husband.

'No, I don't mind at all,' she smiles, donning a rather colourful seventies-style beach hat and positioning it low to block out the sun. Everything about her is colourful. And, though this addition seems very in vogue, I have no doubt that it is not a retro fashion purchase but a Mary original.

'My ex is American and though no longer together we are still on good terms. We still speak occasionally on Facebook and meet when there is a family gathering. He is a good father. Well, he needs to be. He is the father of my five now grown-up children and he married twice again after we split up and had five more children. Father of ten. Can you imagine?'

Bizarrely, I can. We have had so many children in the house over the years that I feel that I am 'mother' many times over.

Mary, who I know has one of those pure hearts, will always do what's right – especially where children are concerned, so I don't doubt that they are on good terms, whatever might have happened between them to cause the split.

She picks up her story where she left off on the hospital journey. After the experiences at a strict Catholic boarding school, at twenty-one years old Mary went to New York in the 1960s to join the Women's International League of Peace and Freedom, a prominent feminist group advocating peace through women's leadership. On her first night after travelling by boat from Southampton to the States, she went to Harlem to hear Malcolm X speak. She stood in the crowd where Malcolm X was standing on the podium waiting to make his speech. He leaned into the microphone and said, 'I ain't speaking 'til the white chick leaves.'

'That day changed me for good. I turned and walked

away without looking back. I walked down to Harlem to find a cab. And I decided that no child in my care would suffer because they are in the minority.'

It was through peace demonstrations that Mary met her husband Jim, who was a Vietnam draft resister, and key political activist in the protest movement.

'In fact, he ripped up his draft notice and burnt it publicly at a demo in Washington Square. He ended up in prison as a result.'

I think my jaw must be dropping open as she talks about this other life that she has led. I feel as if I am drinking in a real, live history lesson. I find the whole thing fascinating.

Their worlds and political ideals coincided, Mary explains, and they married soon after. Almost immediately Mary fell pregnant with twin girls; later she had another girl and they moved to Pennsylvania, knowing full well that Jim would be arrested at some point, and choosing their home because the penitentiary wasn't too far away.

'Within a week of setting up our new lives, the FBI came knocking at the door and arrested Jim. He served a long and hard sentence – made much tougher because the other prisoners as well as the guards did not like draft dodgers.'

Mary looks away from me and out towards the horizon beyond the waves as she says quietly, 'That prison sentence broke him. He lost much of his spirit and ended up drifting from one woman to another looking for solace.'

It's not just a history lesson, it's a shocking personal tragedy.

When their marriage fell apart, Mary came back to England with her girls and after a lot of work and moving about living in caravans and saving up she got in at Ruskin, Oxford to study social work and help with the women's movement there. She remarried and had two more children. Her next husband was an organic farmer who set up a chain of successful organic shops across the UK.

'He made a great deal of money before he forgot his principles.' She pauses for a moment.

Mary left him too, now with five children to care for.

'Alongside working full-time in social work,' she smiles.

And I thought I had things tough. As she tells me about each of the children they all sound as if they are interesting people – who have each inherited Mary's powerful desire for change and to do good in the world, manifested in different ways. I run out of words, which is unusual for me, and there is a lull in our conversation as we both reflect. I look across the beach, wondering how many more of the silver-haired people enjoying the sun around us were involved in radical political movements in the 60s and 70s. When I was young I didn't think anyone over the age of fifty was capable of having a radical anything. There must be a whole generation looking like pensioners who have lived through some of the most dramatic post-war changes that have shaped our nation. I enjoy the idea that I am on the beach in the company of someone – and others around us no doubt – who has seen so much of the world and been part of some key moments in history, challenging ideas and rocking the status quo.

Jacob points out to the sea again, and it is clear that he wants to try his luck once more with the waves. If I'm honest, I'd prefer to sit here and chew the cud with Mary, but here are forms of sensory play beyond what I can provide in my kitchen – and I must seize every opportunity. It's also time for another application of sun lotion. I worry that his pale skin will turn pink in this sun. He has been starved of vitamin D and has an unnatural whiteness to his limbs.

We do another trip to the water's edge, me hopping about looking as though I'm dancing a Tarantella while trying to support Jacob on his Bambi legs. We make a right pair. This time Jacob goes into the sea as far as his chest. What progress from those tentative steps when we first arrived! It's another measure of his determination. Next time I think he will make it up to his chin. We dry off, and begin to pack away.

There is no doubt that those humble cheese sandwiches have left me hungry.

Next I do something naughty – without Mary's permission, I ask the boys if they would like an ice-cream.

'Yes please,' chirrups Ben, giving his grandmother a sideways glance. Jacob joins in with a sibilant 'essssss'. And how can I resist? I hold Jacob's hand as we walk across the pebbles to find patches of sand to stand in. This is one of my favourite places, even though I'm not a beach person – or at least not a pebbly-beach person.

We make it to the first ice-cream vendor, but I move onto the second. Why do I do this? I have no idea. When I'm on holiday I never eat at the first restaurant I come to, probably missing out on a very good experience. I'm not sure why I do that, but onto the next ice-cream place we go. We order ninety-nines with flakes. I ask Mary if she would like one too. Her eyes light up just as the children's do. We sit on the little stone wall by the beach and enjoy our treats. It's a lovely finish to our time here. The boys look happy: Jacob is singing something and humming through the monstrous mess of ice-cream that is imploding around his face. He has got some idea that he must lick off the dribbles running down the side of his cone but isn't managing it very successfully – and is perfectly happy in the struggle. I look at his face and see a change. There is a confidence here, further awakening, and though he is leaning against the wall rather than sitting on it, he is standing up straighter and taller than he has been.

I look at the time, fully aware that later this evening I'm taking Jacob to the hospital to see the MRI scanner.

Mary notices me look at my watch. I have loved our day and remain proud of the enforced spontaneity but I want to get back before the other children get home from

242

school. I also need to pop into the supermarket to get some additional bits for their tea. Sometimes a few cans of spaghetti on toast will do and it sits easily with Lily's vegetarianism. It's definitely time to be in the car, and the sugar rush will stave off my own hunger for now.

Within minutes of Mary pulling away I turn my head and see that both boys have fallen asleep.

'Good,' says Mary when I point it out. We can talk.'

She suddenly adopts a very serious tone. 'I've put Jacob on two national adoption registers. I used one of the wonderful photographs you sent me as his profile picture.'

'You know I have the copyright on that,' I laugh.

Mary goes on to say that she has met one couple who put themselves forward. 'They live in the district, but I don't think they're right for our Jacob.'

I ask why she thinks that.

She tightens her lips and her face hardens a little. 'I didn't feel the love. They were from a private fostering agency. The agency were very keen to introduce us and market them to me but, no, I'm not feeling it. I know that expensive long term placements are good business for an agency, and I didn't pick up that they had the experience needed to live long term with a boy like Jacob.' She sighs. 'They wouldn't meet his needs.'

Mary pauses. 'Now is it right or left here?'

She didn't seem to have any trouble with directions on the way – and I realise that she is feeling awkward.

'Look, my manager has asked me to ask you if you would adopt Jacob,' she says, blurting it out all of a sudden.

I feel a wave of sickness and frustration. 'Mary, we couldn't look after Jacob long-term. Our lives are not geared up for that.' I'm surprised that she has asked.

Mary smiles. 'I know that. But I had to ask. My manager is looking only at the cost and in-house fostering or adoption is the cheapest option. But no, you have a young family and work commitments and your house isn't geared up for a child with disabilities.'

I feel sad, but also mightily relieved that Mary is not putting pressure on us. She is sensible and cares for the children far more than the managers seem to.

'There is another couple, from the north east, who have expressed an interest. They have come via a different route.' Mary explains that they are from one of the well-known charities, not an agency, though it means that they do also come with a big cost.

'My manager is already smarting because I've arranged to visit the couple at their home.' It will require an expensive overnight excursion that the manager didn't want to fund. Mary explains that he has suggested she talk to them online, and that they could do a virtual tour of their home.

'But I'm not having any of that, thank you very much. I've booked my train tickets and I'm going to meet them in person. This is about what's best for the child, not for the service's coffers.' Mary reminds me that she used to be a manager in her old job in another county.

'So I do understand some of the pressures that he's under. And that's one of the reasons I stepped down from it, because it became all about money and not what's best for the children.'

I suggest that the focus on cost, in my experience, has been a false economy that only delays important changes to a child's life for the better. 'And when the cheap option fails, as it usually does, there is no choice but to fund the now even more expensive plans.'

Mary makes a face. 'It's the business model that managers want, unfortunately.'

I ask how often her manager comes out to meet the children.

She laughs. 'In my experience? It hasn't happened so far.'

I know that Jacob could never stay with us long term. It simply isn't possible. That hasn't stopped me from considering it, of course, but my brain is beginning to make the adjustment to accepting it.

We drive on. Mary changes the subject and returns to talking about her own childhood experiences of growing up in a faith boarding school. I ask her what she now thinks about boarding schools.

She looks very serious for a minute. 'I hate them, actually.'

Wow. I wasn't expecting her to be quite so frank.

'They can be abusive and they cover things up.'

I am really saddened by this, and by the way she speaks. Sad because something terrible must have happened to Mary to make her this reactionary to the boarding school system. She suddenly laughs though, and tells me about Mass and going into the chapel twice a day to hear the missal.

'Missal?' I ask, seizing on the unfamiliar word. 'That sounds Jewish to me.'

'Maybe. But it's Catholic.'

As somebody who did not grow-up with religion in my life I actually know very little, and as with most life experiences I want to know more. I ask Mary to describe the chapel ritual.

'Oh, being woken at 6am, pulling back the beds to air, washing our faces in freezing water, getting dressed into stinking hideous clothes and filing down to the chapel to line up and take it in turns to kneel and receive holy bread and wine from the priest. The host.'

I ask why the priest is called the host and she laughs.

'Not the priest, the bread. But I don't know why it's called that. I've never really thought about it to tell you the truth. It just was.'

I listen to Mary and play back what I think she has just told me. 'So, you're woken up really early, while it's still dark in winter. There's no breakfast?'

She nods her confirmation.

'Then you queue up to kneel in front of a man

– who's speaking in Latin, a dead language that you don't understand?'

'Indeed.'

'Then you kneel down and take holy bread from this man while your head is at the same level as his groin?'

Mary shrieks. 'Oh my, I've never thought of that before. The whole thing is totally bonkers, isn't it? Weird. Beyond weird, actually. What were they doing? What were we thinking?' She finds my interpretation of events quite amusing, and I'm glad to provide some light relief for reflection on what was evidently a traumatic time.

As we drive closer to the house I ask Mary if I can run into the shop and get four tins of spaghetti. From the checkout I can see across to the car park where Mary is talking to the boys. They must have woken up, sensing that the journey has stopped for a few minutes. I have to confess to being slightly disappointed that they are awake. I want to know more about Mary's childhood and the dogma of Catholicism as she experienced it. My old best friend from Portsmouth grew up in the Catholic faith and suffered from guilt about everything, though the guilt never stopped her naughtiness: she just felt bad about it. I find the whole thing fascinating. It's something I truly don't understand. If we get the chance I will be sure to ask Mary more, but now is not the time.

My thoughts begin to shift towards children and hospitals.

Chapter Ten

After I have cleared the table and stacked the dishwasher, I begin to prepare for Jacob's trip to have the MRI scan. Lily, spotting an opportunity that there may be an outing about to happen, begins to circle. She stands in the kitchen doorway.

'So, where are you going?'

'I'm taking Jacob on a visit to see the MRI scanner so that he isn't too freaked out tomorrow when he has the scan.'

'Jacob. Of course. Why can't I come?'

I am slightly shocked by her response. I wasn't expecting that. I haven't seen it as anything that she or the others might be interested in. I explain that it is a trip for Jacob. 'And anyway, I thought you'd be happy painting on your canvas boards in your bedroom.'

I'm really shocked by what comes next.

'You care more about him than you do about me. You prefer him to any of us. You haven't had a second for the rest of us since he arrived. He's your favourite.'

Well, that takes the wind out of my sails. I didn't see that one coming – but then I never do with Lily. The boys have not been through the trauma that Lily has experienced in early life, they have a much more stable inner core. When Lily feels threatened she can seem quite bitchy and nasty. I know her well enough to just try and ride it out, let it pass. But it gets to me, and I find myself feeling cross. I know that this is irrational because I have found myself feeling cross with all the children, and it's none of their faults. I tell myself to be lovely to her and remind myself that Lily just feels a little insecure. I am about to sit down and reassure her properly when I notice the time. I have forty-five minutes to get to the hospital, park and find the MRI scanner, and I feel the stress mounting.

Lily looks at me with her big saucer eyes. They are narrowed a little, so that I can see her anger, and just in case I haven't quite got the message she is wearing a challenge in the thin line of her lips. I know this face. I know she could blow up at any minute and then my timings will be out completely.

'Can you wait until I get back for us to finish this chat properly?' I ask.

'You won't though, will you? You are all over him, fussing about. You'll be busy with something else he needs when you get back, and you'll have forgotten about me.

'No, Lily, I promise...'

'Anyway,' she cuts me off. 'He's not as bad as you think he is. He's playing you.'

For the second time in the space of a few minutes I am floored. Wow. I totally wasn't ready to hear that. Lily has an agenda here. We are in for a long, drawn out argument. Nothing I say will go unchallenged and uncriticised. I look at the clock again and think about what to do. Lloyd should have been home an hour ago but there is bad traffic at Newbury so he is late.

My neighbour Jean has kindly offered to watch the others while I am at the hospital, just until Lloyd gets back, but I'm panicking now. One look at the determined set of Lily's jaw confirms that a storm is brewing and I know it's not fair to leave her with Jean. Not that Jean can't handle herself: an ex teacher will certainly not be impressed with the tsunami of abuse and swearing that can pour out of Lily's mouth when she is in one of her more complicated moods.

'And my anxiety's back. Not that you would notice. Or care.'

Uh oh. I'm going to have to handle this carefully. I'm constantly having to unpick the threads of Lily's angry self to find out what is really bothering her.

'Anxiety? What do you mean?' I can't deal with this now. If I let her come she will win, but if I leave her here then I just have visions of Jean having to call the emergency duty team (EDT) out of hours desk. They will only advise in ways that 'hold' the problem until office hours. Once, when we looked after a seven-year-old girl, she had a severe trauma meltdown and began chasing Vincent with a kitchen knife and turned over all the chairs in the kitchen while screaming, 'Get off me!' even though no one was anywhere near her. The EDT support offered was to call the police. Fair enough. She was wielding a knife. Except that when I called the police, they kindly told me that she is the corporate responsibility of the local authority and as she was only seven years old, it was social services who needed to deal with the situation – they had proper, grown-up criminals to chase after. I didn't blame the police and felt guilty about wasting their time, but once you get caught up in an EDT call you feel obliged to do what has been suggested. I decide that the hypothetical scenario of Jean having to call EDT because Lily is in a bad place is not worth the energy and stress, and so I agree to take her with me.

'Lily, you *can* come on this occasion, but I expect your behaviour to be excellent. So, quickly get ready and don't make me late.' Punctuality is one thing that is very important to me and I am determined to teach all my children about the importance of it as a fundamental part of good manners. When I lived in Portsmouth there was a popular quotation that, because I associate it with that part of the world, I assume has a naval origin: *If you are late you waste my time; if you are early you waste your own time.* The message is to be on time. I am also conscious that the MRI department here are doing something out of hours for our benefit in addition to the medical appointment tomorrow, so I would be even more horrified to find myself late for our allotted time.

Jean will let herself in to the house after I text goodbye. It's a good arrangement that suits everyone. She never sees the boys: only when they come down for food. She enjoys babysitting, especially since Vincent showed her how to use the Firestick. She is talking about getting one herself and paying Vincent to teach her how to use it.

Lily quickly cheers up, and even begins to help me. The pouty teenager from just a few minutes ago has left the room and a charming child has replaced her. There is no sign of the 'anxiety' she is claiming.

'Can you go and get Jacob for me, and walk him into the kitchen?'

Having got her way, she acquiesces immediately. There are no second guesses needed over where to find him. He is lying on the floor next to Vincent, attempting Minecraft. Learning fast, he has built a weird house out of squares that he can't wait to show Lily – generally recognised as the expert in the Allen household since she has a whole Minecraft village on her computer.

While I'm packing up a tote bag with snacks and drinks, I call out to Lily to bring an activity along too. 'Use your imagination – something to entertain Jacob in case there's time to kill.'

We've all been there, stuck in a waiting room for hours.

I have done it so many times that I have this bit off to a fine art. One is always prepared with something to do.

I return to the sitting room and there they are: beautiful children all at peace – as if the earlier outburst had never happened and if Lily was best friends with Jacob rather than seeing him as some sort of nemesis. She has cheered up enormously, but we definitely need to do a little more work on how she might successfully get her point across without holding me to ransom. I think under other circumstances that could be called bullying. But it's a job for another day. The skills we need to teach our children are endless but most go towards helping them become lovely, kind, rounded people who can earn a living and hold down a job and a relationship.

Jacob has twigged that he is off out again, and loves the idea. He is ready with far less fuss and a good deal of excitement, a lopsided grin plastered across his face.

'Grab the car keys, Lily, from the standing man in the hall.'

We all walk out the back door through the garden and into the garage. I put Jacob's new seat in the back of the car; Mary has left it by my car because I had completely forgotten about it. It's exactly the same principle as a regular car seat but bigger, with good support for his neck and head. I fiddle about getting it into position safely, and encourage Jacob to get in and help me put the strap across. Children love independence and Jacob is no different – he is thriving because he is learning from the others. Lily sits herself in the front seat of course. The rule is that the oldest child on the journey can ride shotgun.

By the time we get to the hospital Lily has sung the whole of the Beatles album, with Jacob on backing vocals – an echo behind. Lily clearly loves it, though now doubt this would not be admissible evidence in front of her friends. She is still on catch-up from missing many normal childhood events such as singing along to parents' favourites, watching Disney classics and Pixar animations, and the opportunity to basically 'be a child'.

We park the car with no trouble, and when I offer Jacob his chair he says, 'No, I want to walk.' A full sentence, with proper grammar and syntax. Lily holds his hand and I realise that I haven't taken full notice of his growing vocabulary and linguistic development. Wow, he really is whizzing through his milestones. To my great relief I can see that the MRI centre is on the ground floor, second on the left after the Friends of the Hospital shop – very close by. Both children clock the various delights on display as we walk by the shop. Jacob holds his arm out and points to the shelves of sweets and crisps. I ignore it, just as I do for the older children and realise that this too is something of a development. A few days ago I might have responded, like you would when a baby reacts to something. We are all beyond that now – milestones for me as well as Jacob.

We walk into the MRI reception.

The man on the desk looks quite officious, but then to my surprise he looks at us and holds out his arms as though he is the maitre d' at a top restaurant. 'Welcome Jacob, you are our very special guest this evening.'

I am so impressed!

The waiting room is completely empty aside from us. We sit down and almost as soon as we do a nurse in smart blue trousers and matching top appears from a doorway to collect Jacob.

'This is Lily,' I say. 'Is it okay if she comes along too?'

'Of course it is. The more the merrier. Hello Lily!'

I'm utterly overwhelmed by the loveliness of the staff. We follow her through double swing doors into a sort of ante-room. She explains, in her best child-friendly English, that this is where Jacob will change into an outfit 'which looks a little bit like mine does.'

I watch the children's faces as they hang onto her every word. The nurse explains the lockers to put away the clothes you have changed out of. 'Some people come in on foot and some come in on a bed with wheels.'

Lily puts her hand up like she would if she was at school. I find this so endearing and almost forgive the earlier shenanigans. 'Do you have to pay to use the locker?'

The nurse reassures Lily that it is free and as far as she knows the NHS have not started charging for lockers. Then she looks in my direction. 'For now at least.' She is only half-joking and I respond with my solidarity face and a conciliatory eye-roll.

We walk through more white swing doors into a series of confusing little corridors full of complicated equipment. I can tell both children are seriously enjoying this experience – who knew that this might pass for a night's compulsive entertainment? Of course Lily wanted to come. I see it now. Both children have missed out on so much that even a simple bus ride into town or an unexpected car journey can be a big excitement. We walk into a much bigger space and there it is: the MRI machine. The nurse, whose name is Jo, introduces Jacob to Marques the radiographer. Marques is dressed in a similar fashion to Jo, but his outfit is a deep green to contrast with her blue. Both Jacob and Lily stand looking at the big white machine and in unison give a wide-eyed, 'Wooah.' It is as though they are seeing the lunar module, and actually, even to me, it doesn't seem far off.

Marques makes a point of shaking first Jacob's hand and then Lily's. I'm glad I brought her. She may be getting taller and older but she still loves things like this. And why wouldn't she? These wonderful professionals are making them feel very special.

'Did you bring a teddy with you, Jacob?' Jo asks.

Oops no, that's my fault. I didn't think. Note to self for tomorrow. But I needn't worry: Marques comes out of his area with a large purple monkey called Maisy. They talk Jacob and Lily through the whole experience, and use Maisy as a model. It is brilliant and, though I know this is intended for Jacob's benefit, I too feel so much better. I have been having nightmares about him screaming and feeling scared. I never know what has really happened to these children and my mind has learnt over the years of experience that if you think it was bad then it was probably worse.

After a wonderful half hour of humour, explanation and reassurance, and an experience that I didn't think could get any better, Jo brings out a small box. I recognise the Lego logo immediately. She gives Jacob an MRI scanner to build. I am amazed, but apparently Lego was commissioned by the hospital to make toys to help children understand what will happen to them for certain procedures. It is truly astounding. My impression of the NHS, this hospital and its wonderful staff continue to rise – and they were at a high level to begin with. What a tremendous bunch they are. I am so full of love for them and what they have done for Jacob that I think I'm going to burst. I manage to hold it together enough so that we can all say goodbye, and they tell us that their colleagues, Sally and Ross, will be in tomorrow to meet Jacob.

On the way out, I hear Lily say, 'You're so lucky. I wish I was having a scan.'

By the time we arrive home, Lloyd is standing in the kitchen drinking a coffee. I walk in holding Jacob's hand, which is the first thing he is surprised by. He gives me a raised eyebrow, acknowledging that some miracle has occurred in the last few days.

Lily cannot wait to tell him about the scanner and her new friends Marques and Jo. 'And look at the Lego they gave Jacob!' Like me, and Lily, Lloyd is blown away with the generosity of the toy, but also the depth of thought and understanding that has gone into that act. I get over-excited all over again as I tell my story about how blooming marvellous the staff were. 'And I would fight any government who tried to take it away from us,' I add for good measure.

Lloyd, who is well used to my opinions on greed and corporate takeovers, nods and finally has the chance to say, 'Hello Louise.'

It is always like this, and we are both used to it. I smile and greet him in return. 'And how was your trip?'

'Oh, you know. The work was fine but the traffic was horrendous. It took an age to get through it.'

I feel Jacob's hand tighten round my fingers and take the hint, moving away from boring adult chit-chat. We can do that when they're in bed. By now after all our adventures today it's really quite late so I instigate the 'it's nearly your bedtime' conversations. I take one look down at Jacob and decide that he can have a shower in the morning. He has had a busy day and if he doesn't go to bed soon I'll never get him up in the morning for his MRI. Lloyd has now drunk his coffee and is heading towards the wine rack. I will have to make a fuss of him and ask about his work event when I have got the children to bed.

Jacob shows Lloyd the Lego box. Lloyd sits down and asks Jacob if he would like to build it.

'I think he's...' I was going to say, 'had enough excitement for one day', but they haven't had the chance for much bonding time yet.

I sigh. Maybe not to bed just yet.

Chapter Eleven

The next morning I'm anxious, in spite of all the reassurances that last night's experience brought. I can feel it in my stomach and bones.

Lloyd is still asleep; the business trips are hard work and even though I have mocked the level of impact of the socialising dinners and drinks, it's still work and Lloyd complains that he never sleeps properly in hotels, even though where he stays is usually at the upper end of the luxurious scale, not like some of the budget accommodation the University put me in when I was away overnight for a training session. No swanky five stars for me. The place my colleagues and I stayed in was so rough that I found dirty toenail clippings in the bed and there was barbed wire around the car park – you know the sort you see in films about penitentiaries. So I know what he means about preferring your own pillow.

The children are up and rushing about with the usual chorus of 'where's this?' and verse of 'where's that?' with an improvised 'Who hid my tie?' thrown in for good measure.

Children are universal in their preference for blaming someone else before they have looked properly.

I do my 'Oh, is that *child* looking?' routine and find the items within seconds. Lily seems okay-ish, though I detect a hint of a sulky atmosphere in her replies through the door. I wonder what's brewing there and when she doesn't emerge, instinct tells me to go back up to see what's taking her so long.

I knock on the door, then open it gently. To my horror, with only a quarter of an hour before departure, Lily is in bed with the duvet pulled over her head. I'm stressed anyway and I know if Lily senses my stress she will go for the jugular. It's all part of the attachment disorders we traumatised children act out. I include myself because I'm sure I haven't come out of my own childhood unscathed. I also know that Lily comes from a background that was deceitful and manipulative and when I've challenged her in the past about some of her behaviour, I have regretted it.

'Strike while the iron is cold' is definitely today's mantra with Lily. I don't have time to go into battle – which is what we have done in the past. On occasion she has stood in her room screaming like a banshee, shouting that she hates me – loudly enough for passers-by ask if we need help, and I can only assume they must have thought I was committing murder. But not today little Madame Lily, I haven't got the time and I am old enough to play the games better. I pull back her curtains and open the window. Calmly and kindly, but with a dash of authority, I say, 'Can you tell me what's going on, Lily?'

She makes a sort of moaning sound.

I hate these scenarios, which I suspect we will do again and again until she has learnt to rethink her pattern of behaviour. It always goes like this: Lily displays passive aggressive avoidance. Then, if I say anything at all to challenge it, she zooms from 0-100 on maximum throttle within a second. Sometimes she can seem totally out of control – which of course, in many ways, she is. I can't reason with her when she is like this. She can't hear me through her trauma and so it is wasted breath. I also don't want the shouting this morning because Lloyd needs his rest. And I know, too, that if I don't deal with it effectively she will think it's okay to always behave like this to get her own way. I remember a social worker saying to me, 'See the child, not the behaviour.' The two things are very separate. What good advice that was – but it's not always easy to enact.

I establish that she feels sick and has a bad leg – an interesting combination of symptoms which explain why she can't get up. Hmmm. I'm not convinced, but I need to get Jacob to the hospital.

'Okay, Lily. You can stay there until I get back, and then you can get up, shower, tidy your bedroom, vacuum the sitting room and do all your homework.'

I'm not at my most sympathetic because I suspect that

the root cause of this is jealousy. But I am not going to give her a hard time. I know that the boys used to feel jealous of the attention I gave to her when she first arrived. I believe most things settle down and they will find their place.

'If you are a good girl I will pick up a salted caramel muffin from the café in the hospital,' I offer as an olive branch.

Lloyd's asleep so I leave him a quick note explaining the situation.

Downstairs both boys find me and, with a child's radar for any injustice, demand to know why Lily isn't going to school. I resist offering an easy white lie about feeling ill – because in our house feeling ill is not a good enough reason to miss school, as they well know. *Being* ill is a reason.

'I think she is having trouble with Jacob and the amount of attention he needs right now,' I explain.

To my horror, they both agree. 'Yes, he's your favourite child.'

Wow. If you want to stick the knife in, that's definitely the way to do it. Next I'll hear complaints from Lloyd and the dogs. I give them my best 'you're being ridiculous' eyebrows and just about stop myself from flouncing out of the kitchen, but the wind has totally been taken out of my sails. I set my shoulders back and concentrate on the next stage of today's mission: to get Jacob organised. But where is Jacob? When I open the door to his room he's not in his bed.

I don't call out his name because I'm still conscious that I don't want to wake up Lloyd, but blimey living with a family can feel like a comedy show sometimes.

Enter stage left, Jacob. Actually, not quite, but he has got himself to the loo and is sitting on it with his shorts down around his ankles swinging his legs. He looks incredibly pleased with himself. I stand by the door and put my hands on my hips.

'You are a very clever boy.'

'See?' says Vincent, walking past at that moment with the air of a prosecuting attorney in his final summing up.

Deep breath. I help Jacob with the rest of his morning ablutions and let him make his way down the stairs which he now does on his bum, a new technique. I remember the boys doing this until they became more confident. Jacob has got this! Life is so busy that I have not yet recorded every little milestone in Jacob's My Story book, converted from one of my hard-backed sketch books. I must remember to update it with these little moments. Officially the social workers are meant to do this and they call it Life Story Work, but I struggle with the term. Other children don't have to do it and it shouldn't feel like 'work'. I have taken a zillion photos of Jacob both on his own and with the other children and now Lloyd's back I can add him too.

I have to confess I have bought some rather splendid outfits for Jacob. He is now the proud owner of a Minecraft t-shirt and hoodie, which I will have to surgically remove from him at the hospital. Last night when I checked on him he was wearing the hoodie in bed. I had to pull back the covers or he may have boiled alive. I notice the time. There will be no updating of the My Story book this morning. We shall have to be quick!

I do the usual 'pre-flight' checks before departure: throw things into the dishwasher, give surfaces a cursory wipe to suggest some semblance of order, and call the dogs in from the garden to put them in their bed. Lloyd isn't a natural dog person. None of his family are really, apart from his now grown-up daughter who was probably influenced by the time she spent here. But away Dotty and Douglas go. I don't want them barking every time they see one of their furry friends walk by the window with their owners – a favourite pastime when I'm not around.

Jacob and I head out to the car, a simple exercise for most people, and certainly for us it has become far more straightforward than those initial helpless days. Jacob has begun to hold my hand quite naturally, as I do his. I catch myself standing with one arm out opening and closing my hand so he knows to connect his hand to mine. He can make the few steps out to the car with support – we don't need to get him into the wheelchair each time now. We chat away as I plug him into the car seat – again, something that wasn't possible just a few weeks ago. He is clutching his Lego model proudly and seems to be looking forward to his expedition.

I drive off to the hospital and watch in my mirror as

Jacob quietly sings along to *Yellow Submarine*. The journey gives me time to think. I wonder how Mary is getting on with the list of essential requirements for Jacob. It's been a little while now and I feel that there is the ever-present danger of Jacob and his needs being sucked into the vortex of 'decision making' at Children's Social Care. I have known foster carers ask for essential items to help their children with education or life skills, and they have waited until the child became a teenager. Due to the bureaucratic layers of the institution, nothing happens quickly – unless it's an event that might damage its reputation. One of my friends (who adopted a little girl a few years ago) has been taking her daughter to see a sensory play therapist and can't stop raving about her. I have all her details and, after talking to her at length on the phone, I know this would be amazing for Jacob. How much better for this kind of work to be carried out by a professional and not just an enthusiastic foster carer.

I do not feel nervous at all, and I doubt very much if Jacob is. He is still running his fingers over the Lego model of the MRI scanner. He has gained some weight and looks sturdier. Mind you, we are definitely one of those households where we offer you food as soon as you've walked through the door, and no one leaves hungry, including me, so I suppose that should come as no real surprise. I'm the main protagonist in that particular plot, residue of my own childhood starvation experiences. I look in the mirror, look at my new second chin developing, and sternly tell myself, 'No'. I have spoken to others who grew up with food issues, and the effects are long-lasting into adulthood.

As I park the car in the hospital car park, I remember that I can claim back the petrol and parking for today's and yesterday's appointments. Yesterday the car park fee was eight pounds. If I add up the petrol and car park fees, it comes to around forty pounds: nearly one quarter of my allowance for Jacob. Sometimes I think the people who devise these allowances use the same model they created in the 1970s, or don't actually have anything to do with the raising of children and the reality of what that costs.

Jacob knows exactly where to go. We pass the Friends of the Hospital shop and once again I notice him glance in at the goodies. I tell him that if he's good he can choose a smoothie and cake from the café on the way out. The same man is sitting behind reception, and I wonder whether he has even been home or had a break, but he beams at Jacob and remembers his name.

'Good morning Jacob. And how are you today?'

To my delight Jacob says, slowly, 'Good, thank you. And you?'

That little understanding of social nicety in returning the inquiry makes my heart melt. As does the receptionist's reply.

'All the better for seeing you.'

Could these people be any nicer? We head off to waiting

area two as directed and find a couple of seats next to each other. A tall, slim, older woman, dressed in white today, comes out to call Jacob. Her name is Sally, but we knew that from last night. Firstly Sally has to weigh Jacob, which he thinks is an excellent game. I'm right about his weight: it's gone up quite significantly according to his 'blue' book that all children in this part of the world get. He was weighed a few weeks before he came here by the local authority nurse. If children are not at school they come to your house to perform this measure. His weight was just under 15kg. Today he's weighing in at over 16kg.

'This is wonderful,' I smile, although Sally probably has no idea what I am so pleased about. I ask what his weight should be.

She squints at her chart. 'Around 17 to18 kilograms, I should say.'

Well, we aren't far off that and our trajectory is good. My smug smile remains.

Next we head off to the room with the lockers and dress Jacob in his fetching, sky-blue suit. He is giggling the whole time, enjoying every minute and all the attention. Every day he seems to become bolder and reveal his character more and more. Our little gang heads towards the MRI room. Truth be told, it would be more accurate to say that Jacob *leads* us all up to the MRI scanner as though he is the magnetic resonance imaging technologist and Sally is the patient.

I say hello to Ross, who smiles at me and says, 'I'm Dave. Ross is off today.' I want to explain that Marques told us last night it would be Sally and Ross but before I can apologise, Jacob has leapt in.

'He-llo Dave. I'm Ja-cob.'

Dave takes his cue and says, 'Hello Jacob. I'm very happy to meet you.'

I love how Jacob is negotiating these 'ordinary' meetings and exchanges with considerable aplomb.

'Right then, Jacob,' Sally says. 'Time to climb up onto the bed.'

Jacob accomplishes this with no fear or hesitation.

'The Lego model was a brilliant idea,' I tell Dave and Sally.

They smile but are switching to technical mode and need to concentrate now as they go about their work. Sally brings in a chair for me to sit on. While she is busying herself with this she explains that there is an American man's voice who will instruct Jacob's breathing. We all practise the process: in and out, deep breath, hold, let go. I feel confident that Jacob understands. I sit next to him with his teddies all around, wondering now if they were for his benefit or mine, and squeeze his hand softly at every instruction to help guide him through. I don't need to. He knows exactly what to do. Even better, Sally has provided him with some stunning bright blue headphones so he can listen and watch *The Lego Movie 2*.

They have thought of everything. This is a walk in the park.

It takes an age in that space tunnel, and though I watch carefully, Sally gives nothing away about what she may or may not be seeing as the MRI takes its images. Afterwards she helps me to manoeuvre Jacob to a standing position. I slip his camouflage crocs on and hug him for his bravery. He merely giggles in response. We say our goodbyes to Sally and Dave and the lovely man at reception and head over to the promised cake counter to buy some treats. Jacob chooses an iced mango and passion fruit smoothie and a gingerbread man, and I get a caramel muffin for Lily for when we get back.

Outside the hospital foyer are a couple of wooden benches. We sit down there while Jacob has his drink and cake. It's a nice day and I don't want too much crumb carnage in the car if I can avoid it. I get my phone out of my bag and see a text from Lloyd: How much longer are you going to be? Lily is not in a good place and I need to work.

Great!

My heart sinks, and I speculate about what the atmosphere is like at home. I know Lloyd has a lot on and always has a million things to do after a business trip. And it isn't fair: Lily *should* be at school. She's feeling insecure and jealous and sometimes when she gets into these moods her behaviour can be quite vile and difficult to handle. I take a deep breath and try to remember all the things I have learnt in training and from fellow foster carers and adopters. Still, I know it's not much good. I am going home to a bad atmosphere, tension and conflict.

I enjoy the peace for as long as I can as we drive home. I notice I have been doing forty in the sixty mile zone, literally dragging my heels. I hate a tense environment. When I was a child our house was thick with toxic atmosphere. The anger and negativity was so heavy you could just feel it when you walked through the front door. Why would anyone want to walk into that? And how have I managed to recreate it in my own home?

I park outside the front in order to be close to the front door for Jacob. I want to enter my house through the front door rather than the back. I need to remind myself that I am in charge today. As I put my bag on the floor next to the standing man, Lloyd comes out to greet me, not with a kiss or a hello. He tells me of some awful behaviour from Lily.

'First she came down for breakfast and made a mess everywhere. When I politely asked her how she was she said, and I quote, "Fuck off, none of you want me anyway". It's not exactly what I want to come home to.'

'I see.'

Lloyd, like many dads, male adopters and foster carers that I know, believes that his 'busy' overrides mine and the needs of the children. I have seen normally reasonable men become less reconstructed when a child interferes with their living. I get this. I do. I am always trying to figure out the best way to do my work and balance things too. So I hate moments like this. My heart sinks further and I watch Jacob's smile drift away from his face.

I hate it. I hate it. I hate it!

One of my very good foster friends, Andrea, often says, 'I don't know how you do it with a husband to keep happy as well.' Andrea is a widow, and has been for years. She looks after sexually exploited girls. She has five of them ranging from nine to twenty years old. She is one of my favourite foster carer friends, and regularly laughs out loud as she points out the absurdities of the lives of some of us who have to negotiate our way round partners and birth children. Today is going to be one of those negotiating days. I need to keep the peace here. I need for none of the children to feel unsettled.

I need to support Lloyd first, who is still ranting.

'It's totally unacceptable, I'm not being told to fuck off in my own home. And I have a deadline that I *must* meet.'

How did they get to the swearing stage, I wonder, suspecting that I haven't heard the whole story. We all have an inner child, all of us. We all have an inbuilt response to any feeling of 'it's not fair', and Lloyd's button has been firmly pressed this morning. I closed mine down years ago after looking after so many children who genuinely felt that 'life' itself was not fair. I realised then that it was right at their age to feel like that, but not at our age. Still, Lily provoked a similar response in me last night and this morning, so I know that my inner child remains too, but I continue to try to suppress it. But I also know that Lloyd and I will argue about this. Emotionally, I am the polar opposite to Lloyd on this one. The children are the children. Adults should have worked their stuff out years ago, or at least maintain a semblance of control over it. But we can do the arguing later. For now I hold Jacob's hand and smile at Lloyd. 'I'll go and have a word in a minute. After I've settled Jacob down.'

I move past him.

'Oh, and the scan went really well. Thanks for asking,' I add, unable to resist. And, yes, momentarily letting my own inner child rise to the surface.

I choose low-maintenance parenting and take *The Lego Movie 2* back out of my bag to put on again for Jacob. He is delighted and, I hope, not affected by the atmosphere in the house. I mutter multiple expletives under my breath as I get it set up. I know it's wrong to swear in front of children, so none are discernible but they make me feel a bit better.

I walk towards the kitchen to make a coffee and brace myself to see Lily.

Poking my head tentatively round the door, I see she is under the duvet. I also note that her room looks like a poltergeist just burgled it. Deep breath.

'Hi Lily, how are you?'

I get no reply.

'Lily?' How are you?' I try again.

Still nothing.

She has pulled her curtains back into darkness, something which I loathe. I usually walk through the house moaning that we don't need lights on in the day and that it looks like someone's died if you leave the curtains closed in the daytime.

I say a version of this to Lily who has gone to the effort of moving her head to expose her hair at the top of the duvet.

'I wish I *was* dead.'

After such a positive start at the hospital, I feel myself slipping into a spiral of discontent – as so many parents of children who are struggling with something do. I know what this is about, but I don't know how to fix it. I know she is profoundly jealous of Jacob and I know she has riled up the boys to share a sense of her perceived injustice. I avoid saying anything that will cause a flare-up and instead go for a mild, 'If you get up, shower and dress you can come downstairs and have your muffin.'

I know this girl and I know how much she likes these muffins. I walk away satisfied that my ploy will work. And my little feeling of success is not unfounded because, sure enough, an hour later (because Lily, like the boys, has evidently heard somewhere that showers are to be stood under for half an hour at least) she appears. Amazing! She comes into the kitchen in top-to-toe black clothing.

Carefully selected no doubt as an outward reflection of her mood.

I push the muffin plate towards her.

'Would you like a hot chocolate to go with that?' I ask.

She doesn't look up but mutters a sullen 'yes'.

I jump in with a quick 'Yes?' the tone of which she recognises because she quietly responds, 'please', although the pleasantry is accompanied by a snarl of anger. Okay, so this 'sickness' definitely has nothing to do with her stomach. We have confirmed that at least.

I fill the kettle and leave Lily to 'enjoy' her muffin. I stick my head round the sitting room door to check on Jacob. He is happy as Larry, whoever Larry might be. I return to Lily and sit down opposite her, hoping that she might be reachable in the aftermath of her sugar rush.

'Lily you know that I, that we both, love you very much. You are now here, with us, and this is your *home*.' I put emphasis on the final word but deliberately avoid using the fluffy unicorn term 'forever home' as no one knows what forever is, or indeed can be sure that anything is forever. In fact, nothing is forever. 'You are here,' I repeat, 'but Jacob will be moving on to an adopted family or specialist foster carers as soon as Mary finds the right people. That could be any time now.'

She looks at me and says, 'Hot chocolate?'

The consonants are exaggeratedly drawn out. The little minx.

'Would you like to try that again?' I say.

She rolls her eyes and delivers an exaggerated, 'PLEEAAASSSSSE!'

I make the drink and put it down in front of her, smiling and maintaining outward calm in spite of wanting to scream.

Lloyd chooses this moment to walk in. 'Oh good. Have you cheered up then?'

The chair screeches on the floor as Lily stands up, takes her muffin and walks off in an enormous huff.

'What's wrong with her now?' says Lloyd as he moves towards the coffee machine. 'Was it something I said?'

Give me strength.

Chapter Twelve

The next morning, just before dawn, I'm in my studio checking my emails. Between Jacob's needs and Lily's shenanigans I'm finding late nights and early mornings the only time when I can get on with some work and be productive.

I'm also currently deciding what to do on a portrait commission. It's of two women. They married a long time ago, back when it was still considered a 'thing'. They are a true inspiration: one was a ward sister, the other was in the army. Both are now happily retired and enjoying life. They asked me to paint them in extremely expensive dresses. I had to add the dresses and 'finished' the portrait late last night before I went to bed. As the sun rises this morning and gives me the clarity of actual daylight I can see that there is still much to do.

I stare at my laptop to see what came in yesterday. I didn't get a chance to check at all with everything that was going on. There is a flurry of emails from social workers and other children's professionals. I think I'll deal with those in a minute, after I've had another coffee. I scan down looking for agent, editor and gallery – my three main emails of interest as that's how I earn my living. One email is from my editor, Jo. It's a friendly 'how's it going?' which I know is actually her lovely way of saying 'there's a looming deadline'. I have a quick panic which fires me up to get moving. It's not even 6am but I go for coffee number two. The dogs can stay in bed for now. I don't want to be disturbed yet. If I get distracted I will go off course.

Shuffling back to the studio I open the security-protected emails from the local authority. I think more about Jacob and how soon we might hear the (hopefully, good) news from his MRI scan.

I also contemplate what I am going to do about Lily. I see that Dara has been busy with a new group of siblings in a new placement. They are taking on five children! I know that Dara will have their back, but they are going to need a hell of a lot of resilience. Sadly, there are not enough foster carers for the numbers of children coming into the care system so I salute and support anyone new. I also let out a big sigh for those poor carers who are just about to take on a sibling group. I tap an email back saying I will call her later this morning, keeping my wording highly professional. I would never indicate the closer working relationship I believe we share in an email or work text. There are some social workers I know I will be true friends with in the future, like Dara – but that can't fully happen while we have a working relationship, just in case a situation arises that will compromise it.

The next email is from Mary, who I know plays the system with impeccable sophistication. She reminds me that Jacob is her last placement before she retires and that she will do everything she can to do right by him. I scan my eyes further down her email and read *I think I have found a family for Jacob*. My eyes read the words a few more times. If Mary thinks it, then it must be so. I am so happy for him. There is happiness, but I also feel sad at the same time. This is the hardest part of this work. I have grown so close to him and he has become so much a part of our lives that feeling pain is inevitable when children move on. *STOP, Louise*, I remind myself sternly. This is not about me and represents the very best outcome for Jacob. He is going to need the best love and care he can to keep fulfilling this blossoming potential. I want to know who they are. I know there is no way Mary would set Jacob up with a bunch of lemons, but you know, she might just need a second opinion.

Further down the inbox is an email about booking my training. Some of it is developmental, but some is mandatory and has to be repeated every three years. Blimey, that came around quickly: it's apparently time Lloyd and I both renewed our first aid and attachment training. I scan down the list looking for the nearest and shortest sessions. As an ex-university lecturer I know the truth about what influences subject selection by learners! I smile to myself as I realise there *is* a first aid session in three months' time, very near to where I live. Tick.

I go back to my editor's email and as I take on board her gentle nudge to get back to writing, I also think about the research I have been doing into alternative therapies for Lily. I worry that if she can't break this cycle of learnt behaviour it will really prevent her moving forward. She must have been so scared at times in her past that she gets defensive if she feels threatened.

I have been through a lot with Lily. She was not in a good state physically or emotionally when she first came here all those years ago. It will take years for all that fear and anxiety about being hurt to dissipate. My main concern is that she learns new ways of thinking that don't put her right back where she was all those years ago. I need to quickly send an email to Lily's social worker. She has been with us so long now that reporting any behaviour concerns actually feels like betrayal. I carefully write a bland email asking if we could explore some more 'My Story' work or perhaps some counselling for Lily.

I put 'counselling' with a tentative question mark. I hate having to hand her personal experiences over to the local authority but later on, if something did happen to her, we would all need to have a clear narrative trail that we can refer to. It's so hard for looked-after children. Lily is full of hormones and often shows the same behaviour that any teenage girl would go through, just sometimes it feels more.

She needs support to unravel all those emotions. Sometimes I have to accept the hard truth that I am not enough. She needs to talk to someone else. But sitting down with a new adult, often a complete stranger, and telling them your deep, innermost feelings as therapy is also problematic. It just won't happen for most children and young people I know. Most of us need to feel safe and relaxed before we can be truthful.

One particular girl I knew was sent to therapy after a suicide attempt. She told her therapist that she was scared of clowns and spent all six sessions talking about why she hated them. In fact, the girl was not scared of clowns, she just didn't want to talk to the therapist and it filled the time. I can imagine Lily pulling a similar trick, and I wouldn't blame her. I wonder if something creative, or maybe sensory, would help Lily. If that's the case then it would mean paying for it myself. By the time it goes through the banana slug of the system without someone like Mary to take knowing shortcuts, Lily will have left home – or worse. I hope for her, as I do for all the children, that they know how to have safe, good friendships and relationships based on trust and equity rather than need.

Too much reflection this morning, too much to think about – still, I feel as though I have achieved a few things. I look at the clock. I've got an hour before I need to wake them all up for school, and I gleaned from Lloyd yesterday that he could do with a bit longer in bed this morning.

Though I don't remember being left alone to have a lie-in myself, I think, rather ungraciously. I push my quiet anger about all the domestic work that goes unrecognised and unpaid to one side and work on a chapter, choosing words over the painting this morning. Soon it's 7am and time to wake my scholastic sleeping beauties.

I get in the shower quickly before they come to, then it's a free for all.

Jacob has tuned in perfectly with the household timings. He certainly has gained a huge amount of confidence. As I get dressed I can hear the now-characteristic 'Weeeze,' that he uses so endearingly in the mornings as he is waking himself up, more insistently when he wants me to come. I love it. I might change my name by deed-poll to 'Weeeze'.

I finish my make-up and hair while singing in relay to Jacob – knowing that the other children will complain of bleeding ears. Finally, I go in to see Jacob who is beaming at me, as always. I pull up his roller blind and the sun bursts into his room, touching the top of his head. He levers himself up, resting on one arm, which I have not seen so far – good, another development. I sing inside with that cheering sight before me. I am also thrilled in the knowledge that Mary has found a long-term foster family to look after him. I remember what my adopted mother used to say about children born with disabilities. 'Poor little buggers, we never know what happens to them. They can be so used.' Apart from the 'weird' irony in her wisdom, I have always felt a concern for a child with disabilities as yes, I suppose they can be 'used', but they can also suffer by not being given the chance to shine in ways that others would never have credited them for, or even by being written off altogether as the first doctor did with Jacob.

I feel so warm and content with my domestic bliss that I could be in a 1970s advert for Fairy Liquid. But we all know that these moments are fleeting. I offer to help Jacob from his bed but he ignores me and gets out without too much bother. He stands almost straight and I want to cry but don't. The poor boy will think I'm sad about his achievement and he must never think that. He is still wearing a nappy overnight, so we sort all that out.

'Can I hold your hand?' I ask as we ready ourselves to go down. This is for my benefit as much as his: my legs still go cold when he's near the stairs; a reaction so primitive that it can't be explained.

Jacob looks up at me and nods a yes to my request, but I can sense that he is keen to get moving and today I wonder if his acquiescence is because he knows that *I* need to hold *his* hand to feel safer.

At the bottom of the stairs I let go of his hand and watch the dogs launch themselves towards him. He does a very slow spin, but full of laughter. Isn't that what we should all aim to see on the faces of children? Joy.

In the kitchen he pulls his chair out. We need to do some work here because the chair makes an excruciatingly grating scrape sound as he drags it on the flagstone floor. He sits on his chair with ever-increasing efficiency and swings his legs round under the table. My my, this young man has his feet firmly under the table in every sense, and I see clearly that this is what's threatening Lily. I remember when she began to feel safe she used to follow me everywhere, even to the loo. If I worked in the garden she would be a few feet away. If I went in to get something she would be right behind me. Then, one day I looked round and she wasn't there. She had finally accepted that I wasn't going anywhere and was not going to hurt her or let her be hurt. As much as I was relieved that my shadow had moved away, I remember that I also missed it.

I open the fridge door to get the milk and offer a choice of cereal from the big cupboard to Jacob. He enthusiastically points at the Coco Pops.

I let him, of course.

I am keen that he continues to gain weight and that he not only gets to choose for himself but has that choice validated. He didn't know how to make a choice when he first arrived, but I try not to dwell too much on those early life-experiences. My imagination does enough with the little that I do know.

While I get the bowl and spoon I distract myself from impending MRI results by thinking more about Lily and what I can do to help her through this. Jacob is needy, of course, and she is old enough to understand that. I also consider what I can do to reduce the impact on the boys. They didn't have her levels of adversity in early life and, without wishing to sound harsh, they have little scope to complain too much.

Just as I pour the apple juice into a glass for Jacob I remember how dehydrated Lily was when she came to us. I'm not a doctor or nurse but I am pretty sure that dehydration can cause poor moods. Lily was never given water when she needed it, or much to drink at all. Conversely, I fussed over the boys so much they couldn't go thirsty. The children's nurse once told me that Lily's body doesn't recognise when it's thirsty. I wonder if, because I have been – as Lily says 'distracted' with Jacob – I haven't kept a close enough eye on what she is drinking. She takes a water bottle to school every day but I can't monitor that. I think that if I buy a new snazzy water bottle she will more likely keep her levels up. It's not the whole explanation, but it could be a contributing factor to her recent behaviour.

I add 'water bottle' to my shopping list and make a mental note to contact the school nurse at Lily's school too. I smile at Jacob who is humming as he eats. I start telling him what our plans are today. 'We're going to the big supermarket, the one that has the cars outside for children to ride in.'

He looks so excited and I am so full of hope for him. I wonder who these long-term foster carers are. I have been doing this long enough to know that a local authority would prefer the cheapest option, which would be adoption. But I also know that unless the adopters are millionaires it's specialist long-term foster carers who will take him. They will need as much support as they can but Mary knows all this too, with bells on, which is why I know this little man will be safe.

I hear my phone ping and with an element of confusion I squint and try to remember where I left my 'static'. It's still in my shopping bag under a pile of receipts that I need to recycle. Just in time I grab it and speak. It's the local GP surgery and our lovely doctor. He's film-star attractive and garners quite a bit of female interest locally. I know some women who have faked needle phobias to have his attention.

'Hello Louise, Dr Miller here.' Doctors always sound well educated, especially on the telephone.

I reciprocate with my very best telephone manner. 'Good morning Dr Miller, how are you?'

'I'm fine, thanks. I just need to feed back the MRI results.'

I take him off loud speaker immediately and look at Jacob through the entrance of the kitchen as he smiles back at me. My own smile fades as I hear the doctor's next words.

'It's not good news, I'm afraid.'

Chapter Thirteen

I stand still, frozen at the other end of the line. Dr Miller stops speaking. There is a long pause. Time goes in slow motion for a moment.

'Louise, can you hear me? Are you okay?'

I can do nothing else but stand in the middle of the kitchen looking at Jacob.

I can't reply. I don't trust my mouth to form words. I feel only an inhuman sound building up inside me. It is as if a cloak of utter despair has been placed around my shoulders. Anyone who has heard the words 'it's not good news' knows how the bottom falls out of your world. I realise that I am physically sinking too. Somehow I am actually down on the floor in the kitchen, though I don't remember getting here. Jacob is looking at me strangely.

I pull myself right back up with a sharp tug. This isn't about me, this is about Jacob — and now, more than ever, this little fella needs the adults around him to be just that, adults! I step into the role I'm best at: being a pragmatist. I metaphorically roll my sleeves up and ask Dr Miller to continue as I wave to Jacob, smile cheerfully, and step out of his earshot.

'There are problems showing up in the scan. It's early days of course, but they are severe. What we see resembles spina bifida, or maybe a hormone problem. Either way, it's not good. The MRI takes a picture of the spine and it looks like there is damage – a hole, if you like. We have no idea about a cause as yet. It could be something to do with the physical conditions he has experienced, we just don't know. I'm afraid that we need to ask you to come back to the hospital.'

Dr Miller is very experienced. He keeps talking to fill the gaps as I try to process what I am hearing. I have no real idea what spina bifida is, but it sounds scary. The words are ugly and brutal and I don't know what to do with them.

'He needs to have more scans, another MRI and a CAT scan so that we can really see what's what. I have already referred Jacob for a full musculoskeletal examination. You will need to book the scans as soon as you can. Do you still have the number?'

I remember that the letter from the hospital is on my desk and say on autopilot, 'Yes, I'll do that now.'

My stomach clenches as I think about what lies ahead for Jacob. All the progress he has made. It can't all be for nothing. It can't all be in my head. I have pictured a trajectory that sees him going to a mainstream school and riding a bicycle and doing everything that his foster siblings can do. In my dreams he has crossed the finish line of a marathon with his arms in the air and a gold medal around his neck.

'But he's been getting stronger. Every day he's been getting better. He's been walking and taking himself to the loo.' I can hear the pleading tone that my voice has taken on.

'I bet he has, and that's wonderful to hear, Louise. And there is more work we can do to build on all the good that you've already started. But Jacob will need surgery to close the hole in his spine, and it may be that his nervous system is damaged too, which explains the weakness in his legs. He might never walk unaided, Louise, you need to prepare yourself for that possibility.'

'Never?'

'At this stage, we don't know. But, looking at his records and more importantly the gaps in his records, and knowing from you about his past, there are many questions that need answering. I think that young Jacob is just a tad too young to help us with all the answers for now. We need to know what damage has been done.'

Just as I think things can't get any worse, Dr Miller changes direction. 'How is Jacob's vision?'

'Fine, I think.' My response is automatic, and then I remember my observations of his drawing and mark making: it always leans heavily to the left. So does my own work, actually, which is why I spotted it in the first place. Not as much as Jacob's, his is much more pronounced, but I know my leanings in writing and drawing are to do with my neuro divergence and are related to my dyslexia.

'Why?' I swallow, detecting something else in Dr Miller's tone. 'What else could be wrong?'

'If there is a problem with the spine, of the degree that we think we are seeing, then there is a possibility that the retinas have been affected too.' I hear more words that I don't understand and don't want to understand. Something that sounds like 'subluxations' and he repeats 'vertebrae' several times in a way that I don't like.

'Can you tell me one thing, doctor? If it is what you think it is, is it degenerative?'

There is another long pause on the end of the line. I know our family doctor well enough to imagine him pulling his glasses up to his forehead to rub his eyes. I have sat in his room with many children over the years and I know that he does this when he feels sad or exasperated.

'More than likely, I'm afraid, yes.'

Another pause.

'Louise, are you still there?'

'Yes, I'm here. I'm just struggling a little to deal with what you have told me.'

I thank him, though it feels somewhat ironic to be saying thank you for the news I have just heard. I say goodbye and stand quietly for a few seconds to straighten out my

thoughts and get ready with the big smile that Jacob is used
to seeing when I enter the room.

I do not fail him.

'How is the most amazing boy in the world?' I ask.

He giggles. Oh, how I have come to love that sound.

'After I've cleared up and put out the washing we'll
head off to the shops and see the cars. What do you think
of that?'

The world is working against me today as my phone
rings again almost immediately. It's Mary.

'Hi. Louise. How are you?'

Her greeting is punctuated by pauses. She knows!

'When did you find out?' I demand.

'About two hours ago.'

I know that Mary officially starts work at 9am, but
actually she will have been working since 7am or perhaps
earlier. I grab a saucer from the rack with my spare hand
and grab four biscuits from the jar by the microwave and
put them on the plate. I park them next to Jacob, grab a
drawing book and pens from the cupboard in the garden
room and put those next to him as well. I hunt for the
colouring book while telling Mary that I am setting Jacob
up with some art stuff.

'Of course, what else would you do?' she laughs.

'I'm relieved to hear a laugh,' I tell her.

Mary tells me that she suspected all along that this
would happen, that my reports of his progress were too

good to be true in the long term. 'I know you wanted it all to be down to delay, but it was very unlikely. I've seen it before when a child with problems receives good care for the first time. They feel safe and get better. All that progress masks the real issues lurking beneath.'

'But what if he doesn't get better? What if this is it for him, a life in a wheelchair and other problems?' I say, conscious that my voice has risen in pitch. I have found my way to my studio now so that Jacob can't hear me.

Mary clears her throat. 'It is what it is, Louise, and now that we know we can help him properly. Now as you know, I have been working with this couple from Northumberland, the ones I told you about who are specialist foster carers with one of the big charities.'

I try to take it all in. 'They look after two other children who have profound disabilities. They know exactly what they are doing and do it because... well, because they do. They're bloody incredible.'

'Did you know them already?' I ask, suspecting an element of typical Mary-magic going on here.

'Umm yeah, umm maybe,' she hedges. 'Oh alright. They have a girl and boy. I know the girl a little. She is over eighteen now and was one of my best friend's cases a few years ago now. So I know how amazing these people are. We can trust them.'

I ask about the next stage.

'I'm on it. I'm catching a train today. It looks like an

eight-hour journey so a good opportunity to catch up on some of that dreaded paperwork that my manager is breathing down my neck for,' she chuckles.

I know she doesn't give a fig about what her manager thinks.

I get back in the kitchen. Jacob is drawing what I think is a bee. I'm not entirely sure but it's lovely and his tongue is sticking out while he is concentrating.

It isn't long before my phone rings again as I knew it would.

'Hi Dara.'

'Hi Louise, how are you?' Just as I knew straightaway from Mary's tone, I can tell from her voice that this time the news hasn't travelled to her yet. Jacob is engrossed, so I head outside. I go on and explain all the information from Dr Miller and Mary, as concisely as I can.

Dara takes it all in, as if every piece of news is to be savoured and chewed into tiny pieces before swallowing.

'Oh Louise, it will be okay,' she consoles.

'You're not allowed to say that,' I jump down her throat. 'None of us are. In all the training we are told never to raise expectations.'

Dara pipes up, 'Oh sod that.' In her dulcet Eastern European brogue it sounds wonderful, and exactly what I need to hear.

I remember to ask Dara how the fledgling foster carers are getting on. 'The ones with the sibling group of five?'

'They are almost dead,' she laughs ruefully. 'I told them not to take this referral but the children's social worker was very good at persuading them that they would be fine. I'm not sure that even you would be fine with this load – and guess what? They're not.'

She pauses for a quick breath. 'They look a hundred years older and the male foster carer told me that he hadn't washed for five days in a row because he hadn't had time.'

'Wow,' I say. 'Why do you guys do this to people?' I'm only half-joking.

'It's not me, Louise, as you well know. It's the decision of the children's social worker and the placements team.'

I sigh and say, as I always do, 'Follow the money, honey.' Dara may have me on one of my favourite themes, and I am happy to be distracted from thinking about Jacob.

Because today I feel without direction or motivation. I guess I'm in a bit of a spin from the news about Jacob. Lily is also still worrying me. She came down this morning informing me that she has 'severe anxiety' having completed an online anxiety questionnaire recommended by a friend. She's using this old trick again. I feel out of my depth today and wonder if what I said to Lily in response was the right thing – it just came out. 'You can't measure your feelings from what is basically a pub quiz.' I am quietly becoming fed-up with everyone and their uncle jumping on the mental wellbeing band wagon for children and young people. All the questionnaires and slogans are not helping Lily, that's for sure. Just before I sink into deeper and more negative thoughts my phone goes. It's Mary. What now?

'Me again. How are you doing?'

'I'm afraid I'm not in a good place today, Mary.'

'I didn't think you would be. That's why I'm outside with a box of cakes from your lovely local bakers.'

Jacob has only just had his breakfast, but since when has that been an issue for a child who is being offered a fresh chocolate éclair? Jackson and Vincent, who are both reconsidering their ideas about me preferring Jacob to them, set up their old Thomas the Tank train set for Jacob last night in the garden room.

'Would you like to go and play with the train set?' I ask Jacob. He is off his chair in a flash and manages the steps across the kitchen and the step down into the garden room. He has learnt to 'coast' using the furniture to support him, but he is making his way otherwise unaided. *See?* I want to scream at anyone who will listen. *What does that say to your diagnosis?* Mary waits until Jacob is settled at the blue train tracks with Henry and the Fat Controller in his grasp. Douglas and Dotty spy an opportunity to chase trains and settle down with him.

'I'm retiring after everything is settled with Jacob and his new foster carers. He will be my last case.'

I knew this was coming, so it is no surprise, but it feels like a crashing loss to the profession, and to me.

'Tell me a little more about what they are like,' I say, to stop myself from making an impassioned plea to Mary to keep going.

Mary obliges, describing a quiet, modest couple who live in a big bungalow with plenty of space inside and out for Jacob.

It's what I need to hear, but I feel weirdly at a loss. I'm happy for him, truly, but I don't want him to leave, and don't want him to leave knowing what I know about his life chances given this latest medical news. I really am not in a good place today. It is one of those days when you dislike the world and nothing seems right. Sometimes when I feel this way, the emotion serves to stoke up the fire in my belly to work even harder for children and young people who are, through no fault of their own, vulnerable. Today I feel more defeated.

Mary ploughs on. 'Their names are Jennifer and Andrew. You'll like them. They both have grown-up children from other marriages. They met while working in a nursing home for disabled children. Andrew used to work as an engineer and was very good at it, but decided that he needed to do something more meaningful with his life. Jennifer has worked with 'complicated' children all her working life.'

Mary doesn't physically make the inverted commas but I can hear them in the emphasis she uses.

'They are probably some of the most experienced

carers I have ever met.' She smiles. 'And not only that, they know how to navigate their way through the system.'

That always makes me feel better. Not like those poor new foster carers of Dara's who may well stand down after what will be an utterly overwhelming experience: then we lose more carers. I have complete faith in Mary's choice. She knows what she is doing and I also know that she and her fellow 1970s graduates are like a mafia working in children's social care, making sure that the system relates to their original belief that children matter. I would love to know what their curriculum was like compared to now. Mary has told me that she feels 'over the hill' and her colleagues see her as outdated. She has been my – and Jacob's – champion throughout all of this, and I need to let her know that.

'What's next?'

Mary tells me about an opportunity for us all to take Jacob to meet them.

'Jennifer's aunty left her a small holiday home near the beach, halfway between them and us, and has suggested that would be a good place.'

It's a bit of a drive but I don't mind. It's a thoughtful way to make it happen. And anyway, when I was a girl I wanted to be a long distance lorry driver, mainly because of the Yorkie advert. And it sounds perfect. 'We could take Jacob and the other children to meet everyone.'

'Along with the other two children in their care,' Mary agrees. 'Both with significant disabilities.'

It's all good. It all sounds right. It's all for the best.

We tuck into the chocolate eclairs and talk about Mary's retirement plans. I listen, feeling very happy for her, but at the same time like I'm losing a friend. This woman represents what social work should be about, acting in 'the best interest of the child' – as quoted from the Children Act 1989.

I have always been actively interested in other people's lives. My own life has been riddled with unusual circumstances and strange things, so I like to talk to others about their pasts. Mary was previously forthcoming about growing up in a Catholic boarding school with nuns. This experience is so far removed from everything I know that I am keen to return to the subject.

'Tell me more about that convent school of yours.'

'Which bits do you want to know? That I had to clean a hundred pairs of shoes every night?'

'Wow, that's awful.'

'On the contrary, it was one of the good bits. Standing alone, away from the nuns and their preferred, fee paying girls was a relief.'

'How long were you there?'

'I went to the school at five years old and was expelled at sixteen.'

'Expelled? Oh blimey, why? What did you do?

'Well...'

'Because I was expelled too,' I blurt out.

'That tells you something, doesn't it?' Mary laughs. 'And we still treat children as criminals if they get into trouble at school, without questioning that the school may be the trouble.'

I nod my head.

'My older sister was a scholarship child, like me – but there the resemblance ended. She was compliant and well behaved. Her way of surviving, I guess. But where I was expelled for my attitude, she swallowed it whole. At 18 years old she became a nun.'

Mary has a sister who is a nun? I can't imagine anyone less nun-like than the woman before me.

'I've never understood. Neither of us had any other real experience of life but I knew that how I was being treated was wrong and degrading, whereas she accepted it.'

I ask what becoming a nun meant for their relationship.

A little more anger creeps in her voice 'They never let me say goodbye to my sister. They told me that she now belonged to them.'

'Not even able to say goodbye?'

'Oh, it gets worse,' she says, grimly. 'A few weeks later the school had a jumble sale. I went along with some cash I had saved. I noticed that the nuns were selling all my sister's possessions and I was horrified. I asked to buy her sewing basket. They said no.'

I'm outraged on Mary's behalf. 'What an absolutely horrible thing to say and do. That just seems vindictive.'

Melting éclair in my mouth leaves me articulating my rage in the most dignified manner.

'Yes, doesn't it?'

I notice a glint her eye.

'You got that sewing box though, didn't you?'

'Yes, I did – eventually. They didn't want to sell it to me but I had the money so they had to – and there was no way I was going to back down. I bought it and took it home to our mother who was glad to have it.'

'I take it you didn't send your own children to boarding school?'

'No.'

'Back to the task in hand,' Mary says. 'Let's book our day to meet Jennifer and Andrew.'

'Have you sent *all* of Jacob's medical information to them? Even the latest stuff?' I ask, a little more sharply than I intend, wanting to make sure that they really do know exactly what they are taking on.

'What do you think?' Mary smiles. Of course she has.

There is never any time like the present as far as Mary is concerned. She calls them directly and before I know it I'm on speaker phone to them. I can hear the warmth in their voices and I feel warm in return about the whole business.

I can see through the window that Jacob is now lying on his side in the garden making 'Swooossh', 'beep beep' and 'whoo whoo' sounds. Around him today momentous decisions have been made.

Chapter Fourteen

We are in a kind of limbo, the in-between time as we make arrangements for the different phases of Jacob's departure. The most important of these is meeting Jennifer and Andrew tomorrow. I keep myself busy working on my portrait of Jacob. I have spent some time sketching him and taking photos, and in the time period between now and him moving to Northumberland I can do the main bulk of the work. I love the fact that all the children leave with a painting of themselves: it's my gift to them and something I hope they will keep forever.

Lily has been better since we announced the news about Jacob's new family. Perhaps there is safety in knowing that Jacob is moving on, but I still think it's her dehydration that prompts the poor mood. And so Lily finally met the school nurse today. The first few appointments Lily was left in reception waiting but the nurse never showed up. I was furious. This is not how children claiming to have anxiety should be treated. Today the appointment finally happened, but things didn't go the way Lily expected them to, and it feels as though it has done more harm than good.

The nurse told Lily that 'self-harming is a coping mechanism', as though it were a piece of advice – and Lily is, rightly in my opinion, upset. Lily tells me that she had not intended to hurt herself. 'I've never even thought about self-harming.'

'I'm glad to hear that.'

'But it seems that it's almost *expected*,' she explains tearfully. 'It's what you have to do. I've got anxiety. The questionnaire told me. But I don't want to hurt myself.'

'I'm sure that's not what the nurse meant. She wasn't encouraging you to self-harm.'

But she was, perhaps inadvertently, sowing a seed that self-harm is an option, and for that I am irate. How has it come to this? How can a vulnerable teenager be made to feel that this is the only way forward in order to cope? It is almost as if she is being encouraged to do it. Not to mention the self-diagnosis of 'anxiety' from a silly online quiz. My head is in a spin again. I don't have all the answers (or any of them, it feels like sometimes), but I have learnt to stop, take a deep breath and count to ten before I pick up the phone or send an email.

Accordingly, I send a less-irate email than I might otherwise have done, one that is much blander than my original version, a heavily watered-down draft of what I would actually like to say to the school and the nurse. You never can be quite sure if correspondence will come back to bite so I choose my words very carefully. There seems to be a gaping great hole in the strategies for raising awareness of mental health issues for children and young people, and in the resources available to meet the need – and young people end up seeking advice in the wrong places. So now we are sitting in the surgery waiting to see a doctor. The lovely Dr Miller is not available, but we have secured an appointment with a locum.

Lily sits up straight, but she is unusually quiet and so I do my best to explain what is going on – but they are my words, not hers. The doctor, who seems to lack any compassion, tells Lily that she 'looks alright'. Oh, well, that's fine, then. Because it's really easy to 'see' inside someone's head.

'It's not serious enough to be referred to CAMHS (Child and Adolescent Mental Health Services),' he shrugs and smiles, as though I should be happy about that. 'Children need to have attempted suicide to get that appointment,' he explains, 'and we're not quite in that league.' Self-harming and now suicide. What is it with these people? Perhaps that's *why* the medical people keep mentioning self-harming – as a way of moving up the waiting list.

Blimey we live in a strange and weird world.

In some ways though, it's had the desired effect. Lily has had something of a scare, but I hope for now she can stay away from the mental health service and just grow at her pace. I need to keep it all in perspective and not let my own emotions become entwined with hers to complicate matters. I am feeling sad because I am going to be saying goodbye to a special boy who has firmly established a permanent place in my heart, if not my home. She is struggling with emotions that she doesn't understand. I place a big glass of water in front of her and instruct her to drink it down, which she does very obediently.

She has moved from being cross with my nagging to now glowing when I make a fuss over her. The subject of water intake is a good way to do this. She needs to feel loved and cared for, and this is a quick win.

'Better?'

She nods.

'No more online quizzes, okay?' I raise an eyebrow.

She shakes her head.

'We're going to do this properly. We've got this.'

In the morning we leave to take Jacob to meet his new family. I notice the heavy quietness in the car. The peculiar mix of happiness and sadness that this occasion represents. The children aren't fully aware of Jacob's medical prognosis, so they don't bear that weight, at least. He is wearing a nappy for the journey. Bowel and urinary incontinence are symptoms of the spina bifida, and although he has much more control than when he first came to us, he can't manage on a journey like this. We haven't had the tests that will confirm the vision problems, or possible build-up of fluid on the brain, but there are likely to be some severe, residual learning difficulties either way. I did a lot of wishful thinking, it seems, but I am now coming to terms with a new, adjusted reality for Jacob.

The car journey is three and half hours – long enough to be arduous, and I know I will also be driving on the way home. I'm used to it and don't mind. Lloyd finds it more stressful and can get grumpy if he drives so I tend to do most of it. Not driving also allows Lloyd to catch up on his sleep. He manages to nod off with an ease that I find bewildering – and envy slightly. I just can't do that. I think it's a hangover from all the necessary, heightened vigilance from my own abusive childhood. I have to stay awake as a passenger – just in case. Just in case of what, I don't exactly know. I feel okay, I think. Emotional, but I have a good feeling about today.

The children are all fine sitting in the back, embracing the distraction of a road trip. The boys have their headphones. Lily is sitting next to Jacob, all sign of her resentment gone. In fact she is tickling him, which is so sweet. The miles disappear and we are soon driving along the narrow lane that Jennifer described – a road that does not appear on the sat-nav. There are a number of log cabins in a circle with a wonderful grassy area in the middle set up with picnic tables, a basketball hoop and a football goal. It's an idyllic little area, and the way the cabins are set out to be inward-facing suggests community and sharing. I drive onto the grass and spot a couple of people waving at me.

They point to a parking position. We all get out of the car and the children stretch their legs while checking out the area. Jennifer walks straight up to me and gives me a huge hug. That's it: I'm good for nothing and burst into tears. I point at my face and shrug and Jennifer just hugs me all the harder.

Lloyd smiles and walks up to Andrew. They shake hands and Andrew gives Lloyd a friendly slap on the arm. I like the fact that they are both so tactile. These are my kind of people.

Outside the cabin the other two children – Nick and Sandy – are waving to us. The boy looks about eight and the girl is late teens. They all beam and call out to Jacob – who is excited. He immediately heads over to them and starts talking, introducing himself to Nick as 'brother' which makes us all laugh. It is with a heavy heart that I allow myself to acknowledge the limp when he runs a few paces. I've pretended it wasn't there, but knowing what I now do about his prognosis, it seems it's more pronounced now. I was blinded to these things when I got myself wrapped up in the miracle of all the progress he was making.

My children are impressed that Jennifer and Andrew know all their names without being introduced – and are handed drinks and snacks on arrival. These people know instinctively how to make us feel welcome. Within minutes the children are playing French cricket in the field. Nick asks Vincent to push his wheelchair. Vincent looks afraid for a moment but has no choice other than to oblige. He soon gets the rhythm of the game and soon he and Nick are wheelchair running all over the field, cheering and laughing as though they are winning Olympic gold. Jacob soon wants his wheelchair too, so that he can join in the fun – and Lily volunteers to partner him in a game whose rules seem to be implicitly understood by all the kids without explanation, though it seems to me that they must be continually evolving and adapting. Whatever – it works.

The afternoon we spend together is relaxed and reassuring. We get to know each other a little. I learn that Jennifer and Andrew have been coming here for years. They know all the other families – who also appear at various times to play with the children. At one time I count fourteen children on the field, all chasing around. It helps that the weather is good. We sit in the sunshine with Jennifer and Andrew and a number of their neighbours – who are also friendly and accepting. Lloyd and Andrew share barbecuing duties, and somehow an apparently endless supply of burgers and sausages are distributed among the group. The children remain at the centre of the experience always. It is a really lovely experience and I am energised by the warm glow that comes from the people as well as the sun.

We talk a little about the logistics and practicalities of Jacob's transition. We will take him back for his second

MRI scan so that we can get his diagnosis moving. I tell them about the helpful NHS staff on his previous visit.

'Jacob won't mind going back there at all.'

'One of our grown-up children, Emma, will look after Nick and Sandy while we drive down to collect Jacob.'

We set a date for a few weeks' time. I suggest that they stay overnight at ours as it's too far up and down the country to do in a day.

Jennifer squeezes my arm. 'Thank you, that's very kind. But we really don't want to put you out and, as a fellow mum, I know how much extra work it would be. So, don't worry.'

I smile to myself and think of all the visitors we have had over the years who accept the hospitality but never even to offer to help wash-up. These are genuinely thoughtful, kind people but at the same time they are no pushovers. I get from them that they are strong, no-nonsense people who will advocate for Jacob – as they already do for Nick and Sandy.

Jacob points up to the sky as we pile ourselves back into the car.

'What is it, Jacob?' I ask.

'Amen bird,' he says.

And he's right. Our prayers have been answered. I won't cry now. I won't.

It's another three days before the bombshell drops.

PART THREE

Mary

I

Mary sipped at her latte, savouring every second. No bloody green tea this morning, thank you very much. She needed this.

Callum's viciousness in his little act of sabotage – blocking the specialist foster care – was beyond belief. Mary thought some unkind thoughts about her manager. She compared him to a succession of small, furry animals: a rat, a weasel – but the comparisons were too favourable. Finally she found the fit: he was a snake, she decided. A dirty, slithering serpent. Venomous, deceitful and cowardly – hiding in the long grass. There had to be a way through this, though. Jacob Tillyard deserved better. Why did people have to be so obstructive? It was the nuns and the sewing box all over again. The irony here was that Callum was incriminating Jennifer and Andrew with the same kind of accusation that had seen Jacob removed from the Hallidays in the first place.

She hesitated before picking up the phone. There was no way Louise was going to take this well. She was going to have to know sooner or later, though.

'Louise, it's Mary. How are you?'

'I'm good, thank you. Still on a high from our meeting with Jennifer and Andrew. How about you?'

'Alright.'

Except that the way Mary said the word indicated that she was anything but, as Louise soon detected.

'You sound as though you might be having a bit of a morning.'

'You're not wrong. Something's happened.'

'Jacob?'

'Yes, indirectly. Not his condition,' she added quickly, knowing how much Louise was preoccupied with Jacob's health.

She heard Louise let out a breath of relief at the other end of the line.

'There's no easy way to say this, so I'm just going to come straight out with it. Jennifer and Andrew have had a number of allegations made against them.'

'Allegations?' Louise's voice sounded bewildered. 'What sort of allegations? They can't be true, whatever they are.

They're lovely people. I met them. We had a lovely time.'

'They are lovely people,' Mary said, firmly.

'So what happened?'

'Okay. A social worker from here was sent out to their holiday home. It's routine, as you know – to check them out.'

'To spy on them.'

'You said that, not me.'

'This social worker has brought back evidence that they are drinkers and are irresponsible, and that they cannot look after Jacob.'

Mary heard Louise swear out loud. Very loud, indeed. She used a chain of rude words to express utter disgust. It also sounded as though she might be kicking something. 'Calm down, Louise. What's that noise? Don't take it out on an inanimate object. That's not going to achieve anything.'

'Hang on. I know exactly what's going on here,' Louise said. 'They don't want to pay them the fee, do they?'

Mary groaned. 'I told you they were expensive because of this national agency transfer business.'

'Christ, Mary. We've been here ourselves. We've had a couple of allegations made against us in the past, all unproven. I'm so angry! I know what it's like to experience an allegation that is corrupt, and, trust me, so many are! I know what it can do to a foster family and the children. When we had the nasty fake allegation, the social worker said that she was going to have to interview our other foster children and birth children to see if they were safe. It was bloody awful.'

'I hear you, Louise. I know this is unlikely to be true, but the managers will say that there's no smoke without fire, and it's going to take some time to unravel.'

'I want more detail. When did they spy on them?' Louise demanded.

'The day you were all there together,' Mary answered quickly.

More expletives found their way down the phone line.

'There are some photos of your gathering – and then some of the recycling bin. Apparently everyone was drinking around the children.'

'You what?' Louise's voice was irate. 'Are you actually serious? You can't be, because if you are, then I think my head might explode.'

'Look, stay calm. Talk me through what happened.'

'It was a barbecue. A social occasion. I didn't even have a drink because I was driving.'

'Can you think back? Who did?'

'Jeez, I don't know. Lloyd may have had a beer. Andrew had one, I think. People had a few beers and glasses of wine, I suppose. It was a wonderful day.' Louise paused suddenly. 'Can I see the photographs?'

'Officially? No.' Mary smiled. 'But look. It might be easier to go through this in person. Are you home later?'

Mary made an arrangement to be at Louise's by lunchtime, giving her more time to see what she could do to begin to fix things. She drummed the side of her now-empty mug thoughtfully and picked up the receiver again. Some days the Scottish croft still seemed a long way off.

Next on her contact list was an old friend, a lawyer who was always good for a brainstorm and some sage advice.

'Can I send you something?' Mary asked. She quickly outlined the list of allegations, filled her friend in on the context and sent off the photographs.

Her friend called back within a quarter of an hour.

'In my professional opinion? It sounds to me that they just want to save money and don't want to pay the charity acting as an agent for this specialist foster care.'

'How sound is the evidence against them?'

'Photographs look damn incriminating, if I'm honest. That's a lot of empties in the recycling. You know how these things work.'

'But it's the best care for him. The boy will have a great life if he goes to these people.'

'Ha. As if social care has ever had anything to do with the best interests of children…But, if that's the case, then you'll find a way to 'Mary it', won't you?'

Mary parked outside Louise's house. She wasn't surprised to see that Louise was looking out for her.

'I've been thinking and thinking,' Louise said, before Mary could get through the door.

'Me too. But first, how's that coffee machine?' said Mary, figuring that today's healthy eating project had also been sabotaged, so a second good coffee couldn't hurt.

'Whoops. Some holiday snaps just slipped out of my hand,' she said when they were settled in the kitchen.

Louise reached for the photographs, making an innocent whistling sound as her hand shot out.

'I knew it.' Louise narrowed her eyebrows. 'It's so underhand!'

'What can you tell me?'

'This can't be admissible evidence,' Louise said. 'This is the recycling bin for the whole site! It's communal. I know, because I offered to help clear up. I remember one of their neighbours telling me that in the morning they would have to walk the green bins to the gate at the end of the field. Where's my calendar? It was a Sunday, the last day of the week – and they'd had a whole week of being on holiday there and relaxing. That's why the bins were full. Not our stupid party. Come to think of it, I don't think I saw Jennifer drink any alcohol at all.'

Louise was angrier than Mary had seen her.

'It's not fair. The consequences for Jacob – and Nick and Sandy and Jennifer and Andrew – are huge.'

'Right. So are you happy to write a little statement about the bins – and the fact that Jennifer didn't have a drink all afternoon?'

'Too right I am. I'll add that I didn't have a drink either.'

'If you like; it can't hurt.' Or at least that's what Mary thought. Louise composed her email while Mary looked on, outlining the day in detail, and making sure that she was clear about the specifics of the recycling bin.

'Thanks, Louise. Take care. Keep your phone charged and keep an eye on emails. This gives us at least a fighting chance.'

II

But worse news awaited Mary when she logged onto her laptop back at home.

In the short time she was with Louise, the accusations had escalated, and now, to her horror, Louise Allen and her husband were also included within them. Similar suggestions about alcohol consumption and not being fit to look after children were being hurled around. Mary knew that this was absurd, but she also knew that it was exactly the charge on which she had had Jacob removed from the Hallidays, his previous carers, in the first place. This put her in a very tricky position.

Louise would also have seen it by now. She was copied in to one of the emails. Mary wasn't surprised when her phone went a moment later.

'What the actual f-?'

'I know I've just seen it. Calm down, Louise. They've got nothing.'

'Jesus Christ. I don't know if I can do this. Lloyd is going to snap. I don't think he's recovered from the last allegation against us. The way they treated us was appalling. We nearly gave up fostering. I think we would have if it hadn't been for Lily. She sees herself as part of the family. We *are* her family. If we resigned she would be thrown back into the care system and neither of us could do that. We went back to panel and were reapproved for her. I don't think I can do it again.'

'We both know that this is to keep Jacob in the county and use cheap, local and probably not specialist foster carers. Like you did when you made the choice for Lily, think about Jacob here. Put him first. His life would no way be as good as it will be if he goes to Northumberland. You've got to stay strong for him, Louise. Between us, we'll sort it.'

It was time to go back to where the whole story began. Mary pulled out Jacob's file and went back over the first case notes. The file was now thick with medical information and the updates from both the Hallidays and the Allens, Jacob's carers since being removed from Five Stones Farm nearly six months ago now. Mary had felt that there was something very wrong about the information that had been collected all the way along, and in spite of all the progress that Jacob had made, still couldn't shake the feeling that she was missing something. Something important. Like a detective investigating a cold case she went back over every detail, as though she was seeing it for the first time. She noted again the lack of birth certificate, the lack of schooling, the lack of any evidence that Jacob had ever existed. It seemed impossible in this day and age, but somehow it had happened. She read the words of the RSPCA officer, Anna, who had first discovered Jacob, lying in a dog basket beneath the kitchen table, and had written an extensive account of what she had found. She pictured the scene. Three generations of women: Jacob's mother, Daisy, young and healthy but with learning difficulties, unable to take care of her disabled child; Myrtle Prenderghast, her grandmother, elderly and infirm, requiring round the clock care; and in the midst of both of them, poor Betty Tillyard, trying to run a farm all by herself – those poor animals. It was hard trying to read between the lines of very few words. It was a nightmare situation, a dark tale of a woman being torn in different directions. And yet.

'I wonder...' She went back to the laptop and pulled up the newspaper reports. The case had made a bit of a splash at the time. She stared hard at the photographs of the farm, and of the women.

Another thought occurred to her. She did some online research into Jacob's condition – the causes of spina bifida. They were multiple: a mixture of genetic, nutritional, and environmental factors were all suspected in playing a role. Insufficient intake of folic acid in the mother's diet was a key factor. 'Well, I'll be damned,' she said out loud, looking back at the photographs once more.

'This isn't worth the paper it's printed on,' she added,

waving the file in the direction of one of her cats, who didn't stop to interrupt the licking of his paws.

Something did not add up and Mary was determined to get to the bottom of it. Though it was already well into the afternoon, Mary got herself organised for another road trip – back out to Five Stones Farm.

III

Darkness was falling as Mary crossed the Downs, and Mary's thoughts were darker. Given the squalid conditions of the place and the way that Jacob was found, there was no chance that Jacob could have stayed at Five Stones Farm, but how could Jacob's mother, and grandmother – and great-grandmother – bear to see him go without putting up a fight, or at least getting involved? Daisy had learning difficulties, yes, but that didn't explain why she didn't want to continue to be in his life. It saddened Mary as much as it angered her, but she thought she had an inkling about why.

She parked her car just inside the broken gate. The shape of the farmhouse lurched out of the gloom. Nothing much had changed but the season. There was a chill in the air; winter was calling. Mary walked up to the front door, nearly twisting an ankle in the pitted, puddled yard. There was an aroma of sour milk and boiled cabbage that reminded her of dinner in the convent boarding school, a piece of her own history that was preserved with memories as sour as the smell.

'Hello' she called, reaching to knock on the front door. 'Mrs Tillyard, are you there? It's Mary Waters from Children's Social Care.' The ill-fitting door swung open with her touch, to reveal Betty herself, standing at the top of the stairs. She was silhouetted eerily against the moonlight.

'Oh, it's you. I wondered when.' Mary detected a hint of resignation in Betty Tillyard's greeting.

'I have some updates on Jacob – I thought you might like to know how he's getting on.' It was not untrue; just not the whole reason Mary had made the journey.

'Come in. You'd better sit down.'

Betty picked up a candle from the window ledge and led Mary into the kitchen.

Mary generally described her home as 'rustic' which was a euphemism for 'not always tidy', but this level of filth and decay was beyond uninviting. Many of her colleagues took their own mugs and tea bags out to visits with them but this had never been Mary's way: she was a firm believer that if someone was polite enough to offer refreshments then she should accept. She thought she might make a rare exception this evening, though, when Betty offered to put the kettle on.

Mary sat opposite Betty at the huge battle-beaten kitchen table, so old it had holes along the middle to keep eggs. Perhaps it might once have been the cook's kitchen table in the big house that used to run the estate, but now it looked too large for this humble space.

'Why are you really here? Is there something wrong with Jacob?'

Whatever else she might be, Betty wasn't daft, Mary judged.

'I won't beat about the bush, Mrs Tillyard,' she said, holding Betty's gaze. 'I know that Daisy isn't Jacob's mother.'

Betty, strong for so long, suddenly seemed to deflate. She put her head down towards the table and her shoulders convulsed. She began to cry. The sound filled the room, primal and raw.

Mary remained at the other end of the table, knowing this was what Betty needed to do. When the keening began to subside, Mary leaned in to offer support.

'How did you know?' Betty was still in that uncontrolled, shuddering stage of post-crying.

'Take your time. You've had this bottled up a long time.

'I was 53 years old and my husband had just died,' Betty said. 'There was a man who managed us tenants and we had a...' she paused. 'A friendship, you might call it.'

Mary nodded. She knew all about 'friendships' like these.

'I didn't even know I was pregnant. And my friend was long gone before I found out. With the stress of Frank's death I weren't eating right anyway. I didn't know I was eating for two. I thought having babies, all that malarkey, was long behind me at my age. Then when Jacob came, it was clear that he wasn't... right. Just like Daisy wasn't right all those years ago. It was just easier to pretend it was Daisy's child. It would have made more bloody sense if it was. I just knew that I'd done wrong by him, but there was no way of putting it right.'

There was no point in telling Betty Tillyard that not having the right diet, not having enough folic acid during her pregnancy, had likely led to Jacob's spina bifida − or that other age-related factors might have contributed to his health problems.

'What a weight you've carried, Betty.'

'Aye.'

'But I do have some good news.' Mary told Betty about Jacob's new foster placement and what a lovely life he was having and going to have.

It produced the first small smile Mary had seen from Betty's careworn face.

'And we can get you some more help here, you know. There are all sorts of services you can access to help with Daisy, and with your mother.

Betty looked tired. She nodded slowly.

They sat silently together at the table for a while: two women at similar stages in their lives, both having to move on and make their reckonings for peace of mind, albeit in very different spheres.

'How about writing Jacob a letter, explaining what happened?' Mary suggested, eventually.

'That would be terrible thing to do to the boy.'

'For who?'

Betty shook her head.

'Betty, it's time for the truth. For everyone's sake.'

Betty seemed to be wrestling with the idea, but remained unconvinced.

'Why? What good will it do him?'

'To have freedom,' Mary said. 'Freedom to spend the rest of his life not guessing – and not feeling that anything was his fault.'

After an age, Betty moved her head slowly in the slightest of nods.

'You're right. Yes, you're right.'

Both women locked gazes for a moment. Mary got her A4 notepad out of her bag and dug around for a pen while Betty sat at the table with her hands clenched in front of her.

'What do I say? Where do I start?'

'Whatever you want, in your own words,' Mary said, simply. 'Now, can I talk to Daisy?'

The next afternoon, at the office, Mary could sense that there was something afoot. Whispers amongst colleagues and flashes of brightly coloured paper gave the game away. Here we go, thought Mary, knowing that they were getting ready to 'celebrate' her retirement. She pulled out Jacob's file. From her bag she pulled out Betty's letter to Jacob, and went to the photocopier to make a copy. She put the copy into Jacob's file which was on its way to Northumberland looked after children's team. The original, Mary put back into her notebook and into her bag. Tomorrow she would send it recorded delivery to Jennifer and Andrew so when they felt Jacob was ready, one day in the future, they could show him Betty's letter.

Summoned by Callum to the front to receive her retirement present, Mary politely stood up to the smiles of colleagues. There were some underwhelming words from her manager to account for a lifetime in the profession.

Mary left the office early on her last day, but instead of going home, she waited inside her car without turning on the ignition. She didn't want to do this in Callum's office, she wanted neutral territory. Callum didn't pull the same long shifts that some of the others did. It was nearing five o'clock. He'd be out of there at a minute past, Mary was sure of it. She waited in the gathering gloom.

'Thank you for earlier, but I'm not quite done,' she announced, flinging open her car door when Callum approached his own vehicle a few moments later.

'What? What are you talking about?'

'Daisy Tillyard is no more the mother of Jacob than I am. We've had this all wrong from the start. I've been back and spoken to Jacob's sister.'

'Jacob's sister? Jesus Christ, don't tell me there's another child?' Callum's face was a picture of fear.

'Not another *child*. The wrong mother. Daisy Tillyard is actually Jacob's sister. The mother is the one we thought was the grandmother of Jacob, Betty Tillyard. She is actually his mother. I went back today and got the whole story. She had an affair with a farm hand and fell pregnant. Her husband was already dead and she was in her late fifties. She kept the pregnancy hidden and did nothing to protect the baby she was carrying. No folic acid, no iron, no check-ups, no nothing. Then told people, when the child came, that it was Daisy's. The shame – and the need to carry on working and running the farm – meant that Jacob was just left to fester in the dog basket with a bottle of milk thrown at him now and then. All stuff that should have been investigated by us – by *your* department.'

Callum backed away slightly, looking over his shoulder to see if anyone else was around to hear this sensational story.

'I really don't think that...'

'Christ, Callum,' said Mary, allowing the uncharacteristic blasphemy to slip from her. 'You didn't even have the right mother! Betty Tillyard was grieving and suffering post-partum depression, and we did nothing. How do you think that's going to look? Don't try and wiggle out of this one. There's nowhere to go.'

'Mary, you're emotional because of your retirement. And I know that you have got involved personally in this case,' Callum started to say.

'How dare you? Every case is personal! How can it not be? We're human beings.'

'What I mean is-'

'I'm not sure that I *care* about what you mean. I'm retired, remember. But this is down to *your* incompetence. Mistakes were made, Callum. Be in no doubt about that. And, I don't expect any more resistance.'

'Resistance? I'm not sure that...'

'Oh yes, resistance. And if you don't want others to know about how poorly this was handled by YOUR department, then I suggest you make sure that the ridiculous allegations against the Allen family and the Northumberland couple are withdrawn with immediate effect – because, let me tell you, it gets worse.'

Mary went on to outline her theories about the other abuses suffered by Jacob, none of which had made their way into his file.

By now, darkness had fallen entirely, but the moon shone brightly. Mary watched as an ashen-faced Callum put his car keys back in his pocket and retreated back to the office. Mary picked up the phone to give Louise the good news – her final official action as a social worker.

AFTERWORD

Louise

Saying goodbye to Jacob was hard. He brought so much into our lives, but we weren't geared up to look after his needs long term.

My ignorance of disabilities like Jacob's meant that I had previously not thought to do so. I'm ashamed of that and now think very differently. We all grew through the privilege of spending time with Jacob.

I was full of fear for his future, but I needn't have been. Jennifer and Andrew fulfilled their promise of being wonderful carers. I am in regular email contact with them and get updates and photographs of Jacob, Nick and Sandy. They are a fantastic little group of siblings. Nick and Jacob are a right pair. They are brothers through and through, who look out for each other no matter what. They even look uncannily alike, and are regularly mistaken for birth brothers.

Jacob has defied all the professionals' prognosis and

predictions and goes from strength to strength. Being told he can't do something just spurs him on all the more. I know that Jennifer and Andrew are the main reason for this. They are quiet, unassuming people. I have seen their dedication and commitment to all their children and know that, though gentle, they both have nerves of steel.

I was recently sent a photograph of Jacob receiving an award from his school. Thanks to the continual advice and support from Mary (even long after she retired), Jennifer and Andrew managed to keep Jacob in a wonderful school for young people with disabilities where he is understood, supported and thriving. The photograph I have of Jacob shows him walking from his wheelchair up the steps to the podium with the biggest smile on his face. The award was given for a speech he delivered about what it is like being disabled in an able society. We've seen the recording of him doing the speech. The boys, Vincent and Jackson, cheered him on.

'Go, Jacob, go Jacob.' I can hear them now.

Lily was also moved by Jacob's speech. She made him a painting and wrote a wonderful letter that we sent in the post. Funnily enough, she misses Jacob more than anyone. I wonder what they taught each other.

The local authority funding the school fees celebrated Jacob's massive achievements by trying to get Jacob into a mainstream state school. But Jennifer and Andrew, with the support of Jacob's fantastic social worker from

Northumberland, stuck their heels in and refused to move Jacob.

The nasty allegations against Jennifer and Andrew – then us because I tried to support them – knocked us all. I often wonder how social workers and their managers expect us to do our best for the children when we are under attack in this way. To be honest I'm not sure if I can forgive that manager and that young ambitious social worker for spying and lying. This work is all about trust and we all ended up with a sour taste in our mouths. Jacob nearly lost out on the best place for him. What that experience did do though was galvanise a relationship built on 'having each other's backs'.

Something Mary taught me was to refer to the Children Act above all else. It exists for a reason: to protect the rights of our most vulnerable children and the most compelling clause is about doing what is *in the best interests of the child*. (Though even that was written back in 1989 when mobile phones and the perils of the internet were but science fiction – in itself it could do with a radical overhaul.)

Children's Social Care can feel like the Wild West of our public funded services. Too much goes unregulated – and though it could be argued that it *was* regulated, I offer the notion that you can only collate data from things that are measurable. The whole system exists on fragile foundations: immeasurable things like emotions and relationships, and sometimes secrets and lies. How can you measure that accurately, if at all? The whole sector needs to be brought into the 22nd century, ahead of its time. But the 21st century may be too much to ask at the present moment: the big broken machine keeps on limping through the next set of problems without contingency or foresight. And yet, people who think as I do are amassing in numbers and gradually achieving platforms to talk about what it feels like for the child in the system, and the adults who have left it – which can only be good news and spurs me on.

Children suffering from emotional and physical pain find themselves being pushed through a faceless factory of children's social care where everyone and their dog seems to think they know what's best for them – and children in care have no choice but to be part of it. This is what lights the fire in my belly every day to do the work I do. If politicians, managers and all the other great and good genuinely knew *that pain* they would not do things the way they do currently. Terrible things go on in our society, in all societies, but since when did we let so much greed and bad practice go unchallenged around children and young people? I believe it's because people don't really know how bad it is and perhaps the Thrown Away Children series goes some way to help point out some of the injustices. I believe that most people are good. Look at how wonderful and law-abiding most of us have been in our series of lockdowns (though we can't say the same for some of our leaders). So, we need change for the good.

We have a Minister for Children. A big job, especially when you think there are approximately 12.5 million children and young people under the age of 18 years in England alone. We also have a Minister for Prisons. There are approximately 84,000 people in prison and did you know that approximately 26% of those prisoners come from the care system? In England we have around 100.000 children under the age of 18 years in the care system right now. I know what you're thinking: why then haven't we got a Minister for Looked After Children? I'm sure that if we did then the Minister for Prisons would have a bit of an easier job. From every angle it feels like the great and the good don't get it – or don't care. If you know me by now and have read my other books you know that I try to say it 'as it is'. I have no interest in seeking favour with the people who run this system, and I see no benefit from getting excited or shouting about a few attempts to fix one or two tiny little aspects of the broken factory. It won't do. It isn't enough.

So, with that liberated thought in my head and heart I continue to question the bleeding obvious, to follow the money and to consider who is really benefitting from children's pain and misery.

I know that trying to look after any child in a system that is effectively broken and under resourced is challenging, but what Jennifer and Andrew – and Mary – have collectively shown me is never to give up: to keep going and not stop until you get what the child needs. I hope my new caution around social workers and their managers fades – and I think it will. I only have to think of the love and effort both Mary and Dara gave to the children to remember that there are good people in the system.

Throughout the telling of Jacob's story I make some serious points about the financial situation for foster carers – both for those who work for independent agencies and those who work directly with local authorities. The lockdown situation of 2020 exacerbated all those pinch points: when the additional costs of feeding foster children rose dramatically while they weren't in school and were combined with loss of income from parents like me not being able to complete my working day while home-schooling, all those financial considerations were brought to the fore.

I dread to think how much we have supplemented the allowances over the years, and perhaps more than ever in recent months. That's why I struggle to understand why there are still foster carers who come into this for the money. Jacob's first foster carers, the Hallidays, are characterised as taking on Jacob for the financial reward he brings. I don't personally know any foster carers who 'do it' for the money; they are not the ones I choose to be friends with, at any rate. But I know of agencies that are less scrupulous, like the one that Jacob is first served by. I have also been into foster homes where the carers boast several holidays a year away from the foster children – perhaps I, or somebody like me, will have them for 'respite' while they are away. Or that financial division can manifest in other ways. I saw one woman open her food cupboard that was divided very clearly into two sections. I could see that her foster children had the cheaper food while she and her husband and birth sons had the best food. I looked after one of her foster children whilst she went on a month-long cruise over Christmas, and he couldn't believe it when I gave him a big cooked breakfast in the mornings the same as I gave all the children. Everyone will get the same in my house and no one should feel that they are in any way 'lesser'. But it evidently does happen.

But it is also a fact that the budgets in children's social care come directly from us, the taxpayers. And, since the onslaught of the commissioning of private companies to buy up the system, much more of the money is going to chancers looking to make a fast buck – operating unseen amongst individuals and organisations who are ethical and deliver good work. Those without scruples see the constant supply of vulnerable children coming into care (and post Covid these numbers are unimaginable and unprecedented) as income generation, and the increasing limitations of local authority services as the opportunity. Even though paying to outsource services previously done in-house is more expensive and harder to monitor and regulate, the commissioning keeps going on. Those of us who see this live with the despair that it has been allowed to happen. People abuse children – and that goes for their budgets and resources too – because they can.

I also have very genuine concerns about some of the labels that are bandied about and applied to children. Many of the children who are in the care system have been hurt not only by the abuse that they have suffered, but by the system itself: a system which is under its own severe financial pressures that results in shunting children around while pinning all their issues on attachment-related issues or other disorders. Like me, Mary has very little time for a lot of what she sees as the rot talked around the emotional wellbeing of the children. Given her years of experience, she believes a lot of children's anxiety is actually caused by the system itself. There is such a long waiting list for children to receive any therapeutic support that someone like Mary just rolls her eyes in despair. This is something that really needs to be aired nationally and internationally. As one doctor recently said to me when I presented her with another tragic young teenager, 'What are we doing to our children?' Personally, I don't think it's a good idea to keep talking about, prodding and probing and second guessing the mental health of children and young people. I think it's the adults, those who have the most unresolved issues, that push them onto the children. Nothing is going to improve for children's mental health until we, the adults, admit that we should do the 'work' on ourselves first. We must know ourselves before we dump our rubbish on children and young people. I hear rhetoric like 'heal' and 'repair'. Think about that for a minute. That's pretty problematic when most adults I meet have their own 'stuff' going on. As an ex-looked after child who hid under the radar from children's social services, I celebrate my early life experiences and see them as gifts that have helped shape me and made me who I am. If we aim to 'heal' and 'repair', whose models are we using exactly? I would hate to think that acts of therapy become acts of social control – where we expect children and young people to behave and be just as we want them to.

I remain in contact with Mary, whose determination and strength have inspired Lloyd and me in ways that are difficult to calibrate. I am so glad to have her at the other end of the phone when I want to run something by her. I love hearing the snort and 'Phaa, that's utter rubbish' that are a likely to response to any nonsense that comes along.

Anna, the RSPCA officer who first found Jacob is – can you believe it? – a social worker now. She retrained a few years ago and, as far as I know, is a very good one. Apparently she never got over the idea that the animals were rescued without question while Jacob was left to live in more than unsatisfactory conditions. She, like so many good women and men I know, has that drive to keep questioning, to keep pushing, to never give up.

Thank you for reading my books; it means the world to me. I didn't mean to become a writer. As many of you know I am dyslexic and missed a lot of school because of my own situation. I have a lot to say. I've seen and know too much. I feel a need to get the stories and information out to you so that you know too. We all have a responsibility for all our children.

The children are more than worth it.

Also in the series

Stella's Story
Louise Allen

*"Stella is just like a tiny bird. This is my first impression of her.
A quiet little sparrow of a girl."*

In the first of a new series *'Thrown Away Children'*, foster mother Louise Allen
tells the true story of Stella, a young girl scarred by an abusive past.

Named for the lager that christened her, Stella's life is characterised by
dysfunction and neglect. Her mother abandons her as a newborn and in the
'care' of her father, Stella is left with no food, water, clothes or warmth.

Louise becomes Stella's foster carer and is determined to give the girl a
better life. But when Stella has a startling response to having her photo
taken, it is clear that the effects of her abuse run deep.

MIRROR BOOKS

Also in the series

Abby's Story
Louise Allen

She doesn't want this baby.
She can't look after this baby.
She will never be able to love this baby.

Little Abby's life begins badly, then just gets worse.

Now foster carer Louise and her family must help her to deal
with the truth about her past, to give her the chance of a future.

The second book in the series
THROWN AWAY CHILDREN

MIRROR BOOKS

Also in the series

Eden's Story
Louise Allen

Ashley is a young single mum who governs her life by astrology and online clairvoyants. One night, unable to find a sitter for her baby daughter, Eden, she leaves her home alone, asleep… locked inside a wardrobe.

It is an action that begins a terrible downward spiral for both of them. When Eden arrives at foster carer Louise Allen's home, she is five years old, she does not speak and her mother is in prison. When she begins exhibiting other disturbing behaviour, including torturing the family pets she loves, it leads Louise to discover the pain and tragic reality behind little Eden's Story.

m
B
MIRROR BOOKS